T0123437

FROM CHURCH HOUSE TO MAIN STREET:
A Scientific Analysis of the Bible

VOLUME 1: THE PHYSICAL
DIMENSION OF THE HOLY BIBLE

EDWARD WAYNE KIMBROUGH

FROM CHURCH HOUSE TO MAIN STREET: A SCIENTIFIC ANALYSIS OF THE BIBLE
VOLUME 1: THE PHYSICAL DIMENSION OF THE HOLY BIBLE

iUniverse books may be ordered through booksellers or by contacting:

iUniverse
1663 Liberty Drive
Bloomington, IN 47403
www.iuniverse.com
1-800-Authors (1-800-288-4677)

Because of the dynamic nature of the Internet, any web addresses or links contained in this book may have changed since publication and may no longer be valid. The views expressed in this work are solely those of the author and do not necessarily reflect the views of the publisher, and the publisher hereby disclaims any responsibility for them.

Any people depicted in stock imagery provided by Getty Images are models, and such images are being used for illustrative purposes only.
Certain stock imagery © Getty Images.

Author Credits: Edward Wayne Kimbrough

Scripture quotations from the Holy Bible, King James Version (Authorized Version). First published in 1611. Quoted from the KJV Classic Reference Bible.

ISBN: 978-1-5320-9713-3 (sc)
ISBN: 978-1-5320-9715-7 (hc)
ISBN: 978-1-5320-9714-0 (e)

Library of Congress Control Number: 2020904388

Print information available on the last page.

iUniverse rev. date: 06/24/2020

DEDICATION

This book is dedicated to the memory of
DR. MARTIN LUTHER KING, JR.
and one of his famous sermons which was
delivered on February 28, 1954, prior to his
involvement in the Civil Rights Movement,
entitled "Rediscovering Lost Values" from
the tape series *"A Knock at Midnight."* This sermon
serves as the foundation for the discussion of Universal
Principles #4 and #5, in Chapter 24, Sections D and E, and
Chapter 30, Section C. Dr. King asserts that to make this world
a better place in which to live, we must go back and rediscover
two mighty precious values we have left behind, and they are:
<u>All Reality Hinges on Moral Foundations</u>
<u>All Reality Has Spiritual Controls</u>

PREFACE

When I retired from the United States Postal Service in 2009, America was experiencing the worst financial crisis since the Great Depression of the 1930s. In the years leading up to this past financial crisis and the years since, there appears to have been a steady deterioration in the attitude of companies toward the long-term welfare of the customers and the public they serve. There is evidence that this attitude is leading us toward another financial crisis which could be more devastating than the 2008-2009 financial crisis.

You have to pump your own gas at the "service" station. Instead of a service technician coming out to fix your computer, you spend hours on the telephone trying to understand someone in another part of the world as they attempt to debug your computer. Instead of being served a decent meal on commercial airlines, as in the past, you are given a tiny bag of peanuts with a soft drink or coffee to wash them down. Companies devise all types of credit card and mortgage banking schemes to engage the public in high-interest, high-risk loans, but then rely on the public and the government to bail them out when they get into trouble. You deposit your money in the bank, and the bank develops gimmicks that enable their computers to siphon money out of your account at extremely high interest rates.

In the past, the bank balances of customers were calculated at the end of the day. Now many banks have eliminated any transaction delays, and overdraft balances are calculated before the end of the calendar day. This means that customers with cash flow problems cannot correct their pending overdraft balances near the end of the calendar day, even when the funds are available to do so, and the banks have the ability to control when deposits are posted to the customers' accounts. Consequently, many banks are able to rack up enormous profits from fees on the accounts of those customers who can least afford it. They have developed a "reverse Robin Hood" strategy, rob from the poor to aid the rich.

Also, in the years prior to 2009, the oil industry was able to continuously raise gasoline prices with very little resistance from our leadership in Washington on behalf of the American people and the other affected industries. In the State of Texas, the price of a gallon of regular gasoline in many places was over $4.00 per gallon, which meant it was much higher in many of the other states. Some families were paying more for gasoline to commute to and from work than the mortgages on their homes, which contributed to foreclosures on many of their homes during the crisis.

The price of gasoline affects virtually every man, woman, and child in this country, because almost all of the products or services we consume require the use of gasoline or diesel fuel at some point in the delivery process. Consequently, our demand for oil is relatively inelastic and the normal market forces of supply and demand do not always apply, because there is very little true competition in the oil market place. That is why the oil companies can charge almost any price they choose when there are no other external price controls.

I was deeply concerned that our leaders appeared to be abandoning basic moral and ethical standards when it came to protecting the people from financial and social predators in the American economy. In order to relieve my frustrations, I had planned to use some of my spare "retirement time" to write letters to congressmen and members of the committees that controlled the industries involved. However, when I started to do research on the internet and elsewhere for my letters, I found that there were many voices already out there that were much louder and stronger than mine, and they did not appear to be having any noticeable effect on the leadership in Washington.

It was then that I decided to write this book, which turned out to be a set of five volumes, in an attempt to pull all of those many voices on the internet and elsewhere together into one place, and instead of just complaining about the problems of humanity, try to offer some common sense solutions. However, bringing those many voices together would not necessarily lead to solutions to these problems, because those many voices represent a very wide diversity of attitudes, opinions, and values.

These diverse attitudes, opinions, and values involve relationships between science and religion, different religious beliefs, different religious denominations, different cultures, different races of people, different lifestyles, and different genders. To unify these many voices, it would be necessary to find **Universal Principles** that would promote peace, prosperity, and survival for all who follow them, no matter their race, gender, nationality, sexual orientation, religious beliefs (belief in God, agnostic, or atheist), economic status, or political affiliation.

It was obvious to me that the only place to look for these **Universal Principles** was the Holy Bible, the Word of God. Therefore, the plan and purpose of this book are to find **Universal Principles** and use them to gather data that will inform you about the nature and potential causes of the problems we are facing, and then offer solutions based on research and input from the many voices. Although our leaders may not agree with the solutions offered, they will not be able to say that there is nothing that can be done. I believe that only an informed American public, through the power of the ballot, can affect any significant improvement in our leadership in Washington. I will attempt to provide factual information for that purpose.

EDWARD WAYNE KIMBROUGH
Houston, Texas
December, 2019

ACKNOWLEDGMENTS

Although the following persons or organizations may not agree with all of the concepts and conclusions I reveal in this book, I want to acknowledge the impact that they have had on my life:

1. My beautiful wife, Wanda Beta Tanner Kimbrough, for her patience, support, and encouragement during the long and demanding process of writing this book. And also, for her legal advice, editing and diligent work in obtaining the initial copyright and working copies of the original concept of this book, which has turned out to be a set of five volumes.

2. My deceased mother, Mary Etta Kimbrough, who in her 92 years of life taught me, by example, how to take care of myself during difficult times and how to deal with adversity. As a single parent, she experienced a great deal of adversity in her life, and her approach to each adverse situation was to pray about it and then "Let go and let God." Over her lifetime I was able to see the ultimate results of many of her adversities, which left her much stronger and victorious.

3. Dr. Robert H. Harvey, my mathematics professor at Knoxville College in Knoxville, Tennessee. Dr. Harvey taught me how to think logically and reason deductively to solve problems. His instruction

and mentoring allowed me, though my background in mathematics and the sciences was very limited when I enrolled, to graduate from Knoxville College with a B. S. Degree in Mathematics and from the University of Tennessee in Knoxville with a B. S. Degree in Industrial Engineering.

4. Rev. Dr. Marcus D. Cosby, my pastor at Wheeler Avenue Baptist Church (WABC) in Houston, Texas and Rev. William A. Lawson, pastor emeritus of WABC. Dr. Cosby has impacted my life enormously by his ability to take scriptural passages from the Bible and apply them, through 2 or 3-point commentary, to the everyday situations we face in life. It often appears that he is speaking directly to me and my situation. I have well over 400 of his sermons in my note files and those 2 or 3 points in his messages still come to life when I review my notes. Rev. Lawson inspired me to refocus on the development of my spiritual values and family values during the early 1990's and thereafter. He married my wife, Wanda, and I in 1998.

5. Dr. Ed Young, the Senior Pastor of Second Baptist Church in Houston, Texas. Dr. Young has been a great inspiration to me by his ability to help me understand difficult passages of scripture and his ability to apply scriptural doctrine to specific spiritual, family, and social situations. His television ministry and CD tapes about prayer, marital relations, raising children, and the redemptive process have been very beneficial to me and my understanding of the Bible and in my personal life. His clear explanation of the redemptive principles of Conviction (acknowledging our sins), Confession (confessing our sins), Repentance (feeling remorse for our sins and asking those we have offended for forgiveness), and Forgiveness (forgiving those who have offended us) has been of great benefit during my search for the **Universal Principles**.

6. Rev. Joel Osteen, the Senior Pastor of Lakewood Church in Houston, Texas. I am inspired by the way Rev. Osteen uses biblical principles to promote a positive attitude as we deal with adversity and as we strive to reach our goals in life. His television ministry has given me consistent encouragement to continue to strive to reach the goals that I have set for my life. I believe we will all achieve our greatest successes in life when we are able to continually improve

our character by practicing **Universal Principles** that place us in alignment with God's word and God's will as we live our lives.

7. The late Mr. Bill Britt and Mr. Rex Renfrow, who have major distributer networks within the organizational structure of the Amway Corporation. They changed my whole outlook on life. The principles they developed for their distributer networks linked biblical principles directly to success in business and success in life. They promoted a reading program which, in addition to the Bible, included success books such as, "Think and Grow Rich" by Napoleon Hill, and "What You Say is What You Get!" by Don Gossett and cassette tapes that celebrated the successes of the distributers within their networks.

Although I was not a successful Amway distributer, their reading and tape program had the following impacts on my life: (1) they added a new dimension to my faith which inspired me to develop and complete unifying principles for my life and set personal life goals on May 5, 1992; (2) they provided access to books that inspired me to continually work on my personal life goals, even during very difficult times; and (3) they inspired me to start reading and listening to the Bible on a regular basis.

In about 1992, I purchased cassette tapes of the King James Version of the Bible, narrated by Alexander Scourby, and listened to them sequentially on a regular basis as I commuted to and from work. Over the years, the cassette tapes became damaged, and I replaced them with CDs by the same narrator, to which I continue to listen. The biblical knowledge I gained from these tapes gave added meaning to the spiritual messages I listened to in church and elsewhere. And, as I observed the conditions that currently exist in this country and the world, this biblical knowledge also gave me the inspiration to write this book. The scriptural references in this book come from the King James Version (KJV) of the Bible.

I would also like to acknowledge the major contributors to the content of this book, which was made possible by the endless sources of information from the Internet and some biblical reference books that I have been using as part of my Bible study since 1992. The Open Bible Expanded Edition (OBEE), (Boa, et al. (1985), *The Open Bible, Expanded Edition, KJV*, Nashville: Thomas Nelson Publishers), is the major source of the following information. The "Biblical Cyclopedic Index" helped me find scriptural references about specific issues; the "The Greatest Archaeological Discoveries" provided information about the impact of archaeology on Biblical and secular history; and the "Christian's Guide to the New Life" (CGNL) provided information about God's covenants with humanity and the four institutions created by God.

The book entitled "All Scripture is Inspired of God and Beneficial" by the Watch Tower Bible and Tract Society, (Watch Tower Bible and Tract Society of Pennsylvania (1963), *"All Scripture is Inspired of God and Beneficial,"* First Edition, Brooklyn: Watch Tower Bible and Tract Society of New York, Inc., International Students Association), provided a detailed explanation about the measurement of Biblical timelines. They provided a description of how time is measured from different perspectives, how their "Chart of Outstanding Historical Dates" from the Bible was developed from biblical and secular history, and a detailed description of Old and New Testament prophecies that have since been fulfilled.

Their "Chart of Outstanding Historical Dates" is the foundation for the timelines of all of the biblical events presented in this book. Although some of their timelines differ slightly from secular timelines, their detailed descriptions of time provide a basis for historians to further verify the impacts of different secular calendars on the time measurement of biblical and secular history.

There are several websites that have also contributed substantial content to this book. The website entitled "Bible Gateway" at https://www.biblegateway.com/ (38) was the source of most of the King James Version (KJV) biblical references throughout the book. The website entitled "BibleHub" at https://bibleatlas.org/ (2) was the source of our analyses of ancient places in the Bible. The website entitled "Got Questions" at https://www.gotquestions.org/ (3) provided the foundational analysis for many of the interpretations of the parables of Jesus in Chapter 18.

The website entitled "Adherents.com" at https://www.adherents.com/ Religions_By_Adherents.html (7) provided a list and size estimate of the 22 major religions of the world, and the website entitled "Religious Tolerance" at http://www.religioustolerance.org/ (6) provided detailed information about the beliefs and practices of most of these 22 major religions, which were used to compare biblical principles to the principles of the other major religions of the world in Chapter 9.

The websites at: https://www.allaboutscience.org/ (16), https://www.allaboutcreation.org/ (16), and https://www.allaboutthejourney.org/ (16) provided foundational material that was used primarily in our discussion of the physical (scientific) dimension of the Bible. The website entitled "Wikipedia" at https://www.wikipedia.org/ (1) provided numerous articles and support material that was used throughout the book.

Although these individual websites contributed significant content to the book, the overall content of the book includes information from many other books and websites, which are referenced in the chapters where their content is used. The "Book References" at the end of Volume 5 of this book will attempt to list most of the books and websites used in the preparation of this book and the approximate locations where their content was used. Each website URL link will have a reference number beside it as shown above, so it can be easily located on the reference list.

The ten symbols (images) that represent the **Universal Principles** are under license from Shuttlestock at https://www.shutterstock.com (35) and are listed at the end of the book references in Volume 5. The remaining symbols and images were developed by me from a public domain image and a contract with Logoworks at https://www.logoworks.com, the company that helped to finalize the design for the overall symbol of the **Universal Principles**.

Book Table of Contents

Introduction

The Scientific Method will be used to search for Universal Principles in the Holy Bible

Volume 1 – The Physical (Scientific) Dimension of the Holy Bible

Volume 2 – The Spiritual Dimension of the Holy Bible

Volume 3 – The Prophetic Dimension of the Holy Bible

Volume 4 – The Social Dimension of the Holy Bible

Volume 5 – Bottom-line Conclusions and Recommendations

INTRODUCTION

In this year of 2019, it appears that our nation is facing a leadership crisis, a spiritual crisis, and a social crisis. We face a leadership crisis because the founders of this nation designed our government to be a government of the people, by the people and for the people. But instead, we have a government of the special interests, by the special interests, and for the special interests. Our elected politicians appear to be controlled by an institutionalized system of bribery where leaders are chosen based on the amount of money they can raise to discredit their opponents, rather than the ideas they have for the advancement and prosperity of the nation.

And legislation is passed or not passed based on the power of money and lobbyists who dominate the decision-making process at the committee level where laws are written. Politicians appear to have more loyalty and allegiance to the political parties they belong to and the special interest groups that keep them in power, than the nation and the people they are elected to serve. We need **Universal Principles** to help us find leaders who are accountable to the American people.

In our government, the House, Senate, and White House currently work like the Three Stooges. When the party of two of the Stooges is in power, the party of the third Stooge looks for ways to be heard by the other stooges, otherwise they must find ways to maintain the checks and balances on power between the Executive and Legislative Branches.

As a consequence, we have a stalemate and gridlock in Washington which strangles the progress of the nation, because each party has its own agenda and there is no unity. Instead, the House, Senate, and White House should work like the Three Musketeers. They should have **Universal Principles** that will allow them to work as one, like the Three Musketeers, for the well-being of the whole nation. We the people also need **Universal Principles** that will help us to identify and elect more Musketeers and transform the Stooges into Musketeers, who are able to work in unity for the benefit of everyone.

We must be aware of what Scripture teaches us, "And if a kingdom be divided against itself, that kingdom cannot stand. And if a house be divided against itself, that house cannot stand" (Mark 3:24-25). In order to strengthen our democracy and address our problems, we must have **Universal Principles** that create transparency. That transparency should expose the events and conditions that negatively impact our lives as a nation, investigate and analyze to determine the truth about those events and conditions, and establish common sense principles and laws to respond to those events and conditions, because evil cannot survive under the light of the truth. The constitution of the United States, represented by the flag, gives every citizen the unique authority to change the direction of our nation, without internal revolution, through the enormous power of the vote.

We face a spiritual crisis because we have abandoned many of the principles that this country was founded on. The Declaration of Independence reads as follows:

> "We hold these truths to be self-evident, that all men are created equal, that they are endowed by their Creator with certain unalienable Rights, that among these are Life, Liberty and the

pursuit of Happiness. That to secure these rights, Governments are instituted among Men, deriving their just powers from the consent of the governed,"

It seems evident from this document that the founders of this nation acknowledged that there was a Creator of the universe. However, there is a continuing controversy among scientists about the origins of life on earth between the theory of evolution and the theory of creation, and it appears that the theory of evolution is the current scientific view concerning the origin of life on earth. As a consequence, our children are being taught that life on earth evolved from a single organism as a scientific fact, when there is no clear scientific evidence to support this theory.

However, the Bible provides a detailed account of creation, including names and places, and it gets no mention in scientific textbooks. In fact, scientific discoveries continue to provide evidence that the universe was created at a specific point in time by intelligent design. This book will conduct a scientific analysis of these two theories by use of the scientific method for further consideration by scientists and theologians.

The goal of this book is to search for **Universal Principles** that provide concrete evidence that the Bible is not just a religious book; it is a scientific book that teaches us how the universe was created; it is a social book that teaches us how to live peaceably with our fellow human beings; it is a prophetic and historical book that reveals how God has worked in the past to fulfill His promises to humanity, and it is a spiritual book that teaches how God has revealed His will and purpose for humanity.

It is my hope that the **Universal Principles** we discover will make it obvious that the teaching of the Bible should be an option, but not mandatory, in all public and private educational institutions. However, the teaching of the Bible should not be mandatory for anyone, unless it is their chosen field of study. And everyone should be free to worship as they please or to not worship at all, but we must make a clear distinction between the issues that involve the separation of <u>church and state</u>, versus the separation of <u>God and state</u>. We need **Universal Principles** that will let us know as a nation if we are in alignment with God's will, so that we may continue to be the recipients of God's blessings and God's grace and mercy.

We face a social crisis because in many cases we do not treat other people the way we want to be treated and we do not treat the life of every human being as sacred. This applies to relationships between police and the communities they serve, relationships within ethnic groups, relationships between the races, relationships between religious organizations, relationships between companies and other organizations, and relationships between nations.

We need a set of **Universal Principles** that transcend all of our differences and allow us to work together for the common good of humanity. We need **Universal Principles** to deal with the proliferation of abortions by providing guidelines and support that will allow the stakeholders to make better decisions. We need to establish systems that will allow citizens and law enforcement officials to work together to identify and resolve issues relating to illegal immigration, crime, and family problems. We need **Universal Principles** to help fugitives from justice, drug dealers, drug abusers, gang members, prisoners, and corrupt government officials to repair their lives and become law-abiding and more productive citizens.

Inside this book is an analysis of the twenty-two (22) major religious groups in the world with 500,000 or more adherents, including non-believers. The two largest of these religious groups are Christianity and Islam with about 52.5% of the total adherents in the world. The problem with comparing these two groups is that their adherents do not have a consistent set of beliefs. According to the website, <u>http://philvaz. com/apologetics/a120.htm (39)</u>, there are about 33,820 Christian denominations in 238 different countries. And there are at least two or three different sets of beliefs among the adherents in Islam.

It is hard to imagine how so many different Christian beliefs can come from the teachings of the one man, Jesus Christ. It appears that some church doctrines are driven by church tradition and not by the Word of God. We must find a way to move from tradition to submission and trust God to do the rest. The purpose of this book is to conduct a scientific analysis of the Holy Bible to find **Universal Principles** that we all might be able to agree on and live by in the Church House and on Main Street.

This book is divided into five volumes which deal with questions that we might ask about the Bible, the origins of the universe, or the issues covered by the application of the **Universal Principles** to our social institutions. The first four volumes of the book deal with the four dimensions of the Holy Bible.

Volume 1 deals with the Physical (Scientific) Dimension of the Bible. It seeks to answer the questions: How did we get here? How old is the universe? And who are our Ancestors?

Volume 2 deals with the Spiritual Dimension of the Bible and seeks to find **Universal Principles** from God's Word that teach us how to live according to God's will.

Volume 3 deals with the Prophetic Dimension of the Bible. It provides a historical record of how God has worked through the Nation of Israel to pre-determine the events of life, to pre-determine the conditions that surrounded the events of life, and to judge humanity based on their responses to those events and conditions of life.

Volume 4 deals with the Social Dimension of the Bible. It defines the four social institutions created by God: the family, human government, the Nation of Israel, and the Church, and investigates ways the **Universal**

Principles discovered in Volume 2 may be applied in those four social institutions.

Volume 5 summarizes the bottom-line conclusions and recommendations from the scientific analysis of the first four volumes and the four dimensions of the Bible, and it defines the meaning of the symbols that will be used to represent the **Universal Principles**. It includes a Comprehensive 8-Year American Recovery Plan (ARP) developed from the **Universal Principles**, which addresses all of the major problems faced by our nation and the world. This **ARP** is designed to return the power of government to the American people by establishing a legislative action plan with timetables to address the major issues we are facing as a nation.

The reader can go to Volume 5 and read the conclusions and recommendations reached about a question or issue, and then go to the other volume and chapter that deals with the details of that question or issue, and see how those conclusions and recommendations were derived. The detailed table of contents for each of the other four volumes is included at the end of Volume 5, so that the reader can quickly find the proper volume and chapter for detailed investigations.

The Scientific Method will be used to search for the Universal Principles in the Holy Bible.

Before we embark on this scientific analysis of the Holy Bible, we need to get an understanding of the **Scientific Method,** which scientists use to perform a scientific analysis. The website, http://www.sciencebuddies. org/science-fair-projects/ (8), provides a very simple definition of the scientific method and the steps involved in its implementation:

> "The scientific method is a process used for experimentation, the exploration of observations, and to answer questions. It is used by scientists to search for cause and effect relationships in nature." The steps of the scientific method are to:

1. Ask a question
2. Do background research about the question
3. Construct a hypothesis about the question
4. Test the hypothesis by doing an experiment on the question
5. Analyze the experimental data and draw a conclusion about the question
6. Communicate the results concerning the question"

The website, http://teacher.nsrl.rochester.edu:8080/phy_labs/ AppendixE/AppendixE.html (9), provides a more classical definition of the scientific method and the steps involved in its implementation:

"The scientific method is a process used by scientists to, collectively and over time, work toward an accurate (that is, reliable, consistent and non-arbitrary) representation of the world. Because personal and cultural beliefs influence both perceptions and interpretations of natural phenomena, scientists use standard procedures and criteria to minimize those influences when developing a theory. As a famous scientist once said, "Smart people (like smart lawyers) can come up with very good explanations for mistaken points of view." In summary, scientists use the scientific method to minimize the influence of bias or prejudice when conducting an experiment or test on a hypothesis or theory. The scientific method has four steps:

1. Observe and describe a phenomenon or group of phenomena.
2. Formulate a hypothesis to explain the phenomena. In physics, the hypothesis may include a causal mechanism or a mathematical relationship.
3. Use the hypothesis to predict the existence of other phenomena, or to predict quantitatively the results of new observations.
4. Conduct experimental tests of the predictions by using independent experimenters and properly performed experiments.

If the experimental tests support the hypothesis, it may eventually be considered a theory or law of nature. If the experimental tests do not support the hypothesis, it must be rejected or modified. The key element of the scientific method is the predictive power of the hypothesis or theory, as tested by experiment. In science it is often said that theories can never be proved; only disproved. There is always the possibility that a new observation or a new experiment will conflict with a long-standing theory.

A scientific theory or law is the representation of a hypothesis, or a related group of hypotheses, which has been verified by repeated experimental tests. In physics scientific theories are often formulated in terms of a few concepts and equations, which are associated with "laws of nature," which suggests that they can be applied universally. Theories and laws that have been accepted by the scientific community become part of our understanding of the universe and become the basis for exploring less well-understood areas of knowledge."

In this scientific analysis of the Holy Bible, a simple and straightforward approach similar to the first definition of the scientific method will be used, that is, of asking a question and using systematic research to find the answer to the question. Specific questions about biblical scripture will be answered by finding all scriptures relating to the question and drawing a conclusion from an analysis of all the scriptures in their contexts. The questions asked will be directed toward the four dimensions of the Bible: the physical (scientific) dimension, the spiritual dimension, the prophetic dimension, and the social dimension as discussed below.

First, the scientific method will be used to investigate the current scientific view of the universe and, based on the discoveries of the past few centuries, attempt to close the gap between the current scientific view of the universe and the prevailing religious view of the universe. Many times, the "Logical Conclusions" that are reached by this scientific approach will not agree with the current scientific view of the universe or the prevailing religious view of the universe. However, the intent of this book and this scientific approach is not to create more controversy, but rather to stimulate a higher level of scientific research and Biblical investigation by scientists and theologians.

Second, the scientific method will be used to investigate the spiritual content of the Bible as it relates to the universe from a macro conceptual point of view based on the eight covenants that God has made with humanity through the Nation of Israel. The purpose of this part of the analysis is to search the Bible for **Universal Principles** that deal with the spiritual issues that divide the religious community into many different denominations, sects, and belief structures. The intent here is to investigate all of the major World Religions in an attempt to find potential areas of agreement on **Universal Principles** of behavior for all of humanity that will promote peace, prosperity, and the survival for all nations.

Third, the prophetic dimension of the Bible will be investigated by studying the history of the Nation of Israel from Abraham to Jesus Christ to show how God has used His covenants with the Nation of Israel to reveal how He predetermines the events of life, how He predetermines the conditions surrounding the events of life, and how He judges humanity based on their responses to the events and conditions of life. The investigative questions will deal with the history of God's predetermined events, conditions, and judgments in the Nation of Israel to fulfill His covenants with Abraham, his descendants, and all of humanity, in the Old and New Testaments of the Bible.

Fourth, the social dimension of the Bible will be investigated by studying each of the institutions created by God: the family, human government, the Nation of Israel, and the Church. Biblical answers to the following questions will be investigated about these four institutions: How did they begin? What is their purpose for existing? What are our roles and responsibilities toward these institutions? And how can the **Universal Principles** be applied in these four institutions?

The express purposes of this book are to:

1. Find **Universal Principles** that will promote peace, prosperity, and survival for all who follow them, no matter their race, gender, nationality, sexual orientation, religious beliefs (belief in God, agnostic, or atheist), economic status, or political affiliation.
2. Utilize those **Universal Principles** to gather data that will inform you about the nature and potential causes of the problems we are facing as a nation and world, and then offer solutions based on research and input from the many voices on the internet and elsewhere.

Volume 1 – Table of Contents

The Physical (Scientific) Dimension of the Holy Bible

Chapter 1
How did we get here? (Theory of Evolution - A Modern Scientific Viewpoint).

A. A Modern Scientific Theory of Evolution

There are two primary theories about the origin of the universe. One theory is the Theory of Evolution, with the hypothesis that the universe evolved over a period of billions of years, which is the current theory promoted by most of the scientific community. The other is the theory that the universe was created a little over 6000 years ago, which is the account presented in the Bible. To get a perspective on the amount of scientific and Biblical evidence that is currently available about these two theories, both of them will be reevaluated using the scientific method described above.

SCIENTIFIC THEORY OF EVOLUTION

Hypothesis:

According to the website, http://www.spaceandmotion.com/Charles-Darwin-Theory-Evolution.htm (21), the basis for Darwin's theory of evolution are five key observations and the inferences that are drawn from them. The great biologist Ernst Mayr summarized these observations and inferences as follows:

A. "Species have great fertility and they produce more offspring than can grow to adulthood.
B. With minor fluctuations, populations of species remain roughly the same size.
C. The food resources for species are limited, but are relatively constant most of the time.
   It may be inferred from these three observations that in such an environment there will be a struggle for survival among individuals in a species.
D. Generally, no two individuals are identical in sexually reproducing species. Variation is rampant.
E. A substantial amount of this variation is hereditary.

From the above observations it may be inferred that in a world of relatively stable populations where each individual offspring must struggle to survive, those offspring with the most favorable characteristics will be more likely to survive, and those favorable characteristics will be passed on to their offspring. These more favorable characteristics will be inherited by following generations and will become dominant among the population over time. This is **natural selection**. If carried far enough, it may be further inferred that natural selection will make changes in a population, which will eventually lead to new species. According to Mayr, "These observations have been amply demonstrated in biology, and even fossils demonstrate the veracity of these observations."

Mayr summarized Darwin's Theory of Evolution as follows:

A. Variation: In every population of organisms there is Variation.
B. Competition: Organisms are in Competition for limited resources.
C. Offspring: Organisms within a population produce more Offspring than can survive.
D. Genetics: Organisms pass Favorable Genetic Characteristics on to their offspring.
F. Natural Selection: Those organisms with the Most Beneficial Characteristics are more likely to Survive and Reproduce."

According to Mayr, "Darwin imagined it might be possible that all life is descended from an original species from ancient times. DNA evidence supports this idea."

"Probably all organic beings which have ever lived on this earth have descended from some one primordial life form. There is grandeur in this view of life that, whilst this planet has gone cycling on according to the fixed law of gravity, from so simple a beginning endless forms most beautiful and most wonderful have been, and are being evolved." (**Charles Darwin**, The Origin of Species)

Experimental Tests:

Before we begin our investigation of the Theory of Evolution of the species, let's consider how many species there are in the world today. According to the website www.currentresults.com/Environment-Facts/Plants-Animals/number-species.php (11), scientists have discovered and described 1,740,330 of the world's species of animals, plants, and algae, as of 2010. Of this total of 1,740,330; 62,305 are vertebrate animals; 1,305,250 are invertebrate animals; 321,212 are plants; and 51,563 are other types of species. According to this same website, https://www.currentresults.com/Environment-Facts/Plants-Animals/estimate-of-worlds-total-number-of-species.

php (11), scientists estimate that there are an additional 5,523,300 species in the world that remain to be discovered and described, bringing the total estimated number of species that currently exist in the world to 7,263,630.

According to the website http://www.wordiq.com/definition/ Theory of evolution (03/09/2011) (36) (**Note:** this website can no longer be found on the internet in 2018), the modern Theory of Evolution of the species is based on Gregor Mendel's theory of genetics and the natural selection theory of Charles Darwin, which states that an extensive process that began over three billion years ago involving simple single-celled organisms has produced the modern species we observe today. The modern scientific community nearly universally accepts this theory of evolution by genetics and natural selection, which assumes that life on earth had a single point of origin and all subsequent life-forms are descendants of a single organism. "This is called the theory of common descent."

The article goes on the say that the modern synthesis of the Theory of Evolution brings together Gregor Mendel's theory of inherited characteristics, now called genes, and Darwin's theory of evolution by natural selection. The definition of "evolution," in the modern synthesis, is the change in the frequency of an allele within a gene pool. The cause of this change in the gene pool may come from a number of different mechanisms, such as natural selection, genetic drift, or changes in the population structure (gene flow). There are three major aspects to the modern synthesis theory: All organisms have a common descent from a single ancestor; there is an origin of novel traits or characteristics in a lineage; and there is a mechanism that causes some traits or characteristics to persist while others die out.

In our scientific analysis of the Theory of Evolution, we will look for evidence that one species can evolve over time into a totally new and different species and the scientific probability that a small number of species could evolve over time into millions of new and completely different species. The Theory of Evolution also implies that the universe and the millions of species on earth were created through random acts of nature and not by intelligent design. To conduct this scientific analysis, we will evaluate the factors and evidence that we are able to find that support the Theory of Evolution, which will be listed below.

1. <u>Microevolution.</u> Small-scale changes in gene frequencies in a population over the course of a few generations is called microevolution. These changes may be due to mutation, gene flow or migration, genetic drift, as well as natural selection (http://www.wordiq.com/definition/Theory_of_evolution (03/09/2011) (36). Microevolution is distinguished by the variation, adaptation, and recombination of existing traits and characteristics within the same species. Random occurrences which change the genome of an organism are called mutations. Mutations can significantly increase the genetic diversity of a species when advantageous mutations are favored by natural selection and disadvantageous mutations are phased out (http://www.biology-online.org/2/14_gene_pool.htm) (12).

   According to the website http://www.allaboutcreation.org/dna-evidence-for-evolution-faq.htm (16), it is very important for the Darwinian paradigm that mutations can corrupt DNA, because changes must be made to a creature's genome over time in order for an organism to eventually evolve into an entirely different organism. However, more than just change is needed for Darwinian evolution, it also needs an increase in genetic information. It does not appear, according to critics, that genetic mutation provides a mechanism for that increase in information to occur. The potential for biological change appears to have genetic limitations.

   As biophysicist Dr. Lee Spetner explains, "...Reptiles and birds are very different. Reptiles have no genetic information for wings or feathers. To change a reptile into a bird would require the addition of...complex information.... I really do not believe that the neo-Darwinian model can account for large scale evolution. What they really can't account for is the buildup of information.... And not only is it improbable on the mathematical level, that is theoretically, but experimentally one has not found a single mutation that one can point at that actually adds information. In fact, every beneficial mutation that I have seen reduces the information, it loses information."

Scientists have discovered that DNA is a nucleic acid that contains the genetic instructions used in the development and functioning of all known living organisms and some viruses. The main role of DNA molecules is the long-term storage of information, which provides the instruction (or code) to the genes in the cells which then determine the characteristics of every living organism on earth. Since the Theory of Evolution is driven by Mendel's genetic laws of inheritance and Darwin's theory of natural selection, microevolution is limited by the genetic laws of inheritance, the DNA that provides instructions to the genes in each cell of every organism, and the three principles of natural selection.

2. <u>Natural selection</u>. Natural selection is based on three principles: (1) the heritable variation within a species; (2) the parents having more offspring than can survive; and (3) the surviving offspring having favorable traits (<u>http://www.wordiq.com/ definition/Theory of evolution (03/09/2011) (36)</u>). Natural selection is a natural mechanism by which the fittest members of a species survive to pass on their genetic information, while the weakest are eliminated (die off) because they are unable to compete in the wild. Natural selection is often termed "survival of the fittest" or "elimination of the weakest." (<u>http://www. allaboutscience.org/evolution-of-man.htm) (16)</u>

The machine that drives evolution is natural selection. When an environmental change occurs, this mechanism causes those organisms that are "abnormal" to survive, making them the "new normal." According to the Theory of Evolution, this can cause an organism over time to change into a totally different form of life. There has been seen in nature some evidence of natural selection, but not to the extent that a species has been changed in a meaningful way. Every genetic mutation of an organism that has been observed by science to change its form or function has resulted in handicap or death. Since organisms that cannot adapt will usually die, it means that a natural ecosystem is vulnerable to rapid change. (http://www.allaboutscience.org/what-is-evolution-faq.htm) (16).

Microevolution and mutation are not in dispute by anybody. It is universally accepted that the hundreds of different domestic dog breeds and wolves, coyotes, dingoes, jackals, and foxes probably all came from an original pair of "dogs." These variations are not upward evolution from simplicity into complexity as supposed by Darwinian evolutionary theory, but variations within a species. These variations are constrained by the genetic code (the dogs do not grow wings and learn to fly) and the variations are always in a downward trend. Genetic information is always lost and no new genetic information is added.

The descendants of the original pair of "dogs" have lost some of their genetic potential, because the original pair of "dogs" would have had all of the potential characteristics of all of their various offspring. Many species have come from the Dog species which in turn have become isolated gene pools. All that science has ever observed is that the original pair of "dogs" would have had all of the potential traits expressed in all of their various offspring. "There is no known process by which genetic information can be added." (http://www.allaboutscience.org/what-is-evolution-faq.htm) (16).

3. Macroevolution (Speciation). The creation of two or more species from one species is called speciation. (http://www. wordiq.com/definition/Theory_of_evolution (03/09/2011) (36). When members of a species mutate to the point where they are no longer able to breed with other members of the same species, the new population becomes a reproductively isolated community that is unable to breed with its former community. The genes of the new population become isolated from the genes of the previous group through speciation. (http://www. allaboutscience.org/evolution-of-man.htm) (16). Organisms who are capable of reproducing but can't reproduce with a member of the same species are deemed another species. (http:// www.biology-online.org/2/14_gene_pool.htm) (12).

Although microevolution (variations within a species) is well documented and observed, macroevolution is not well documented and is therefore highly disputable. Macroevolution is the transition from one species of plant or animal into an entirely different species and involves large or important changes in the basic function of an organism. It can only be the result of a series of genetic mutations, which cannot happen during a single organism's life span. Laboratory observations of every genetic mutation involving form or function have either been fatal, crippling, or self-reversing. For example, the genetic deviations of some bacteria have survived antibiotics better than those without deviations, but died out quickly when the antibiotics were gone. Macroevolution, the variation from one species to another, is the evolutionists' explanation of how the millions of species on earth came into being, but it suffers from a lack of empirical evidence that this process occurs regularly in nature. (http:// www.allaboutscience.org/what-is-evolution-faq.htm) (16).

4. Junk DNA. There are segments of DNA whose functions remain a mystery. Scientists do not know what these segments of DNA do. Darwinists believe that Junk DNA are useless vestiges

from our evolutionary past and are similar to vestigial organs. Opponents of this theory point out that just because scientists do not know what Junk DNA does, does not mean that Junk DNA does not serve an important function. Considering the history of vestigial organs, back in the 19th Century there were dozens of organs which were designated "vestigial" because scientists could not figure out what they did. Those vestigial organs were interpreted as evidence of Darwin's theory, just as Junk DNA is today. According to a list of 86 vestigial organs put together by Robert Wiedersheim, one of Darwin's disciples, scientists have discovered important functions of all but a handful, which remain ambiguous at the present time. (http://www.allaboutcreation.org/dna-evidence-for-evolution-faq.htm) (16).

5. Pseudogenes. According to the website http://www.allaboutcreation.org/dna-evidence-for-evolution-faq.htm (16), scientists believe that pseudogenes are genes which have lost their function through mutation. As John Woodmorappe, a noted scientist and author, explains, "Arguments for shared evolutionary ancestry have been advanced based on the similarities in perceived disablements found in orthologous pseudogenes (counterpart pseudogenes in other primates)." Woodmorappe goes on to say however, "...A close examination shows that this presumed evidence is equivocal. Dissimilarities between the pseudogenes of presumably related organisms are at least as prominent as the similarities, and similarities in orthologous pseudogenes can arise independently of shared evolutionary ancestry."

6. There is an article on the website, http://evolutionfaq.com/articles/five -proofs-evolution (20), by Richard Peacock in which he provides five examples that he believes will support and prove the Theory of Evolution. These five examples are: (1) The universal genetic code; (2) The fossil record; (3) Genetic commonalities; (4) Common traits in embryos; and (5) Bacterial resistance to antibiotics. An analysis of these five examples will be addressed in the following paragraphs.

The universal genetic code. "All cells on Earth, from our white blood cells, to simple bacteria, to cells in the leaves of trees, are capable of reading any piece of DNA from any life form on Earth. This is very strong evidence for a common ancestor from which all life descended." (http://evolutionfaq.com/articles/five-proofs-evolution)(20).

There are at least three characteristics that distinguish living organisms from non-living matter. First, all living organisms are composed of a material known as protoplasm, which has a chemical make-up of proteins, carbohydrates, lipids, water, and nucleic acid. Second, all living organisms are organized into cells, which can range from one cell per organism to billions of cells per organism. And third, all living organisms have a mechanism to reproduce themselves through offspring, because they have a limited life span. (Winchester, A.M. (1964), *Biology and its Relation to Mankind,* Princeton, NJ: D. Van Norstrand Company, Inc. Pages 12-20).

Scientists have discovered that DNA is a nucleic acid that contains the genetic instructions used in the development and functioning of all known living organisms and some viruses. The main role of DNA molecules is the long-term storage of information, which provides the instructions (or code) to the genes in the cells which then determine the characteristics of every living organism on earth. (https://en.wikipedia.org/wiki/Hershey–Chase_experiment)(117)

The analysis of macroevolution (speciation) in Items 3 above revealed that there is no clear scientific evidence that one species can evolve into an entirely new species with a different form or function. The fossil record, as revealed in Item 7 below, does not provide any clear evidence of any transitional species. Therefore, there must be another explanation for the universal genetic code.

Scientists have discovered that all living organisms are composed of protoplasm and cells and that DNA provides instructions to the cells that determine the characteristics of every living organism. Scientists have also determined that all living organisms have genetic commonalities. Since all living organisms are composed of protoplasm and cells, and DNA provides instructions to the genes in the cells which determine the characteristics of every living organism, then DNA, not a common ancestor, must be the source of the universal genetic code.

7. The fossil record. "The fossil record shows that the simplest fossils will be found in the oldest rocks, and it can also show a smooth and gradual transition from one form of life to another." (http://evolutionfaq.com/articles/five-proofs-evolution)(20).

    According to the website, http://www.allaboutthejourney.org/fossil-record.htm (16), Darwin offered the following critique of his own theory of evolution:

    "Firstly, why, if species have descended from other species by insensibly fine gradations, do we not everywhere see innumerable transitional forms? Why is not all nature in confusion instead of the species being, as we see them, well defined? (Darwin, Origin of Species, Page 143)

    But, as by this theory, innumerable transitional forms must have existed, why do we not find them embedded in countless numbers in the crust of the earth? (Darwin, Origin of Species, Page 144)

    Lastly, looking not to any one time, but to all time, if my theory be true, numberless intermediate varieties, linking closely together all the species of the same group, must assuredly have existed. (Darwin, Origin of Species, Page 149)

Why then is not every geological formation and every stratum full of such intermediate links? Geology assuredly does not reveal any such finely graduated organic chain; and this, perhaps is the most obvious and gravest objection which can be urged against my theory. (Darwin, Origin of Species, Page 230)"

Scientists have searched for fossil evidence of past organic transitions since Darwin revealed his original theory, but none have been found. If Darwin's theory of macroevolution were true, in his own words, we should see a large number of fossils at intermediate stages of biological development. Based on standard mathematical models, there should be far more transitional forms in the fossil record than complete specimens. However, I was not able to find any substantial evidence that any true transitional fossil specimens have ever been found. (http://www.allaboutthejourney.org/fossil-record.htm)(16)

8. Genetic commonalities. "Human beings have approximately 96% of genes in common with chimpanzees, about 90% of genes in common with cats, 80% with cows, 75% with mice, and so on. This does not prove that we evolved from chimpanzees or cats, though, only that we shared a common ancestor in the past. And the amount of difference between our genomes corresponds to how long ago our genetic lines diverged." (http://evolutionfaq.com/articles/five-proofs-evolution)(20).

According to the website http://www.allaboutcreation.org/dna-evidence-for-evolution-faq.htm (16), genetic similarities between totally different species are interpreted as DNA evidence of evolution. The fact that the DNA of humans is 96% the same as the DNA of chimps is taken to mean that humans are genetically related to chimps and the two species descended from a common ancestor. Opponents of Darwin's theory point to the fact that there is genetic similarity between all living organisms, and the more similar two different species are, the more similar their DNA should be.

"The DNA of a cow and a whale, two mammals, should be more alike than the DNA of a cow and a bacterium. If it were not so, then the whole idea of DNA being the information carrier in living things would have to be questioned. Likewise, humans and apes have a lot of morphological similarities, so we would expect there would be similarities in their DNA. Of all the animals, chimps are most like humans, so we would expect that their DNA would be most like human DNA."

9. Common traits in embryos. "Humans, dogs, snakes, fish, monkeys, ells, (and many more life forms) are all considered "chordates" because we belong to the phylum *Chordata*. One of the features of this phylum is that, as embryos, all these life forms have gill slits, tails, and specific anatomical structures involving the spine. For humans (and other non-fish) the gill slits reform into the bones of the ear and jaw at a later stage in development. But, initially, all chordate embryos strongly resemble each other. In fact, pig embryos are often dissected in biology classes because of how similar they look to human embryos. These common characteristics could only be possible if all members of the phylum *Chordata* descended from a common ancestor." (http://evolutionfaq.com/articles/five-proofs-evolution)(20).

According to the website https://en.wikipedia.org/wiki/Karl Ernst von Baer (37), comparative embryology has been used by scientists to study and gather evidence of evolution. The Russian scientist, Karl Ernst von Baer, came up with four principles of comparative embryology by observing embryos of different species, which are as follows:

a. **General characteristics** of the group to which an embryo belongs develop **before special** characteristics.

b. **General structural relations** are likewise formed **before** the most **specific** appear.

c. The form of any given embryo does not converge upon other definite forms, but separates itself from them.

d. The **embryo** of a higher animal form never resembles the **adult** of another animal form, such as one less evolved, but only its embryo.

Karl Ernst von Baer inferred from these four principles and the fact that embryos from similar groups of organisms developed in a similar way toward more complex different structures was evidence that all organisms have a common ancestor.

However, the analysis of macroevolution (speciation) in Item 3 above revealed that there is no clear scientific evidence that one species can evolve into an entirely new species with a different form or function. The fossil record, as revealed in Item 7 above, does not provide any clear evidence of any transitional species. Therefore, there must be another explanation for the common traits of embryos.

Scientists have discovered that all living organisms are composed of protoplasm and cells and that DNA provides instructions to the cells that determine the characteristics of every living organism. Scientists have also determined that all living organisms have genetic commonalities. Consequently, when an embryo first begins to develop, the genetic commonalities would probably show up first in the embryo, then the functional commonalities would probably show up next, such as the internal organs, then the very specific features and characteristics related to each species would probably show up last.

10. Bacterial resistance to antibiotics. "Bacteria colonies can only build up a resistance to antibiotics through evolution. It is important to note that in every colony of bacteria, there are a tiny few individuals which are naturally resistant to certain antibiotics. This is because of the random nature of mutations. When an antibiotic is applied, the initial inoculation will kill most bacteria, leaving behind only those few cells which happen to have the mutations necessary to resist the antibiotics. In subsequent generations, the resistant bacteria reproduce, forming a new colony where every member is resistant to the antibiotic. This is natural selection in action. The antibiotic is "selecting" for organisms which are resistant, and killing any that are not." (http://evolutionfaq.com/articles/five-proofs-evolution)(20).

According to an article on the http://www.icr.org/aritcle/do-bacteria-evolve-resistence-antibiotics (17) website, to investigate the evolutionary implications of the acquired resistance of bacteria to antibiotics, we must first distinguish between microevolution (variation, adaptation, and recombination of existing traits within a species) and macroevolution (the appearance of new and different genes, body parts, and traits within a species).

We must then ask the question, does the acquired resistance of the bacteria to antibiotics, this bacterial population shift, and this dominant exhibition of a previously minority trait point toward macroevolution. Since each species of bacteria remained that same species of bacteria, and nothing new was produced, the answer is no.

The article goes on to explain that many genes are present in a given population of bacteria which express themselves in a variety of ways. The genes and traits of the bacteria are freely mixed in a natural environment. When the bacteria are exposed to an antibiotic, most of the microbes die, but some possess a resistance to the antibiotic and are able to survive through a fortuitous genetic recombination.

Over time, virtually all of the surviving bacteria will possess this resistance. As a result, this new population of bacteria has lost the ability to produce individuals with a sensitivity to the antibiotic. During this process, no new genetic information was produced. In fact, genetic information was lost. (www.icr.org/aritcle/do-bacteria-evolve-resistence-antibiotics)(17). This process involves microevolution within a species and natural selection within a species which is very evident in living organisms.

11. <u>Genetic Drift.</u> When a species is split into two or more groups that live in different environments and have no contact with one another, the groups are not able to reproduce with one another. Natural selection in each of the groups will favor them in their different environments which will favor slightly different genes in each group. The difference in the gene pool between the different groups can be very significant over time. If these groups become reunited again, gene migration occurs (see Item 12 below). If they remain **separated**, their genetic differences will become greater over time. (http://www.biology-online.org/2/14_gene_pool.htm)(12).

12. <u>Gene Migration (Gene Flow).</u> As explained above, when two or more groups are separated and are unable to reproduce with one another, *genetic drift* occurs, and their gene pool will differ over time. If the separate groups are brought together again and allowed to reproduce, all of their genetic differences will be merged together again into one group which will create more *genetic diversity* within the group. This is called gene migration or gene flow. (http://www.biology-online.org/2/14_gene_pool.htm)(12).

13. <u>Adaptive Radiation.</u> Adaptive radiation is the microevolutionary change of **genotype** (genetic constitution) and **phenotype** (physical characteristics) of a species from its common ancestor

such that the species becomes more diversified over time. Darwin's experiments with finches is a good example of adaptive radiation. As the offspring of the common ancestor of the finch relocated to different natural environments, the mechanisms of natural selection and changes in the gene pool (microevolution) caused the finches to become more adapted to their new and different environments. (http://www.biology-online.org/2/14 gene_pool.htm)(12).

14. Industrial Melanism. The existence of two or more distinctly different groups of a species that belong to the same species is called polymorphism. Alleles of these polymorphic organisms are governed by the mechanism of natural selection, and in the case of industrial melanism, the genetic differences between these groups in different environments soon become apparent over time. The species called the peppered moth is a good example of the principles involved in natural selection as far as industrial melanism is concerned.

In England during the 1800's, soot would collect on the sides of buildings from chimneys and industries to make them a darker color. The peppered moth was more visible against the sooty buildings, because it had a light color. Predators of the peppered moth could find them more easily against the dark buildings. A new strain of peppered moth came into existence, due to mutations, which was darker in color than the light-colored peppered moth. The darker peppered moth was harder to find by predators in the sooty industrial areas. Consequently, natural selection would favor the darker moths in darker polluted environments and the lighter moths in the lesser polluted areas. (http://www.biology-online.org/2/11 natural selection.htm) (12).

15. Selective Breeding. Today breeders of plants and animals are able to produce organisms that possess desirable traits, such as high growth rate, high crop yield, resistance to disease and

many other phenotypical characteristics that will benefit the organism and the species. When one member of the same species that possesses **_dominant_** alleles for particular genes, such as fast growth and high yield, is crossed with another member of the same species that possesses **_dominant_** alleles for long life and quick metabolism, it is called selective breeding. Since genes for these desirable characteristics are dominant in both members of the species, when they are crossed, they will produce at least some offspring that will show all of these desirable characteristics.

When an offspring is produced that shows all of the desirable characteristics, it is termed a **_hybrid_**, because it is produced from two genetically different parents that produce offspring with more desirable qualities. To replicate this process, breeders continuously track the characteristics possessed by each member and offspring, so that in subsequent breeding seasons, they can selectively breed the members again such that the more favorable qualities will be produced in the offspring. (http:// www.biology-online.org/2/12 selective breeding.htm)(12).

When the allele for each characteristic possesses one dominant and one recessive gene, the offspring will become **_heterozygous_**. To produce heterozygous offspring, most professional breeders will produce **_gene banks_** of specific qualities by a true breeding cross (AAbb with AAbb), which can be crossed with aaBB. This enables the dominant features to be retained in the first breeding group which can be passed on to the offspring in the second breeding group.

This process of selecting parents poses no threat to nature from humanity manipulating the course of nature and is called artificial selection or selective breeding. It has increased the efficiency of many plants and animals through breeding, such as continuously breeding selected cows to produce a hybrid with a high yield of milk. (http://www.biology-online.org/2/12 selective_breeding.htm)(12).

16. <u>In-breeding Depression.</u> The continuous in-breeding and selective breeding of particular favorable genes can cause some of the other genes in the gene pool to be lost forever, which is called in-breeding depression. The breeder may have phased out these other genes due to the breeder wanting other more desirable genes to be present in their gene pool, even though the lost genes may have been important for other important reasons.

This may cause a reduction in the genetic diversity of the gene pool, because many of the organisms acquire similar ***genomes*** as a result of constant breeding with each other. Consequently, breeders need to concentrate on producing more heterozygous offspring to ensure the long-term welfare and diversity of the species. Preserving the genetic diversity of a species and keeping the gene pool of the species as diverse as possible are the most important things to consider. (http://www.biology-online. org/2/12 selective_breeding.htm)(12).

17. <u>Genetic Engineering</u>. The website http://www.biology-online. org/2/13 genetic_engineering.htm (12) defines the process of genetic engineering as the controlling of a particular characteristic of an organism by splicing an area of a chromosome with a gene that controls that particular characteristic of the organism. The DNA sequence and gene are split from the rest of the chromosome by the enzyme endonuclease. For example, a gene may be programmed to produce an antiviral protein and then removed from one organism and placed into another organism. For example, the gene could be placed into bacteria, where it is sealed into the DNA chain using ligase (any of a class of enzymes that catalyze the linkage of two molecules). When the chromosome in the bacteria is once again sealed, the bacteria are now effectively reprogrammed to replicate this

new antiviral protein. Even though genetic engineering and human intervention have actively manipulated what the bacteria actually are, the bacteria can continue to live a healthy life.

Genetic engineering has made it possible for some experimental breakthroughs to occur in recent years, which include the following:

a. Scientists successfully cloned an exact copy of a sheep, named "Dolly," at the Roslin Institute in Scotland. This was probably the first incidence of two organisms being genetically identical and was the first successful cloning of an animal. Later the sheep's health declined and it died.

b. The genetic sequence of a rat was successfully manipulated by scientists to grow a human ear on its back. The purpose of the experiment was to reproduce human organs for medical purposes.

c. An American scientist is currently conducting controversial tests to clone himself.

Due to the complex and microscopic nature of DNA and its component nucleotides, genetic engineering has not been possible until recently. The above examples show some of the potential and controversy associated with this concept.

The article goes on to provide some advantages and disadvantages of genetic engineering:

a. Advantages:

1) People/plants/animals who are genetically prone to certain hereditary diseases could be detected and provided with early prevention measures. Also, the treating of infectious diseases can be initiated by

implanting genes that code for antiviral proteins specific to each antigen.

2) Plants and animals could be manipulated to show desirable characteristics. For example, the genes in trees could be manipulated to absorb more carbon dioxide to reduce the threat global warming.

3) Genetic diversity could be increased by producing more variant alleles which could be crossed over and implanted into another species. For example, it is possible to grow insulin by altering the genetics of wheat plants.

b. Disadvantages:

1) Due to the extremely complex inter-related natural chain consisting of many species linked to the food chain, some scientists believe that the introduction of genetically modified genes into the natural food chain may have an irreversible effect with unknown consequences.

2) There are many moral issues associated with genetic engineering, especially involving religion, which questions humanity's right to manipulate the laws that determine the course of nature.

18. <u>Age of the earth</u>. The age of the earth will have an impact on the time that scientists believe it has taken for the species to reach their current state of evolution. The primary method that scientists use for dating the earth is called Radiometric Dating, which is explained in detail on the website: <u>http://www.allaboutcreation.org/radiometric-dating.htm (16)</u>.

<u>Radiometric Dating – A Brief Explanation</u>. According to the above website, scientists have used radiometric dating as the primary dating scheme to determine the age of the earth. The techniques used in radiometric dating take advantage of the

natural decay of radioisotopes. Atoms that have the same number of protons in their nuclei but a different number of neutrons are called isotopes. Radioisotopes are unstable radioactive isotopes that decay spontaneously.

As they decay, radioisotopes go through various transitional states until they finally reach stability. For example, Uranium-238 (U238) is a radioisotope which will spontaneously decay until it transitions into Lead-206 (Pb206). The atomic mass of these isotopes is represented by the numbers 238 and 206. During the process of transitioning from Uranium-238 into Lead-206, Uranium-238 goes through 13 transitional stages (U238> Th234> Pa234> U234> Th230> Ra226> Rn222> Po218> Pb214> Bi214> Po214> Pb210> Bi210> Po210> Pb206).

In this transitional process, the Uranium-238 is called the "parent" and the Lead-206 is called the "daughter." Scientists believe they are able to determine the age of rock by measuring how long it takes for an unstable element to decay into a stable element and by measuring how much "daughter" element had been produced by the "parent" element within a specimen of rock. This scientific belief is based on three significant assumptions, which are discussed below.

Radiometric Dating – The Assumptions. Although many of the ages derived from radiometric dating are highly publicized, the fundamental assumptions employed in their derivations are not publicized. Following are the three major assumptions for your consideration:

a. The rate of decay of the isotopes remains constant over time.
b. There has been no contamination of the specimen rock (that is, no daughter or intermediate elements have been brought into or leeched from the specimen of rock).

c. One can determine how much daughter was in the specimen rock when it was formed (if one assumes there was no daughter when the rock was formed, and there was daughter at the beginning, the rock would have an incorrect appearance of age).

The fundamental question is: Are these three major assumptions reasonable? Although scientists have not been able to vary the decay rates of isotopes by very much in the laboratory, recent findings seem to indicate that decay rates may have been accelerated in the unobservable past. If these findings are valid, the first assumption that the rate of isotope decay is constant would be considered unreasonable.

(https://www.icr.org/i/pdf/technical/Young-Helium-Diffusion-Age-of-Zircons.pdf)(17)

The website https://creation.com/ (13) has many articles on radiometric dating, but a more recent article at https://creation.com/radiometric-dating-breakthroughs (13) discusses recent discoveries concerning the radiometric dating process. The recent findings concerning accelerated decay rates have been summarized by Dr. Carl Wieland, founding editor of Creation Magazine, as follows: "When uranium decays to lead, a by-product of this process is the formation of helium, a very light, inert gas which readily escapes from rock. Certain crystals called zircons, obtained from drilling into very deep granites, contain uranium which has partly decayed into lead.

By measuring the amount of uranium and 'radiogenic lead' in these crystals, one can calculate that, if the decay rate has been constant, about 1.5 billion years must have passed. (This is consistent with the geologic 'age' assigned to the granites in which these zircons are found.) There is a significant amount of helium from that '1.5 billion years of decay' still inside the zircons. This is at first glance surprising, because of the ease with which one would expect helium (with its tiny, light, unreactive atoms) to escape from the spaces within the crystal structure. There should hardly be any left, because with such a slow buildup, it should be seeping out continually and not accumulating."

"Drawing any conclusions from the above depends, of course, on actually measuring the rate at which helium leaks out of zircons. This is what one of the recent RATE (the "RATE" project stands for, "Radioisotopes and the Age of The Earth") papers reports on. The samples were sent... to a world-class expert to measure these rates. The consistent answer: the helium does indeed seep out quickly over a wide range of temperatures. In fact, the results show that because of all the helium still in the zircons, these crystals (and since this is Precambrian basement granite, by implication the whole earth) could not be older than between 4,000 and 14,000 years.

In other words, in only a few thousand years, 1.5 billion years' worth (at today's rates) of radioactive decay has taken place. Interestingly, the data has since been refined and updated to give a date of 5680 (+/- 2000) years." This entire article entitled, "Radiometric Dating Breakthroughs" by Carl Wieland is at the website: https://creation.com/radiometric-dating-breakthroughs (13).

Analysis of Results:

1. There is substantial evidence that microevolution involving Mendel's laws of heredity and Darwin's theory of natural selection has been and continues to be occurring within the species. However, there is no empirical evidence that microevolution has been able to accumulate sufficient mutations, variations, and adaptations to cause one species to transition to an entirely

new species with a different form or function. This degree of change in which two or more species evolve from one species is called speciation or macroevolution.

Although the modern synthesis Theory of Evolution includes the theory of common descent of all organisms, which would require speciation, there does not appear to be any clear empirical evidence that supports speciation or macroevolution within the species. And it appears from current evidence that <u>microevolution is limited by the genetic laws of inheritance, the DNA that provides instructions to the genes in each cell of every living organism, and the principles of natural selection.</u>

2. Junk DNA are segments of DNA whose functions remain a mystery. The proponents of Darwin's theory believe that Junk DNA are useless vestiges from our evolutionary past and are similar to vestigial organs, which point to a common ancestry for all organisms. Similarly, scientists believe that pseudogenes are genes which have lost their function through mutation and some scientists use them as an argument for shared evolutionary ancestry among organisms. There has been no clear evidence to support these theories of common ancestry, and, as mentioned above, there is no clear empirical evidence that one species can evolve into a new species with a totally different form or function.

3. Some proponents of the modern synthesis theory of common descent have noted that the universal genetic code is very strong evidence that life evolved from a common ancestor. Since the analysis of macroevolution (speciation) in Experimental Test 3 above revealed that there is no clear scientific evidence that one species can evolve into an entirely new species with a different form or function, there must be another explanation for the universal genetic code.

Scientists have discovered that all living organisms are composed of protoplasm and cells and that DNA provides instructions to the cells that determine the characteristics of every living organism. Scientists have also determined that all living organisms have genetic commonalities. Since all living organisms are composed of protoplasm and cells, and DNA provides instructions to the genes in the cells which determine the characteristics of every living organism, then DNA, not a common ancestor, must be the source of the universal genetic code.

4. When Darwin was developing his Theory of Evolution, he offered the fossil record as a source of proof of his theory. As revealed in our analysis of the fossil record in Experimental Test 7 above, Darwin expected the fossil record to show numerous transitional organisms which would reveal the intermediate links of all species in the same group. He noted that the fact that geology did not provide such linkages was perhaps "the most obvious and gravest objection which can be urged against my theory."

Scientists have searched for fossil evidence of past organic transitions since Darwin revealed his original theory, but there is no clear evidence that any have been found. If Darwin's theory of macroevolution were true, in his own words, we should see a large number of fossils at intermediate stages of biological development. Based on standard mathematical models, there should be far more transitional forms in the fossil record than complete specimens. However, according to our information resources and research, there is no clear evidence that any transitional fossil specimens have ever been found.

5. Genetic commonalities have been offered as proof that all organisms shared a common ancestor. For example, humans have about 96% of genes in common with chimpanzees, 90%

of genes in common with cats, 80% in common with cows, 75% in common with mice, and so on. Opponents of Darwin's theory point to the fact that there is genetic similarity between all living organisms, and the more similar two different species are, the more similar their DNA should be. If it were not so, then the whole idea of DNA being the information carrier in living things would have to be questioned.

6. The common traits in embryos has been offered as proof that all organisms have evolved from a common ancestor. The Russian scientist, Karl Ernst von Baer, developed four principles of comparative embryology:

   a. **General characteristics** of the group to which an embryo belongs develop **before special** characteristics.
   b. **General structural relations** are likewise formed **before** the most **specific** appear.
   c. The form of any given embryo does not converge upon other definite forms, but separates itself from them.
   d. The **embryo** of a higher animal form never resembles the **adult** of another animal form, such as one less evolved, but only its embryo.

Since the analysis of macroevolution (speciation) in Experimental Test 3 above revealed that there is no clear scientific evidence that one species can evolve into an entirely new species with a different form or function, there must be another explanation for the common traits in embryos.

Scientists have discovered that all living organisms are composed of protoplasm and cells and that DNA provides instructions to the cells that determine the characteristics of every living organism. Scientists have also determined that all living organisms have genetic commonalities. Therefore, based on von Baer's four principles, when an embryo first begins to develop, the genetic commonalities would probably show up first in the embryos causing them to have a similar appearance, then the functional commonalities would probably show up next, such as the internal organs, then the very specific features and characteristics related to each species would probably show up last.

7. Bacterial resistance to antibiotics is an example of evolution because the colonies of bacteria can only build up a resistance to antibiotics through evolution. This is clear evidence of evolution, but it is microevolution within each species of bacteria, because when each species of bacteria is exposed to antibiotics, each species of bacteria remained that same species of bacteria, and nothing new is produced.

When the bacteria are exposed to the antibiotic, most of the microbes die, but some possess a resistance to the antibiotic and are able to survive through a fortuitous genetic recombination. Over time, virtually all of the surviving bacteria will possess this resistance. As a result, this new population of bacteria has lost the ability to produce individuals with a sensitivity to the antibiotic. During this process, no new genetic information was produced. In fact, genetic information was lost. This is classic microevolution within each species of bacteria.

8. As stated above, there is substantial evidence that microevolution involving Mendel's laws of heredity and Darwin's theory of natural selection is occurring within the species. Following are examples of how microevolution has been impacting the species in the past and how it continues to impact the species as humanity gets more involved in the process:

   a. Genetic Drift. When a species is split into two or more groups that live in different environments and have no contact with one another, the groups are not able to reproduce with one another. Natural selection in each of the groups will favor them in their different environments which will favor slightly different genes in each group. The difference in the gene pool between the different groups can be very significant over time.

b. <u>Gene Migration (Gene Flow).</u> As explained above, when two or more groups are separated and are unable to reproduce with one another, *genetic drift* occurs, and their gene pool will differ over time. If the separate groups are brought together again and allowed to reproduce, all of their genetic differences will be merged together again into one group which will create more *genetic diversity* within the combined group.

c. <u>Adaptive Radiation.</u> Adaptive radiation is the microevolutionary change of ***genotype*** (genetic constitution) and ***phenotype*** (physical characteristics) of a species from its common ancestor such that the species becomes more diversified over time. Darwin's experiments with finches is a good example of adaptive radiation.

d. <u>Industrial Melanism.</u> The existence of two or more distinctly different groups of a species that belong to the same species is called polymorphism. Alleles of these polymorphic organisms are governed by the mechanism of natural selection, and in the case of industrial melanism, the genetic differences between these groups in different environments soon become apparent over time. Certain groups within a species can gain a survival advantage over other groups within the species due to a specific inherited or natural characteristic such as color, size, or location.

e. <u>Selective Breeding.</u> Because of their knowledge of hereditary laws, humanity is able to produce plants and animals that possess desirable traits, such as high growth rate, high crop yield, resistance to disease and many other phenotypical characteristics that will benefit the organism and the species. When one member of the same species that possesses ***dominant*** alleles for particular genes, such as fast growth and high yield, is crossed with another member of the same species that possesses **_dominant_** alleles for long life and quick metabolism, it is called selective breeding.

Since genes for these desirable characteristics are dominant in both members of the species, when they are crossed, they will produce at least some offspring that will show all of these desirable characteristics. When an offspring is produced that shows all of the desirable characteristics, it is termed a **_hybrid_**, because it is produced from two genetically different parents that produce offspring with more desirable qualities.

f. <u>In-breeding Depression.</u> The continuous in-breeding and selective breeding of particular favorable genes can cause some of the other genes in the gene pool to be lost forever, which is called in-breeding depression. The breeder may have phased out these other genes due to the breeder wanting other more desirable genes to be present in their gene pool, even though the lost genes may have been important for other important reasons. This may cause a reduction in the genetic diversity of the gene pool, because many of the organisms acquire similar **_genomes_** as a result of constant breeding with each other.

One of the interesting aspects of microevolution, if one believes the Biblical record of the Great Flood, is that it reflects the evolutionary changes that have occurred in the populations of the world as a result of their descendancy from the eight survivors of the Flood: Noah, his three sons, and their wives. This is also true of the other animals that went into the ark. It should be noted that the dinosaurs would have been too large to fit into the ark and would have been destroyed by the Flood, but one or more of their closely related species might have been small enough to fit into the ark.

9. Genetic engineering is the new frontier in the modern evolutionary process. Breakthroughs in the science of genetics now make it possible for humanity to control a particular characteristic of an organism by splicing an area of a chromosome with a gene that controls that particular characteristic of the organism. The DNA sequence and gene are split from the rest of the chromosome by the enzyme endonuclease.

This new technology has many possibilities for improvements to medical science and the environment, but it also has the possibility to do damage to our ecosystem with unknown and irreversible consequences. There are also many moral issues, especially involving religion, which questions humanity's right to manipulate the laws that determine the course of nature.

10. The primary method that scientists use for dating the earth is called radiometric dating, and based on this dating process, they have estimated that the earth is 4.6 billion years old. The techniques used in radiometric dating take advantage of the natural decay of radioisotopes. Atoms that have the same number of protons in their nuclei but a different number of neutrons are called isotopes. Radioisotopes are unstable radioactive isotopes that decay spontaneously. As they decay, they go through various transitional states until they finally reach stability.

Although many of the ages derived from radiometric dating are highly publicized, the fundamental assumptions concerning the decay rates employed in their derivations are not highly publicized and cannot be tested for accuracy. Although scientists have not been able to vary the decay rates of isotopes by very much in the laboratory, recent findings seem to indicate that decay rates of the isotopes have not been constant over time. An article at the website: https://creation.com/radiometric-dating-breakthroughs (13), entitled "Radiometric dating breakthroughs, describes a recent experiment that estimates the age of the earth to be 5680 (+/- 2000) years old.

Conclusion:

A. There is substantial evidence that microevolution involving Mendel's laws of heredity and Darwin's theory of natural selection has been and continues to be occurring within the species. However, there is no empirical evidence that microevolution has been able to accumulate sufficient mutations, variations, and adaptations to cause one species to transition to an entirely new species with a different form or function such that speciation or macroevolution occurs.

B. None of the species could have existed or evolved before the existence of DNA, because DNA contains the assembly instructions for every living organism on earth. Therefore, DNA must have existed before any species could utilize the laws of heredity to produce offspring that could exercise natural selection.

C. The degree to which a species has been able to adapt to the structural changes to their environment has been controlled by the DNA of that species, and the amount of time that has been available for that adaptation to occur.

D. The evolution of the species has occurred since the beginning of creation, but has always been controlled by and limited by the DNA within each species, which enabled some species to adapt to changes in the environment, while others became extinct.

E. There is no conclusive evidence that the earth has been in existence beyond the timelines presented in the Biblical record of creation.

From this analysis of the Theory of Evolution it may be inferred that:

1. There does not appear to be any clear empirical evidence from DNA experimentation, observation, analysis of fossil records

or any other source that supports the theory that one species can evolve into a new and entirely different species through speciation or macroevolution or that all organisms came from a common ancestor. Therefore, all species must have existed from the beginning of creation.

2. None of the species could have existed or evolved before the existence of DNA, because DNA contains the assembly instructions for every living organism on earth. Therefore, DNA must have existed before any species could utilize the laws of heredity to produce offspring that could exercise natural selection.

3. If DNA and the species have existed from the beginning of creation, then DNA and the species must have been the result of **Intelligent Design**.

4. It appears that the universe is operating like a perpetual motion machine, because the laws of nature and the relationships between the earth, sun, moon, and stars can be measured by mathematical equations, calendars, and clocks which show very little if any change in these relationships over time. The laws of thermodynamics dictate that in a **closed system**, energy and matter can neither be created nor destroyed and that as **usable** energy is consumed by the **closed system**, the quantity of **unusable** energy will increase and the quality of matter and energy within the **closed system** will deteriorate over time.

Since the quality of matter and energy in the universe do not appear to be deteriorating over time (days, weeks, months, years, and seasons have remained consistent over time), then the universe must be an **open system**. If the universe is an **open system**, then matter and/or energy must be supplied to the universe from an **outside source** to keep it from deteriorating over time. If the universe is being supplied with matter and/or energy from an **outside source,** then the continued existence of the universe must be the result of a **Creator** or **Intelligent Designer** of the universe.

5. According to the laws of thermodynamics, even if the earth were 4.6 billion years old and one species were able to evolve by macroevolution into over 7.2 million different species, then there would have to have been some force (**Intelligent Designer**) in the universe to have caused our solar system to exist and function for 4.6 billion years in a manner that would have allowed that macroevolution of the species to occur.

B. How has Darwin's Theory of Evolution Influenced Social, Political and Economic Issues?

What is Social Darwinism?

According to the website, (http://www.allaboutscience.org/what-is-social-darwinism-faq.htm)(16), the idea of Social Darwinism was first promoted by Herbert Spencer, a 19th century philosopher. Social Darwinism is defined as the application of the theory of natural selection to social, political, and economic issues. In its simplest form, it follows the mantra of "let the strong survive," when applied to human issues. Social Darwinism was used to promote the idea that the white European race was superior to other races, and therefore, was destined to rule over all the other races.

The technology, economy, and government of the "White European" was advanced in comparison to that of other cultures at the time that Spencer began to promote Social Darwinism. Because at this apparent advantage in economic and military structures, some argued that natural selection was happening, and the race more suited to survival was winning. Some even extended this philosophy to social welfare programs that helped the poor and disadvantaged; claiming that these programs were contrary to nature itself. Some people use arguments rooted in Social Darwinism to reject any and all forms of charity or governmental welfare.

Social Darwinism, at its worst, was used as scientific justification for the Holocaust during World War II. The claim of the Nazis was that the murder of the Jews was an example of cleaning out inferior genetics. The evolutionary echoes in Hitler's march to exterminate an entire race of people has been noted by many philosophers. The cause of Social Darwinism has been claimed by various other dictators and criminals in carrying out their acts of extermination. Even without these actions, the philosophy of Social Darwinism has been proven to be false and dangerous.

Scientists and evolutionists maintain that Social Darwinism is only loosely based on Darwin's theory of natural selection. However, they will admit to an obvious parallel between Spencer's beliefs and Darwin's theory of natural selection. In nature, the strong survive and those best equipped for survival will live longer than the weak. According to Social Darwinism, those with economic, physical, and technological power will flourish and those without these qualities are destined for extinction.

It is important to note that no credible evolutionists have subscribed to the theories of Social Darwinism, and Darwin did not extend his theories to a social or economic level. The philosophy of Herbert Spencer is only loosely based on the premises of Darwin's work.

However, according to evolutionary theory, nature is a "survival of the fittest" system, which poses some nagging questions: If evolution, through chance, has been responsible for life as we now know it, why should we counter that process? If "survival of the fittest" cannot be applied in what we define as "decent society," then, which is wrong, society or evolution? If neither, then how can we explain morality, charity, and compassion? Why divert resources from the strong to support the weak?

By the time this analysis of the Holy Bible has been completed, we expect to have answers to these questions.

Logical Conclusions: From this historical review of Social Darwinism it may be inferred that:

1. Some countries in the world may believe that because they have social, economic, and political advantages over other countries, they have the natural right to subjugate and rule over other countries by any means necessary.

2. Some organizations within a country may believe that because they have social, economic, and political advantages over other organizations or people, they have the natural right to subjugate and take over or control other organizations or people by any means necessary.

3. Some individuals within organizations may believe that because they have social, economic, and political advantages over other individuals in the organization, they have the natural right to subjugate and rule over other individuals by any means necessary.

4. Some countries, organizations, and individuals may believe that because they have social, economic, and political advantages over others, there is no logical reason for them to help others to succeed, since that would create potential competition for them.

5. Social Darwinism, at its worst, does not appear to consider the need for human beings to be considerate of or responsible for other human beings outside of their own particular family or interest group.

6. In this analysis of the Holy Bible, we will search for Universal Principles that will promote peace, prosperity, and survival for all who follow them, no matter their race, gender, nationality, sexual orientation, religious beliefs (belief in God, agnostic, or atheist), economic status, or political affiliation.

CHAPTER 2
How did we get here? (Theory of Creation — Modern Scientific Viewpoint)

Shortly after I completed a major portion of the research and scientific analysis for the updated Theory of Evolution in early 2010, I began the process of collecting background research data from the Internet and elsewhere concerning a scientific theory of creation, as it relates to the Biblical account of creation. On August 7, 2010, the basic framework for the following hypothesis concerning a modern scientific theory of creation was revealed to me in a dream. Over the next five years I refined this hypothesis and developed the following Scientific Theory of Creation.

MODERN SCIENTIFIC THEORY OF CREATION

Hypothesis:

A. The universe was created during a finite period of time and the earth has remained the same since its creation, except for natural occurrences that are a part of the essential make-up of the universe, some predictable and some unpredictable.

B. All matter, energy and the species on earth are a part of the universe and all matter, energy and the species have been designed with a unique mechanism for their continual survival in the universe, except their survival is dependent upon the predictable and unpredictable occurrences that are a natural or man-made part of the universe.

C. Consequently, the only structural changes that can occur to matter, energy and the species must be the result of their inability to survive the predictable and unpredictable natural or man-made occurrences in the universe, which may cause: (1) the combination or transformation of matter and energy and (2) the adaptation or extinction of the species.

Experimental Tests:

Hypothesis A, B and C (1), the combination or transformation of matter and energy, are supported by the following discoveries and evidence:

1. Albert Einstein's Theory of General Relativity (1915). Einstein summarized his Theory of General Relativity in one sentence: time and space and gravitation have no separate existence from matter, which later led to his theory that the universe is expanding. Einstein summarized his theory of general relativity by the formula: Energy equals mass times the square of the speed of light.

    According to a Public Broadcasting Service (PBS) TV program about Einstein's Theory of Relativity, Einstein's theory describes how space and time tell matter and energy where to go, and matter and energy tell space and time how to look. Einstein's theory was proven by photographs of a solar eclipse which allowed for the precise measurement of the relationships between the sun, moon, and stars, which were predicted by his mathematical equations. (https://en.wikipedia.org/wiki/General_relativity)(118)

    Note: If the movements of galactic bodies within the universe can be measured and predicted by mathematical equations, then the relationships between the suns, planets, moons, and stars within each galaxy must be perpetual motion machines which exhibit some of the same properties as atoms and molecules in the micro environment. If the universe is a perpetual motion machine, how did it get started and why is it not slowing down?

2. Georges LeMaitre's Big Bang Theory which is based on Einstein's Theory of General Relativity (1927). LeMaitre reasoned that if the universe is expanding, it must be the result of an explosion that took place sometime in the past. And if we knew the rate of expansion of the universe, we could estimate when the explosion occurred. He also theorized that there should be some form of background radiation in the universe as a result of the explosion. (https://en.wikipedia.org/wiki/Big_Bang)(119)

Note: This supports the Biblical account that the universe was created at a specific point in time in the past. Even though the universe as a whole might be expanding, our galaxy, the Milky Way, is not expanding, because if it were expanding, Einstein's mathematical equations concerning mass, energy, light and the movements of the heavenly bodies would not be accurate. If the movements of the suns, planets, moons, and stars within our galaxy are not expanding relative to each other, then the expansion that is occurring in the universe must be occurring between the galaxies.

It is also possible that the same natural laws that govern the micro-universe also govern the macro-universe. Just as some molecules in the micro-universe are very stable and others are very unstable, some of the galaxies in the macro-universe may be very stable while others are very unstable. And the Milky Way must be one of the most stable of the galaxies. Consequently, the expansion of the universe must be measured by the expansion of the distance between galaxies rather than expansion within galaxies, which might drastically impact the estimate of when the original explosion occurred (approximately 6044 years from 2018 versus 4.6 billion years).

3. The discovery of cosmic microwave radiation (1965). Arno Penzias and Robert Wilson, employees at Bell Labs, discovered cosmic microwave radiation in the universe in 1965, which supported the Big Bang Theory that the universe was created as the result of an explosion. (https://en.wikipedia.org/wiki/Cosmic_microwave_background)(120)

4. More recent analysis of the Big Bang Theory (1988). Steven Weinberg, winner of the 1979 Nobel Prize for physics, in his book The *First Three Minutes* (New York: Basic Books, 1988), further expands on the Big Bang Theory of the universe. He provides additional evidence that supports the theory that the universe was initially created in a very short period of time by a giant explosion. He also appears to support the theory that our galaxy is 10 to 15 billion years old, based on the rate of decay of various radioactive isotopes such as uranium U-235 and U-238.

Note: The estimate of the age of the universe assumes that the rate of decay of radioactive isotopes is constant and other elemental measurements of test samples are accurate, which has not been proven scientifically. Therefore, it is entirely possible that the rate of radioactive decay can be altered by natural laws and occurrences related to the chemistry of sub-atomic particles which have not yet been discovered, which might be the result of the Principle of Le Chatelier listed below or some other law of nature.

Consequently, science has no clear advantage over the biblical account when it comes to the chronological age of the universe. It is possible that the continued practical study of sub-atomic particles (quantum physics), which includes electrons, positrons, neutrinos, photons, muons, and mesons, may lead to the discovery of and the control of the forces that produce radioactive emissions and radioactive decay. This discovery would make it possible for atomic energy to be as safe to use and control as electricity. The website, https://www.creation.com/radiometric-dating-breakthroughs (13), has found evidence that radioactive decay rates are not constant and do not accurately measure the age of the earth.

5. The First Law of Thermodynamics: Neither matter nor energy can be created or destroyed. The amount of energy in the universe is constant, but energy can be changed, moved, controlled, stored, or dissipated. However, energy cannot be created from nothing or reduced to nothing. (http://www.allaboutscience.org/first-law-of-thermodynamics-faq.htm)(16)

6. The Second Law of Thermodynamics: While quantity remains the same (First Law), the quality of matter/energy deteriorates gradually over time. As usable energy decreases and unusable energy increases, entropy (disorder and randomness) increases. (http://www.allaboutscience.org/second-law-of-thermodynamics.htm)(16)

7. The Third Law of Thermodynamics: While quantity remains the same (First Law), as temperature approaches absolute zero, the entropy (disorder and randomness) of a system approaches a constant minimum (for pure perfect crystals, this constant is zero). (http://www.allaboutscience.org/third-law-of-thermodynamics-faq.htm)(16)

8. The Zeroth Law of Thermodynamics: If two thermodynamic systems are each in thermal equilibrium with a third, then they are in thermal equilibrium with each other. (http://physicsforidiots.com/physics/thermodynamics/)(15)

9. The Law of Conservation of Matter: There is no increase or decrease in the quantity of matter during a chemical change. (Nebergall, William H. & Frederic Schmidt (1957), *College Chemistry*, Boston: D.C. Heath & Company, Page 5)

10. Raoult's Law of Vapor Pressure: The lowering of the vapor pressure of a solvent is directly proportional to the weight of the solute which is dissolved in a definite weight of the solvent. (Nebergall, William H. & Frederic Schmidt (1957), *College Chemistry*, Boston: D.C. Heath & Company, Page 163)

11. Principle of Le Chatelier: If a stress, such as a change in concentration, pressure, or temperature, is applied to a system in equilibrium, the

equilibrium is shifted in a way that tends to undo the effect of the stress. (Nebergall, William H. & Frederic Schmidt (1957), *College Chemistry*, Boston: D.C. Heath & Company, Page 230)

12. <u>Newton's Laws of Motion:</u> First Law –A body continues in its state of rest or uniform motion unless an unbalanced force acts on it; Second Law – The acceleration of a body is directly proportional to the force exerted on the body, is inversely proportional to the mass of the body, and is in the same direction as the force; Third Law – Whenever one body exerts a force upon a second body, the second exerts an equal and opposite force upon the first (for every action there is an equal and opposite reaction). (Metcalfe, John Williams & Charles Dull (1960), *Modern Physics*, New York: Henry Holt & Company, Pages 81-88)

13. <u>The Law of Universal Gravitation:</u> Every body in the universe attracts every other body with a force that is directly proportional to the product of their masses and inversely proportional to the square of the distance between their centers. (Metcalfe, John Williams & Charles Dull (1960), *Modern Physics*, New York: Henry Holt & Company, Page 91)

14. <u>Avogadro's Law of Gases:</u> Equal volumes of all gases, measured under the same conditions of temperature and pressure, contain the same number of molecules. (Nebergall, William H. & Frederic Schmidt (1957), *College Chemistry*, Boston: D.C. Heath & Company, Page 119)

15. <u>Dalton's Law of Gases:</u> The total pressure of a mixture of gases is equal to the sum of the partial pressures of the component gases. (Nebergall, William H. & Frederic Schmidt (1957), *College Chemistry*, Boston: D.C. Heath & Company, Page 97)

16. <u>Graham's Law of Gases:</u> The rates of diffusion of gases are inversely proportional to the square roots of their densities (or molecular weights). (Nebergall, William H. & Frederic Schmidt (1957), *College Chemistry*, Boston: D.C. Heath & Company, Page 99)

17. <u>Boyle's Law of Gases:</u> The volume of a dry gas varies inversely with the pressure exerted on it, provided the temperature remains

constant. (Metcalfe, John Williams & Charles Dull (1960), *Modern Physics*, New York: Henry Holt & Company, Page 207)

18. <u>Henry's Law of Gases:</u> The weight of a gas that dissolves in a definite volume of liquid is directly proportional to the pressure at which the gas is supplied to the liquid. (Nebergall, William H. & Frederic Schmidt (1957), *College Chemistry*, Boston: D.C. Heath & Company, Page 149)

19. <u>Charles' Law of Gases:</u> The volume of a given mass of gas is directly proportional to its temperature on the Kelvin scale when the pressure is held constant. (Nebergall, William H. & Frederic Schmidt (1957), *College Chemistry*, Boston: D.C. Heath & Company, Page 96)

20. <u>Law of Chemical Equilibrium:</u> When a reversible reaction has attained equilibrium at a given temperature, the product of the molar concentrations of the substances to the right of the equation, divided by the product of the molar concentrations of the substances to the left, each concentration raised to the power equal to the number of molecules of each substance appearing in the equation, is constant. (Nebergall, William H. & Frederic Schmidt (1957), *College Chemistry*, Boston: D.C. Heath & Company, Page 228)

21. <u>Gay-Lussac's Law of Combining Volumes of Gases:</u> The volumes of gases involved in a reaction can be expressed as a ratio of small whole numbers. (Nebergall, William H. & Frederic Schmidt (1957), *College Chemistry*, Boston: D.C. Heath & Company, Page 118)

22. <u>Law of Definite Proportions:</u> Different samples of a pure compound always contain the same elements in the same proportions by weight. (Nebergall, William H. & Frederic Schmidt (1957), *College Chemistry*, Boston: D.C. Heath & Company, Pages 24-25)

23. <u>Law of Multiple Proportions:</u> When two elements, A and B, form more than one compound by combining with each other, the weights of element B which combine with a given weight of element A, stand in a ratio which can be expressed by small whole numbers. (Nebergall, William H. & Frederic Schmidt (1957), *College Chemistry*, Boston: D.C. Heath & Company, Page 145)

24. <u>Law of Mass Action:</u> The rate of a reaction is directly proportional to the concentration of each of the reacting substances. (Nebergall,

William H. & Frederic Schmidt (1957), *College Chemistry*, Boston: D.C. Heath & Company, Page 225)

25. van't Hoff's Law of Equilibrium: When the temperature of a system in equilibrium is raised, the equilibrium is displaced in such a way that heat is absorbed. (Nebergall, William H. & Frederic Schmidt (1957), *College Chemistry*, Boston: D.C. Heath & Company, Page 231)

26. Dulong and Petit's Law of Solid Elements: The product of the specific heats and atomic weights of solid elements is very nearly a constant, approximately 6.4. (Nebergall, William H. & Frederic Schmidt (1957), *College Chemistry*, Boston: D.C. Heath & Company, Page 124)

27. Periodic Law: The properties of the elements are periodic functions of the atomic numbers. (Nebergall, William H. & Frederic Schmidt (1957), *College Chemistry*, Boston: D.C. Heath & Company, Page 207)

28. First Law of Electrostatics: Like charges repel and unlike charges attract. (Metcalfe, John Williams & Charles Dull (1960), *Modern Physics*, New York: Henry Holt & Company, Page 388)

29. Coulomb's Law of Electrostatics: The force between two point charges is directly proportional to the product of their magnitudes and inversely proportional to the square of the distances between them. (Metcalfe, John Williams & Charles Dull (1960), *Modern Physics*, New York: Henry Holt & Company, Page 390)

30. Coulomb's Law of Magnetism: The force between two magnetic poles is directly proportional to the strengths of the poles and inversely proportional to the square of their distance apart. (Metcalfe, John Williams & Charles Dull (1960), *Modern Physics*, New York: Henry Holt & Company, Page 467)

31. Faraday's Laws of Electrolysis: First Law – The mass of an element deposited during electrolysis is proportional to the quantity of charge that passes; Second Law – The mass of an element deposited during electrolysis is proportional to the chemical equivalent of the element. (Metcalfe, John Williams & Charles Dull (1960), *Modern Physics*, New York: Henry Holt & Company, Pages 456-458)

32. Hooke's Law of Elasticity: Within the limits of perfect elasticity, strain is directly proportional to stress. (Metcalfe, John Williams & Charles Dull (1960), *Modern Physics*, New York: Henry Holt & Company, Page 180)

33. Joule's Law of Conductivity: The heat developed in a conductor is directly proportional to the resistance of the conductor, the square of the current, and the time the current is maintained. (Metcalfe, John Williams & Charles Dull (1960), *Modern Physics*, New York: Henry Holt & Company, Page 446)

34. Lenz's Law of Induced Currents: An induced current is in such direction that its magnetic effect opposes the change by which the current is induced. (Metcalfe, John Williams & Charles Dull (1960), *Modern Physics*, New York: Henry Holt & Company, Page 492)

35. Ohm's Law of Resistance: The ratio of the emf applied to a closed circuit to the current in the circuit is a constant, which is the resistance of the circuit. (Metcalfe, John Williams & Charles Dull (1960), *Modern Physics*, New York: Henry Holt & Company, Page 457)

36. Index of Refraction: The ratio of the speed of light in a vacuum to its speed in another substance is called the Index of Refraction for that substance. (Metcalfe, John Williams & Charles Dull (1960), *Modern Physics*, New York: Henry Holt & Company, Page 335)

37. Snell's Laws of Refraction: First Law – The incident ray, the refracted ray, and the normal to the surface at the point of incidence are all in the same plane; Second Law – The index of refraction for any two media is a constant that is independent of the angle of incidence; Third Law – When a ray of light passes obliquely from a medium of lesser to one of greater optical density, it is bent toward the normal. Conversely, a ray of light passing obliquely from an optically denser medium to a rarer medium is bent from the normal to the surface. (Metcalfe, John Williams & Charles Dull (1960), *Modern Physics*, New York: Henry Holt & Company, Page 336)

38. Laws of Reflection: First Law – The incident ray, the reflected ray, and the normal to the reflecting surface lie in the same plane; Second Law – The angle of incidence is equal to the angle of reflection.

(Metcalfe, John Williams & Charles Dull (1960), *Modern Physics*, New York: Henry Holt & Company, Page 318)

39. Law of Diameters: The frequency of a string is inversely proportional to its diameter, if its length, density, and tension are constant. (Metcalfe, John Williams & Charles Dull (1960), *Modern Physics*, New York: Henry Holt & Company, Page 292)

40. Law of Lengths. The frequency of a string is inversely proportional to its length, if its diameter, density, and tension are constant. (Metcalfe, John Williams & Charles Dull (1960), *Modern Physics*, New York: Henry Holt & Company, Page 291)

41. Law of Tensions: The frequency of a string is directly proportional to the square root of the tension on the string, if all the other factors are constant. (Metcalfe, John Williams & Charles Dull (1960), *Modern Physics*, New York: Henry Holt & Company, Page 292)

42. Law of Densities: The frequency of a string is inversely proportional to the square root of its density, if other factors are constant. (Metcalfe, John Williams & Charles Dull (1960), *Modern Physics*, New York: Henry Holt & Company, Page 292)

43. Law of Heat Exchange: The heat given off by hot objects equals the heat received by cold objects. (Metcalfe, John Williams & Charles Dull (1960), *Modern Physics*, New York: Henry Holt & Company, Page 236)

44. Kepler's Laws of Planetary Motion: First Law – The orbit of a planet is an ellipse with the sun at one of the two foci; Second Law – A line segment joining a planet and the sun sweeps out equal areas during equal intervals of time; Third Law – The square of the orbital period of a planet is proportional to the cube of the semi-major axis of its orbit. (https://www.physicsclassroom.com/class/circles/Lesson-4/Kepler-s-Three-Laws)(121)

45. Mendel's Laws of Inheritance: First Law – The Law of Segregation: Each inherited trait is defined by a gene pair. Parental genes are randomly separated to the sex cells so that sex cells contain only one gene of the pair. Offspring therefore inherit one generic allele (member of a pair or series of genes) from each parent when sex cells unite in fertilization; Second Law – The Law of Independent

Assortment: Genes for different traits are sorted separately from one another so that the inheritance of one trait is not dependent on the inheritance of another; Third Law – The Law of Dominance: An organism with alternate forms of a gene will express the form that is dominant. (http://www.dnaftb.org/1/bio.html)(14)

46. Quantum Theory: Quantum theory is the theoretical basis of modern physics that explains the nature and behavior of matter and energy at the atomic and subatomic levels. The nature and behavior of matter and energy at these levels is sometimes referred to as quantum physics and quantum mechanics. (http://whatis. techtarget.com/definition/quantum-theory)(18)

47. Seeking of Answers to Metaphysical Questions: Metaphysical questions posed by philosophers like Socrates, Plato, and Aristotle, who lived centuries before most of the natural laws were discovered, may be answered by the natural laws and the principles revealed by this scientific analysis of the Holy Bible. The website: https:// en.wikipedia.org/wiki/Metaphysics (122) defines metaphysics as the traditional branch of philosophy that deals with the explanation of the fundamental nature of being and the world that encompasses it.

Traditional metaphysics tries to answer two basic questions in the broadest possible terms: (1) ultimately, what is *there*? And (2) what *is it like*? The people who study metaphysics are called *metaphysicians*. The metaphysician tries, among other things, to clarify the fundamental notions by which people understand the world, such as existence, objects and their properties, space and time, cause and effect, and possibility. The central questions addressed by metaphysics are as follows:

a. Cosmology and cosmogony. Metaphysical cosmology is concerned with the world as the totality of all phenomena in space and time. Cosmogony is specifically concerned with the origin of the universe. Both attempt to answer questions such as: What is the origin of the universe? What is its first cause? Is its existence necessary? What are the ultimate material components of the universe? What is the ultimate reason for the existence of the universe?"

b. <u>Being and ontology</u>. Ontology is concerned with determining whether *categories of being* are fundamental and in what sense the items in those categories may be said to "be" or exist. It is the investigation of being *in so much as* it is being ("being *qua* being"), or of beings insofar as they exist – and not insofar as (for instance) particular facts that may be obtained about beings or particular properties that belong to beings.

c. <u>Determinism and free will</u>. Determinism is the philosophical proposition that every event is causally determined by an unbroken chain of prior occurrences, including human knowledge, decision-making and actions. It asserts that nothing happens that has not already been determined. The principal claim of determinism is that it poses a challenge to the existence of free will.

d. <u>Identity and change</u>. Identity is the relationship that a "thing" bears to itself, and which no "thing" bears to anything other than itself. Will a change to a property of a "thing" change its identity? If a person were to look at a tree one day, and the tree later lost a leaf, it would appear that the person would still be looking at the same tree after the loss of the leaf. Two theories that account for the relationship between identity and change are Perdurantism, which portrays the tree as a series of tree-stages, and Endurantism, which maintains the same tree at every stage of its history.

e. <u>Mind and matter</u>. As science has progressed in its mechanistic understanding of the brain and body, the nature of the mind and its relation to the body has been seen as more of a problem. Three proposed solutions include: (1) substance dualism with the mind having some of the attributes traditionally assigned to the soul, where mind and body are essentially different; (2) the monistic theory of idealism, which proposes that there is a single universal substance or principle; and (3) neutral monism which claims that existence consists of a single substance that is capable of mental and physical aspects or attributes – which implies a dual-aspect theory.

f. Necessity and possibility. This area involves investigations by metaphysicians of questions about the ways the world could have been. A view called Concrete Modal realism is when facts about how things could have been are made true by other concrete worlds, just as in ours, in which things are different. The idea of necessity is that any necessary fact is true across all possible worlds. A possible fact is true in some possible world, even if not in the actual world.

g. Religion and spirituality. Some of the primary metaphysical questions concerning religious philosophy are: (1) whether there is one God (monotheism), many gods (polytheism), no gods (atheism), or whether it is unknown or unknowable if any gods exist (agnosticism); (2) whether a divine entity directly intervenes in the world (theism) or whether the divine entity's sole function is to be the first cause of the universe (deism); and (3) whether a god or gods and the world are different (as in panentheism and dualism) or are identical (as in pantheism).

48. The predictable occurrences in the universe, which include the rotation of the earth around its axis to create days; the rotation of the moon around the earth to create months; and the rotation of the earth around the sun to create the seasons of the year. These predictable movements of the earth, moon, stars and other cosmic bodies are so precisely ordered that they can be considered perpetual motion machines, which mankind is unable to duplicate on earth and the existing laws of nature cannot totally define.

They are so accurately timed that humanity is unable to develop a clock or calendar that is accurate enough to totally measure their relative movements. They are so predictable that humanity has for centuries used their relative movements to regulate their lives, and recently to launch modern space vehicles to the moon and other planets.

The galaxies that make up the universe are so vast and numerous that they exceed man's imagination. The invisible matter that makes up the elements that exist on earth are so small and precisely ordered that man is still trying to discover the smallest particles of matter (quantum physics). Most of the predictable occurrences in the universe can be described by mathematical equations as demonstrated by the natural laws listed above, which are contrary to a random evolutionary process.

49. The unpredictable occurrences in the universe, which include weather, earthquakes, volcanoes, and viruses, etc. Humanity can only react to and/or adapt to the unpredictable occurrences in the universe, they cannot totally control them. However, the human species has been able to discover vaccines that counteract the harmful effects of viruses and other diseases which have come from the discovery of new combinations of existing matter and energy.

Hypothesis C (2): the adaptation or extinction of the species is supported by the following discoveries and evidence:

1. The discovery of DNA (Deoxyribonucleic acid). In 1952 Alfred Hershey and Martha Chase confirmed DNA's role in heredity in their Hershey-Chase experiment. DNA is a nucleic acid that contains the genetic instructions used in the development and functioning of all known living organisms and some viruses. The main role of DNA molecules is the long-term storage of information. DNA is often compared to a set of blueprints, like a recipe or a code, since it provides instructions to the genes that determine the characteristics of every living organism on earth. (https://en.wikipedia.org/wiki/Hershey–Chase_experiment)(117)

2. The common characteristics of all living matter on earth. Living matter has the following biological characteristics (Winchester, A.M. (1964), *Biology and its Relation to Mankind*, Princeton, NJ: D. Van Norstrand Company, Inc., Pages 12-18):

a. <u>Protoplasm</u>. Living matter is composed of a distinctive material known as protoplasm, which is not to be found in any nonliving matter.

b. <u>Growth</u>. Living matter has a unique and distinctive method of growth which sets it apart from nonliving matter.

c. <u>Cellular organization</u>. Living matter is generally organized into small units known as cells. In some forms there is only one cell to an entire body, while in others there may be billions of cells in each body.

d. <u>Cell respiration</u>. Life cannot be maintained in living matter without the release of energy, which comes from food taken in or manufactured by the organism.

e. <u>Favorable response to environment</u>. Living organisms tend to respond to their environment in a way which is generally advantageous to them.

f. <u>Adaptation to environment through natural selection</u>. All living organisms slowly achieve inherited adaptations to their environment through natural selection, which has four prerequisites: overproduction of offspring; inherited variations within the species, struggle for existence, and survival of the fittest. However, these adaptations are limited by and controlled by the DNA of each species.

g. <u>Reproduction</u>. Since living organisms do not continue to exist indefinitely as individuals, there must be some method of reproducing other living organisms like themselves or their species will become extinct.

h. <u>Death</u>. At some point in time each living organism will die and either be eaten by other organisms or decay and return to the soil.

3. <u>The relationship between DNA, RNA (Ribonucleic Acid) and Proteins.</u> From the website: <u>http://www.bioinformatics.org/ tutorial/ (19)</u>. Basically, DNA is made up of four nucleotide bases which are: Adenine (A), Guanine (G), Thymine (T) and Cytosine (C). A sequence of DNA looks something like this:

"ATTGCTGAAGGTGCGG." The measurement of DNA is according to the number of base pairs it consists of, usually in kBp or mBp (Kilo or Mega base pairs). In the double helical structure of DNA, each base has its complementary base, which means, A will have T as its complimentary and similarly G will have C.

The molecules of DNA are incredibly long. If all the DNA bases of the human genome were typed as A, C, T and G, the 3 billion letters would fill 4,000 books of 500 pages each! The DNA is tightly wound into coils and is broken down into bits which are called chromosomes. Normal human beings have 23 pairs of chromosomes. These chromosomes are further divided into smaller pieces of code called genes. The 23 pairs of chromosomes are composed of about 70,000 genes and every gene has its own function.

Finding out the arrangement of the four nucleotide bases that make up DNA is called DNA sequencing. The sequencing of a DNA is usually carried out by a machine or by running the DNA sample over a gel, otherwise called gel electrophoresis. The determination of the gene's functionality and the position of the gene in the chromosome is called gene mapping.

The Human Genome Project (HGP) involves the careful study and mapping of all the 70,000 genes in the human body. The sequence of the gene is like a language that instructs the cell to manufacture a particular protein. An intermediate language is encoded in the sequence of Ribonucleic Acid (RNA) which translates the message of a gene into a protein's amino acid sequence. The protein determines the trait. This is called the central dogma of life.

RNA and DNA are both nucleic acids of nitrogen-containing bases joined by a sugar-phosphate backbone. However, they have structural and functional differences. Structurally, RNA is single-stranded whereas DNA is double-stranded. DNA contains Thymine, whereas RNA contains Uracil. RNA nucleotides contain sugar ribose, rather than the Deoxyribose that is part of DNA. Functionally, DNA maintains the protein-encoding information, whereas the encoding information is used by RNA to enable the cell to synthesize the particular protein.

Note: These complicated relationships between DNA, RNA, and protein within the cells of each living organism provide evidence that every living organism is very likely to be totally unique and different in some way from every other living organism.

4. The ability of each living species to communicate with others of the same species and their environment in a way that facilitates the survival of the species. This suggests that this ability to communicate for survival is part of the DNA of each living species. Plant species are able to communicate with others of the same or different species by the process of pollination and/or the spreading of their seeds by the environment (wind and water) and other animal species for their survival. Lower animals are able to communicate audibly to facilitate the reproductive process and to hunt for food.

The human species has DNA that is superior to all other living organisms, which gives them the ability to reason and communicate through speech and writing. This also suggests that the human species was able to communicate verbally from the very beginning of creation and had only one language. Because of the ability to reason, the human species is able to rule over all of the other species in the universe. In addition, the human species has a spiritual and creative dimension which gives them the ability to discover and communicate through the hidden forces of the universe and to create new forms of communication.

5. In contrast to the Theory of Evolution, which proposes that all the species have evolved from a common ancestor, the Theory of Creation proposes that all of the species were created at a specific point in time. Each species then evolved over time based

on the limitations of their DNA and their ability to survive the predictable and unpredictable natural or man-made occurrences in the universe, which caused them to either adapt to the changes to their environment or become extinct.

Analysis of Results

1. The fact that the survival of all matter and energy is the result of the combination or transformation of matter and energy can be verified by the natural laws listed above and the fact that all of these laws were an essential part of the universe before they were discovered by humanity, and there are very likely many additional laws remaining to be discovered.

   The structural survival of matter and energy is impacted by unpredictable natural occurrences such as weather, earthquakes, and volcanoes and man-made inventions such as the atomic bomb and environmental pollution. The relationships between matter and energy are so precise that they can be defined and supported by natural laws and mathematical equations rather than the scientific speculation which is associated with the current Theory of Evolution.

2. Since DNA determines the characteristics of every living organism, then DNA must have been a part of the essential make-up of every living organism from the very beginning. If DNA has been a part of the essential make-up of every living organism from the very beginning, then all of the characteristics of living matter have been controlled by DNA from the very beginning.

   From the very beginning DNA has controlled the following characteristics of living matter: it has controlled the content of protoplasm, it has controlled the growth of organisms, it has controlled cellular organization, it has controlled cell respiration, it has controlled the responses of each species to the environment, it has controlled the adaptation of each species to the environment through natural selection, it has controlled the reproduction of each species, and it has controlled the decay of organisms after death.

Therefore, natural selection could not occur before the creation of DNA, because without DNA there would be no production of offspring, no inherited variations within the species, no struggle for existence, and no survival of the fittest, which are the prerequisites for natural selection. However, the fact that all living organisms decay and return to the soil when they die, suggests that all living organisms have some common components of DNA.

3. According to the website www.currentresults.com (11), scientists have discovered and described 1,740,330 of the world's species of animals, plants, and algae, as of 2010. Of this total of 1,740,330; 62,305 are vertebrate animals; 1,305,250 are invertebrate animals; 321,212 are plants; and 51,563 are other types of species. Scientists estimate that there are an additional 5,523,300 species in the world that remain to be discovered and described, bringing the total estimated number of species that currently exist in the world to 7,263,630.

Since every species is defined by its DNA, it would be very difficult to show scientifically how a single organism could evolve into over 7.2 million different species, no matter how many billions of years the earth has been in existence. That original single organism would not only have to overcome the predictable and unpredictable natural occurrences in the universe, but it would also have to overcome the DNA of each species and the natural laws of biology, chemistry, and physics which affect each species. And since many species have become extinct because of their inability to survive their environments, the number of species at the beginning of creation must have been much greater than 7.2 million.

4. The fact that predictable and unpredictable natural and man-made occurrences can create an unfavorable environment for a particular species to survive is well documented. This is evidenced by the

discoveries of species that have already become extinct, such as the dinosaurs, and the 2019 International Union for Conservation of Nature (IUCN) estimate of more than 98,500 species on the IUCN Red List of Threatened Species (https://www.iucnredlist.org/)(40). More than 27,000 of these species are threatened with extinction, including 40% of amphibians, 34% of conifers (evergreen trees), 33% of reef building corals, 25% of mammals and 14% of birds.

Conclusion:

A. The universe was created during a finite period of time, and the earth has remained the same since its creation, except for natural occurrences that are a part of the essential make-up of the universe, some predictable and some unpredictable.

B. All matter, energy and the species on earth are a part of the universe, and all matter, energy and the species have been designed with a unique mechanism for their continual survival in the universe, except their survival is dependent upon the predictable and unpredictable occurrences that are a natural or man-made part of the universe.

C. Consequently, the only structural changes that can occur to matter, energy and the species must be the result of their inability to survive the predictable and unpredictable natural or man-made occurrences in the universe, which may cause: (1) the combination or transformation of matter and energy and (2) the adaptation or extinction of the species.

From this Scientific Theory of Creation, it may be inferred that:

1. All matter, energy and the species (along with their DNA) were created at the beginning of the universe and each species was adapted to the environment in which it was originally created.

2. As structural changes occurred to the environment, as a result of predictable and unpredictable natural or man-made occurrences, each species either adapted to the changes to their environment or became extinct.

3. The degree to which a species was able to adapt to the structural changes to their environment was controlled by the DNA of that species, and the amount of time that was available for that adaptation to occur.

4. The evolution of the species has occurred since the creation of the universe, but has always been controlled by and limited by the DNA within each species, which enabled some species to adapt to changes in the environment, while others became extinct.

5. The human species will continue to make new discoveries about the universe, which will only be limited by their imagination and faith, but the human species will never be able to discover or create anything that is not already a part of the essential make-up of the universe.

6. If all the species were created at the beginning of the universe, then the following is true:

    a. All extinct organisms that previously lived on the earth, such as the dinosaurs, were descendants of the original species from the time of creation.

    b. All living organisms that currently exist on the earth today are descendants of the original species from the time of creation.

    c. Every human being on earth today is a descendant of the original human beings from the time of creation.

7. If all matter, energy and the species (along with their DNA) were created at the beginning of the universe, then the universe must be the result of a **Creator (Intelligent Designer).**

8. If the universe is the result of a **Creator**, then there <u>must</u> be a **Supernatural Power (God)** somewhere who created the universe.

The information presented in this Scientific Theory of Creation will be used in the scientific analysis of the Holy Bible to answer questions, which will be based on the background research from this theory, Biblical evidence, or both, and the background research from the Scientific Theory of Evolution.

CHAPTER 3
How did we get here? (Theory of Creation – A Biblical Viewpoint)

A. How was the Spiritual Universe Created?

1. **In the beginning God first created the heaven (the spiritual universe) and then He created the earth (the physical universe), and when He began to create the physical universe, the Spirit of God moved upon the face of the waters:** <u>"In the beginning God created the heaven (spiritual universe) and the earth (physical universe). And the earth was without form, and void; and darkness was upon the face of the deep. And the Spirit of God moved upon the face of the waters."</u> (Gen. 1:1-2)

2. **When God was ready to create man, He said let <u>us</u> make man in <u>our</u> image and <u>our</u> likeness, which implies that God had others helping Him create the physical universe:** <u>"And God said, let *us* make man in *our* own image, after *our* likeness."</u> (Gen. 1:26)

3. **The tree of knowledge of good and evil was created in the beginning, but at first the knowledge of good and evil was**

only known to the spiritual universe: "And out of the ground made the Lord God to grow every tree that is pleasant to the sight, and good for food; the tree of life also in the midst of the garden, and the tree of knowledge of good and evil." (Gen. 2:9)

4. **The knowledge of good and evil became known by humanity in the physical universe after they sinned by eating the fruit of the tree of knowledge of good and evil, which also means that God gave humanity the authority and ability to use their free will to make decisions whether to obey Him of not:** "And the Lord God said, Behold, the man is become as one of *us*, to know good and evil." (Gen. 3:22)

5. **God had more than one son, and they sinned by marrying the daughters of humanity and having children by them, which lets us know that the spiritual universe includes God's sons:** "And it came to pass, when men began to multiply on the face of the earth, and daughters were born unto them, That the sons of God saw the daughters of men that they were fair; and they took them wives of all which they chose. And the Lord said, My spirit shall not always strive with man, for that he also is flesh: yet his days shall be an hundred and twenty years. There were giants in the earth in those days; and also after that, when the sons of God came in unto the daughters of men, and they bare children to them, the same became mighty men which were of old, men of renown." (Gen. 6:1-4)

6. **There are other scriptures in Job 1:6; 2:1; and 38:6-7 which reveal that God had sons in the spiritual universe:** "Now there was a day when the sons of God came to present themselves before the Lord, and Satan came also among them" (Job 1:6) "Again there was a day when the sons of God came to present themselves before the Lord, and Satan came also among them to present himself before the Lord" (Job 2:1) "Whereupon are the foundations (of the earth) thereof fastened? Or who laid the corner stone thereof; When the morning stars sang together, and all the sons of God shouted for joy?" (Job 38:6-7). **The last**

scripture reveals that the sons of God were there when the physical universe was being created by God.

7. In the following scriptures, Genesis 16:7 and 19:1, angels appeared to Hagar, the concubine of Abraham, and Lot, the nephew of Abraham, which lets us know that the spiritual universe includes God's angels: "And the angel of the Lord found her by a fountain of water in the wilderness, by the fountain in the way to Shur" ... "And there came two angels to Sodom at even; and Lot sat in the gate of Sodom: and Lot seeing them rose up to meet them; and he bowed himself with his face toward the ground" (Gen. 16:7; 19:1).

8. In the following scripture, John 1:1-5, the deity of Jesus Christ is described as him being with God from the beginning of creation: "In the beginning was the Word, and the Word was with God, and the Word was God. The same was in the beginning with God. All things were made by him; and without him was not any thing made that was made. In him was life; and the life was the light of men. And the light shineth in darkness; and the darkness comprehended it not." (John 1:1-5)

9. Colossians 1:15-17 describes Jesus Christ similar to John 1:1-5 as the firstborn of creation and the remainder of the spiritual universe and the physical universe were created by God through his firstborn son: "Who (Christ) is the image of the invisible God, the firstborn of every creature: For by him were all things created, that are in heaven, and that are in earth, visible and invisible, whether they be thrones, or dominions, or principalities, or powers: all things were created by him, and for him: And he is before all things, and by him all things consist." (Col. 1:15-17)

10. Jesus Christ used Psalm 110:1 as evidence that he existed prior to his earthly father David: "While the Pharisees were gathered together, Jesus asked them, Saying, What think ye of Christ? whose son is he? They say unto him, The son of David. He saith unto them, How then doth David in spirit call him Lord, saying, The LORD said unto my Lord, Sit thou on my

right hand, till I make thine enemies thy footstool? (Ps. 110:1) David then call him Lord, how is he his son?" **This incident is also recorded in Luke 20:41-44 and Mark 12:35-37.**

11. **There is another incidence in John 8:57-59 where Jesus told his opponents that he existed before Abraham:** "Then said the Jews unto him, Thou art not yet fifty years old, and hast thou seen Abraham? Jesus said unto them, Verily, verily, I say unto you, Before Abraham was, I am. Then took they up stones to cast at him: but Jesus hid himself, and went out of the temple, going through the midst of them, and so passed by." (John 8:57-59)

12. **In one of his final prayers before going to the cross in John 17:1-5, Jesus refers to his existence with God the Father prior to the beginning of the world:** "These words spake Jesus, and lifted up his eyes to heaven, and said, Father, the hour is come; glorify thy Son, that thy Son also may glorify thee: As thou hast given him power over all flesh, that he should give eternal life to as many as thou hast given him. And this is life eternal, that they might know thee the only true God, and Jesus Christ, whom thou hast sent. I have glorified thee on the earth: I have finished the work which thou gavest me to do. And now, O Father, glorify thou me with thine own self with the glory which I had with thee before the world was."

Logical Conclusion: From the scriptures about God's creation of heaven (the spiritual universe), it may be inferred that:

1. **Language must have existed from the beginning of time because God spoke the spiritual universe (heaven) and the physical universe (earth) into existence.**
2. **When God began to create the physical universe, the Spirit of God moved upon the face of the waters.**
3. **The spiritual universe was created before the physical universe.**

4. The words *us* and *our* in Genesis 1:26 and 3:22 about the creation of the physical universe and God's early encounters with humanity must mean that God was not alone when he created the physical universe.

5. According to Genesis 6:1-4 and Job 38:6-7, God had sons.

6. According to Genesis 16:7 and 19:1, God had angels.

7. Based on the above scriptures, Genesis 3:22; 6:1-4; 16:7; 19:1; and Job 38:6-7, there must be at least three spiritual entities in the spiritual universe: God, God's sons, and God's angels.

8. As one of God's sons, Jesus Christ did not exist prior to the creation of the spiritual universe.

9. According to John 1:1-4 and Colossians 1:15-17, Jesus Christ, as the firstborn son of God, was first created by God and then participated with God in the creation of the remainder of the spiritual universe and the physical universe.

10. According to the testimony of Jesus Christ himself in John 17:1-5, he existed with God prior to the creation of the world, the physical universe.

11. God's other sons and His angels may also have participated with God and His firstborn son in the creation of the physical universe.

12. If there are three spiritual entities in the spiritual universe, then according to the above scriptures, there must be a hierarchy of leadership in the spiritual universe: God Himself at the top level, Jesus Christ the firstborn son at the second level, the other sons of God at the third level, and the angles of God at the fourth level, but Jesus Christ, since his death and resurrection, now has a new status as an intercessor before the throne of God for the sins of the world.

B. How was the Physical Universe Created?

1. **The first day. On the first day God separated the light (Day) from the darkness (Night):** "In the beginning God created the heaven and the earth. And the earth was without form, and void; and darkness was upon the face of the deep. And the spirit of God moved upon the face of the waters. And God said, Let there be light: and there was light. And God saw the light, that it was good: and God divided the light from the darkness. And God called the light Day, and the darkness he called Night. And the evening and the morning of the first day" (Gen. 1:1-5).

2. **The second day. On the second day God separated the waters below (seas) from the waters above (clouds):** "And God said, Let there be a firmament (expansion) in the midst of the waters, and let it divide the waters from the waters. And God made the firmament (expansion), and divided the waters which were under the firmament (expansion) from the waters which were above the firmament (expansion): and it was so. And God called the firmament (expansion) Heaven. And the evening and the morning were the second day" (Gen. 1:6-8).

3. **The third day. On the third day God created dry land and caused all types of plants to grow and multiply:** "And God said, Let the waters under the heaven be gathered together unto one place, and let the dry land appear: and it was so. And God called the dry land Earth; and the gathering together of the waters called he Seas: and God saw that it was good. And God said, Let the earth bring forth grass, the herb yielding seed, and the fruit tree yielding fruit after his kind, whose seed is in itself, upon the earth: and it was so. And the earth brought forth grass, and herb yielding seed after his kind, and the tree yielding fruit, whose seed was in itself, after his kind: and God saw that it was good. And the evening and the morning were the third day" (Gen. 1:8-13).

4. **The fourth day. On the fourth day God created the sun, moon, and stars and the seasons, months, and years:** "And

God said, Let there be lights in the firmament (expansion) of the heaven to divide the day from the night; and let them be for signs, and for seasons, and for days, and years: And let them be for lights in the firmament (expansion) of the heaven to give light upon the earth: and it was so. And God made two great lights; the greater light to rule the day, and the lesser light to rule the night: he made the stars also. And God set them in the firmament (expansion) of the heaven to give light upon the earth, And to rule over the day and over the night, and to divide the light from the darkness: and God saw that it was good. And the evening and the morning were the fourth day" (Gen. 1:14-19).

5. **The fifth day. On the fifth day God created the fish of the sea and the fowls of the air:** "And God said, Let the waters bring forth abundantly the moving creature that hath life, and fowl that may fly above the earth in the open firmament (expansion) of heaven. And God created great whales, and every living creature that moveth, which the waters brought forth abundantly, after their kind, and every winged fowl after his kind: and God saw that it was good. And God blessed them, saying, Be fruitful, and multiply, and fill the waters in the seas, and let fowl multiply in the earth. And the evening and the morning were the fifth day" (Gen. 1:20-23).

6. **The sixth day. On the sixth day God created every beast of the earth after its kind, cattle after their kind, and everything that creeps on the earth after its kind, and God created humanity in His own image, and He created them male and female:** "And God said, Let the earth bring forth the living creature after his kind, cattle, and creeping thing, and beast of the earth after his kind: and it was so. And God made the beast of the earth after his kind, and cattle after their kind, and every thing that creepeth upon the earth after his kind: and God saw that it was good. And God said, Let us make man in our image, after our likeness: and let them have dominion over the fish of the sea, and over the fowl of the air, and over the

cattle, and over all the earth, and over every creeping thing that creepeth upon the earth. So God created man in his own image, in the image of God created he him; male and female created he them. And God blessed them, and God said unto them, Be fruitful, and multiply, and replenish the earth, and subdue it: and have dominion over the fish of the sea, and over the fowl of the air, and over every living thing that moveth upon the earth. And God said, Behold, I have given you every herb bearing seed, which is upon the face of all the earth, and every tree, in the which is the fruit of a tree yielding seed; to you it shall be for meat. And to every beast of the earth, and to every fowl of the air, and to every thing that creepeth upon the earth, wherein there is life, I have given every green herb for meat: and it was so. And God saw every thing that he had made, and, behold, it was very good. And the evening and the morning were the sixth day" (Gen. 1:24-31).

7. **The seventh day. On the seventh day God rested from all His work of creation, and He blessed the seventh day and sanctified it:** "Thus the heavens and the earth were finished, and all the host of them. And on the seventh day God ended his work which he had made; and he rested on the seventh day from all his work which he had made. And God blessed the seventh day, and sanctified it: because that in it he had rested from all his work which God created and made" (Gen. 2:1-3).

Logical Conclusion: From the scriptures about God's creation of the earth (the physical universe), it may be inferred that:

1. **Since God did not complete the creation of the sun, moon and stars until the fourth day, the source of light on the first day could have been the explosions that started the initial cosmic reactions that created the Milky Way and the other galaxies in the physical universe, and God could have divided the light from the darkness by starting the rotation**

of the earth on its axis against the light that was generated by the cosmic explosions.

2. On the second day, God could have divided the waters above from the waters below by first creating the atmosphere (air) around the earth, and then the air would have absorbed moisture from the waters below to create the clouds above.

3. On the third day, the dry land could have been created by earthquakes and volcanoes, and once the dry land had been created, the grass, trees, and herbs would have a place to grow and multiply.

4. On the fourth day, once the explosions from the first day settled down and the galaxies completed their development, the Milky Way would be in place and the earth could be set up to rotate against the light of the sun, moon, and stars, as it is today, to create the seasons, months, and years.

5. On the fifth day, God created the fowls of the air after their kind and the creatures in the seas after their kind and told them to be fruitful and multiply.

6. On the sixth day God created the beasts of the earth after their kind, the cattle after their kind, and everything that creepeth on the earth after their kind. And God created Adam and Eve after His own image.

7. God commanded Adam and Eve to be fruitful and multiply and replenish the earth; subdue the earth; and have dominion over every living thing that moves upon the earth.

8. God gave every seed-bearing plant and every tree that has fruit with seed in it to Adam and Eve for food, and He gave every green plant for food to all the beasts of the earth, all the birds in the air, and all the creatures that move along the ground. It is probable that God did not allow any carnivorous animals in the Garden of Eden that would pose a danger to Adam and Eve.

9. God brought every beast of the field and every fowl of the air for Adam to name (Gen. 2:19-20). It is likely that this scripture only applies to the animals Adam would encounter

in the Garden of Eden and not the more than 7.2 million species in the whole world, because we could only find about 103 animal names in the whole Bible, and Adam could have named this number animals in one day and virtually all of them are still in existence today. (See <u>Exhibit 1</u> at the end of this chapter.)

10. God set aside the seventh day as a day of rest and rejuvenation for the human body and mind. Jesus further clarified the purpose of the sabbath day: "The sabbath was made for man, and not man for the sabbath: Therefore the Son of man is Lord also of the sabbath" (Mark 2:27-28).

11. According to the Timeline of Outstanding Historical Biblical Events, which was derived from the biblical record, the physical universe was created in about 4026 BCE.

12. There does not appear to be any unexplainable conflicts between the biblical record of the creation of the physical universe and the laws and experimental tests presented in the <u>Scientific Theory of Creation</u> in Chapter 2.

One of the secular arguments about creation is that it would take Adam more than a few days to name all of the animals on the earth. Since God placed Adam in the Garden of Eden in the beginning, it is logical that Adam only named the animals that he would encounter in the garden. It is also logical that God would not have placed carnivorous animals in the garden that would have been a danger to Adam and Eve. We were able to find the names of only 103 animals in the whole Bible. Consequently, it is likely that Adam named no more than this number of animals in the beginning and it is entirely feasible this number of animals could have been named in one day.

C. **What was God's relationship with humanity before and after sin?**

1. **What was God's relationship with humanity before sin?**

   a. **God created man in His own image and likeness and gave him dominion over all living things on the earth, and he created them male and female and He told them to be fruitful and multiply and replenish the earth and subdue it, and he gave humanity and all living things herbs, seeds, and fruit for food:** "And God said, Let us make man in our image, after our likeness: and let them have dominion over the fish of the sea, and over the fowl of the air, and over the cattle, and over all the earth, and over every creeping thing that creepeth upon the earth. So God created man in his own image, in the image of God created he him; male and female created he them. And God blessed them, and God said unto them, Be fruitful, and multiply, and replenish the earth, and subdue it: and have dominion over the fish of the sea, and over the fowl of the air, and over every living thing that moveth upon the earth. And God said, Behold, I have given you every herb bearing seed, which is upon the face of all the earth, and every tree, in the which is the fruit of a tree yielding seed; to you it shall be for meat (food). And to every beast of the earth, and to every fowl of the air, and to every thing that creepeth upon the earth, wherein there is life, I have given every green herb for meat: and it was so" (Gen. 1:26-30).

   b. **God planted a garden in Eden and He planted every tree that was pleasant to look at and good for food, and He also planted the tree of life and the tree of knowledge of good and evil:** "And the Lord God planted a garden eastward in Eden; and there he put the man whom he had formed. And out of the ground made the Lord God to grow every tree that is pleasant to the sight, and good for food;

the tree of life also in the midst of the garden, and the tree of knowledge of good and evil" (Gen. 2:8-9).

c. **God put the man in the garden for him to take care of it, and He told the man that he could eat of every tree in the garden, except the tree of knowledge of good and evil, under the penalty of death, and He created the beasts of the field and fowls of the air for the man Adam to name, and He created the woman out of the man, and Adam gave her the name "woman", because she was created out of man, and God commanded that the man should leave his father and mother and cleave unto his wife, and they should become one flesh:** "And the Lord God took the man, and put him into the garden of Eden to dress it and to keep it. And the Lord God commanded the man, saying, Of every tree of the garden thou mayest freely eat: But of the tree of the knowledge of good and evil, thou shalt not eat of it: for in the day that thou eatest thereof thou shalt surely die. And the Lord God said, It is not good that the man should be alone; I will make him an help meet (fit) for him. And out of the ground the Lord God formed every beast of the field, and every fowl of the air; and brought them unto Adam to see what he would call them: and whatsoever Adam called every living creature, that was the name thereof. And Adam gave names to all cattle, and to the fowl of the air, and to every beast of the field; but for Adam there was not found an help meet (fit) for him. And the Lord God caused a deep sleep to fall upon Adam, and he slept: and he took one of his ribs (sides) and closed up the flesh instead thereof; And the rib, which the Lord God had taken from man, made he a woman, and brought her unto the man. And Adam said, This is now bone of my bones, and flesh of my flesh: she shall be called Woman, because she was taken out of Man. Therefore shall a man leave his father and his mother, and shall cleave unto his wife: and they shall be one flesh. And they were both naked, the man and his wife, and were not ashamed" (Gen. 2:15-25).

<u>Logical Conclusion:</u> From the scriptures about God's relationship to humanity before sin, it may be inferred that:

1. By creating humanity in His own image, God gave humanity a spiritual attribute along with their physical attributes.
2. All the living creatures, other than humanity, were not given this spiritual quality, so they do not have access to the spiritual universe and must return to the soil from which they were created when they die.
3. God created woman out of man to be a help mate for man, and it is the man's responsibility to leave his father and mother and find a wife, so that they can become one flesh. This is God's definition of the family, and Adam and Eve became the first family on earth.
4. God commands Adam and Eve, the first family, to be fruitful and multiply, and replenish the earth, which is one of the primary responsibilities of the family.
5. By God giving humanity the authority to subdue the earth, humanity gains dominion over and responsibility for the natural resources of the earth.
6. By God giving humanity dominion over all living creatures, humanity became responsible for the stewardship of all living creatures, including fellow human beings.
7. The tree of life in the Garden of Eden represented humanity's connection to eternal life, and the tree of the knowledge of good and evil represented humanity's connection to sin. As long as humanity obeyed God's command not to eat the fruit of these two trees, humanity would have access to eternal life in heaven (the spiritual universe), and God would teach humanity

how to refrain from sin, so that humanity could be "translated" to heaven when their life on earth was ended. The translations of Enoch (Gen. 5:24) and Elijah (2 Kin. 2:11) give us an idea of how humanity might have been transitioned to heaven and the family of God before the fall of Adam.

8. It is very likely that Adam only gave names to the creatures that he would have access to in the Garden of Eden and not the more than 7.2 million species that were created on Day 4 and Day 5 of creation. As some evidence of this, <u>Exhibit 1</u> lists the names of all the 103 animals that we were able to find in the Bible, and virtually all of them are still in existence today.

9. In the Garden of Eden humanity and the beasts of the field and fowls of the air did not eat meat for food, only herbs, seeds and fruit (Gen. 1:29-30). However, since it is very likely that all the more than 7.2 million species of animals were <u>not</u> in the Garden of Eden at the beginning, it is also very likely that God placed few, if any, carnivorous animals in the Garden of Eden that might be of harm to humanity.

2. **What was God's relationship with humanity after sin?**

    a. Following is the sequence of events that occurred after Adam and Eve sinned by eating the fruit of the tree of knowledge of good and evil. When Satan appeared to Eve (Gen. 3:1-5), he appeared in the form of a serpent and persuaded her to eat the fruit of the tree of knowledge of good and evil and she also gave the fruit to Adam (this is the first instance where humanity exercised their free will): "<u>And the serpent said unto the woman, ye shall not surly die: For God doth know that in the day ye eat thereof, then your eyes shall be opened, and ye shall be as gods, knowing good and evil. And when the woman saw that the</u>

tree was good for food, and that it was pleasant to the eyes, and a tree to be desired to make one wise, she took of the fruit thereof, and did eat, and gave also unto her husband with her, and he did eat. And the eyes of them both were opened, and they knew that they were naked; and they sewed fig leaves together, and made themselves aprons" ... "And the Lord God said unto the woman, What is this that thou hast done? And the woman said, The serpent beguiled me, and I did eat. (Gen. 3:4-7, 13)

b. **God curses Satan and the serpent above all other animals and establishes hatred between Satan and Eve, and between Satan's offspring and Eve's offspring, and Satan's offspring will enjoy limited success and bruise the heel of Eve's offspring, but ultimately Eve's offspring will judge Satan and bruise his head:** "And the Lord God said unto the serpent, Because thou hast done this, thou art cursed above all cattle, and above every beast of the field; upon thy belly shalt thou go, and dust shalt thou eat all the days of thy life: And I will put enmity between thee and the woman, and between thy seed and her seed; it (He) shall bruise thy head, and thou shalt bruise his heel." (Gen. 3;14-15)

c. **God curses Eve and promises to: greatly multiply women's sorrow and conception, which is necessitated by the introduction of death into the human race; in pain women will bring forth children; women's desire will be for their husbands; and their husbands will rule over them:** "Unto the woman he said, I will greatly multiply thy sorrow and thy conception; in sorrow thou shalt bring forth children; and thy desire shall be to thy husband, and he shall rule over thee." (Gen. 3:16)

d. **God curses Adam by: cursing the ground that men need to provide food for the family; thorns and thistles will be mixed with the harvest; men will have to work by the sweat of their brows all their lives to provide food for the** family; and humanity will die and go back to the dust from which they were created: "And unto Adam he said, Because thou hast hearkened unto the voice of thy wife, and hast eaten of the tree, of which I commanded thee, saying, Thou shalt not eat of it: cursed is the ground for thy sake; in sorrow shalt thou eat of it all the days of thy life; Thorns also and thistles shall it bring forth to thee; and thou shalt eat the herb of the field; In the sweat of thy face shalt thou eat bread, till thou return unto the ground; for out of it wast thou taken: for dust thou art, and unto dust shalt thou return. And Adam called his wife's name Eve; because she was the mother of all living. Unto Adam also and to his wife did the Lord God make coats of skins, and clothed them. And the Lord God said, Behold, the man is become as one of us, to know good and evil: and now, lest he put forth his hand, and take also of the tree of life, and eat, and live for ever: Therefore the Lord God sent him forth from the garden of Eden, to till the ground from whence he was taken." (Gen. 3:17-23).

<u>Logical Conclusion:</u> **From the scriptures about God's relationship to humanity after sin, it may be inferred that:**

1. **Because Satan appeared to Eve in the form of a serpent, we know that Satan had the power to appear in different forms to deceive humanity.**
2. **Satan had knowledge of God's plan concerning the tree of knowledge of good and evil and used that knowledge to deceive and tempt Eve. This tells us that Satan may also have knowledge of God's overall plan for humanity and will use it to deceive humanity.**
3. **God curses Satan and the serpent above all other animals and establishes hatred between Satan and Eve, and between Satan's offspring and Eve's offspring, and Satan's offspring will enjoy limited success and bruise**

the heel of Eve's offspring, but ultimately Eve's offspring will judge Satan and bruise his head. This is the first prophesy of the coming of the Messiah.

4. God curses Eve and promises to:

   a. Greatly multiply women's sorrow and conception, which is necessitated by the introduction of death into the human race;
   b. In pain women will bring forth children;
   c. Women's desire will be for their husbands; and
   d. Their husbands will rule over them. Traditionally, this curse has been interpreted to apply to all relationships between men and women; inside the family and outside the family. However, the context of this curse is inside the family unit between husband and wife and not outside the family unit.

5. God curses Adam by:

   a. Cursing the ground that men need to provide food for the family; thorns and thistles will be mixed with the harvest;
   b. Men will have to work by the sweat of their brows all their lives to provide food for the family; and
   c. Humanity will die and go back to the dust from which they were created. Because of sin, humanity dies physically and no longer has direct access to heaven (the spiritual universe).

6. When God drove Adam and Eve from the garden of Eden, He denied them access to the tree of life, which provided them immediate access to eternal life in heaven (the spiritual universe) when their time on earth was ended. Instead, after death humanity's physical body goes back to the dust, and their spiritual nature (soul)

becomes part of the spiritual universe, but does not have direct access to the family of God as before. However, there is evidence that based on their conduct on earth, God might exercise the option to either receive their souls into His family immediately after death, or have them wait in the spiritual universe until the final judgment. The probability that some souls are immediately received into His family after death is evidenced by the translation of Enoch and Elijah and the death and resurrection of Jesus Christ. Others who might have gained immediate acceptance into the family of God might be Noah, Abraham, Moses, Joshua, David, some of the prophets, Daniel, the Apostle Paul, and the twelve disciples, with the probable exception of Judas Iscariot.

7. When Satan introduced sin into the world, he also introduced sin into the family of God, and became an adversary of God and His relationship with humanity. Consequently, it is probable that God cast Satan and all of his followers out of the family of God at the same time He cast Adam and Eve out of the Garden of Eden, but Satan still remained in the spiritual universe (Ezek. 28:13-19).

3. Where was the Garden of Eden Located?

A river flowed out of the Garden of Eden that separated into four branches: Pison in the land of Havilah, Gihon in the land of Ethiopia, Hiddekel (Tigris) in the land of Assyria, and Euphrates: "And the Lord God planted a garden eastward in Eden; and there he put the man whom he had formed. And out of the ground made the Lord God to grow every tree that is pleasant to the sight, and good for food; the tree of life also in the midst of the garden, and the tree of knowledge of good and evil. And a river went out of Eden to water the garden; and from thence it was parted, and became into four heads. The name of the first is Pison: that is it which compasseth the whole land of Havilah, where there is gold; And the gold of that land is good: there is bdellium and the onyx (beryl) stone. And the name of the second river is Gihon: the same is it that compasseth the whole land of Ethiopia (Cush). And the name of the third river is Hiddekel (Tigris): that is it which goeth toward the east of Assyria. And the fourth river is Euphrates. And the Lord God took the man, and put him into the garden of Eden to dress it and to keep it" (Gen. 2:8-15).

Logical Conclusion: From these scriptures it may be inferred that:

1. **The Garden of Eden was located near the ancient lands of Ethiopia and Assyria, and near the Tigris and Euphrates Rivers.**

4. **Why was God displeased with the offering that Cain made?**

The answer to this question might give us knowledge of what God expected in sacrifices and offerings after Adam sinned. Cain brought and offering to God of fruit, but Abel brought an offering of the firstlings of his flock along with the fat, and God had respect for Abel's offering, but He did not have respect for Cain's offering and implied that Cain should have known better: "And in process of time it came to pass, that Cain brought of the fruit of the ground an offering unto the Lord. And Abel, he also brought of the firstlings of his flock and of the fat thereof. And the Lord had respect unto Abel and to his offering: But unto Cain and to his offering he had not respect. And Cain was very wroth, and his countenance fell. And the Lord said unto Cain, Why art thou wroth? And why is thy countenance fallen? If thou doest well, shalt thou not be accepted? And if thou doest not well, sin lieth at the door. And unto thee shall be his desire, and thou shalt rule over him" (Gen. 4:3-7).

Logical Conclusion: From the scriptures about Cain and Abel's sacrifices, it may be inferred that:

1. After Adam sinned, God had prescribed a process by which Adam could atone for his sins, which included the sacrificing of animals, because without the shedding of blood there is no remission of sins.
2. Adam must have taught this process of atonement to his two sons, Cain and Abel.
3. Abel complied with the prescribed process of atonement, but Cain did not.
4. Abel offered the firstborn of one of the animals from his flock; Cain offered fruit.
5. Abel's offering was pleasing to God; Cain's offering was not.
6. Since Adam first sinned, it is probable that God began to use the blood of animals for the atonement of humanity's sins from the very beginning, until Christ died for the perpetual atonement of humanity's sins. This is evident because men were sacrificing animals to God long before the Mosaic Covenant. Noah sacrificed the blood of "clean" animals after the Flood (Gen. 8:20-21). Abraham sacrificed a ram in lieu of his son Isaac (Gen. 22:1-14).

5. How did humanity get so many languages?

Before and immediately after the Great Flood the whole earth had only one language and one speech, and it came to pass that the descendants of Noah traveled to the land of Shinar and decided to build a great city and a great tower to make a great name for themselves in defiance of God, and God determined that they would be able to do all that they imagined, so he confused their language and scattered them over the face of the earth, and the name of the place was called Babel: "And the whole earth was of one language, and of one speech. And it came to pass, as they journeyed from the east, that they found a plain in the land of Shinar; and they dwelt there. And they said one to another, Go to, let us make brick, and burn them thoroughly. And they had brick for stone, and slime had they for morter. And they said, Go to, let us build us a city and a tower, whose top may reach unto heaven; and let us make us a name, lest we be scattered abroad upon the face of the whole earth. And the Lord came down to see the city and the tower, which the children of men builded. And the Lord said, Behold, the people is (are) one, and they have all one language; and this they begin to do: and now nothing will be restrained from them, which they have imagined to do. Go to, let us go down, and there confound their language, that they may not understand one another's speech. So the Lord scattered them abroad from thence upon the face of all the earth: and they left off to build the city. Therefore is the name of it called Babel; because the Lord did there confound the language of all the earth: and from thence did the Lord scatter them abroad upon the face of all the earth" (Gen. 11:1-9).

Logical Conclusion: From the scriptures about the origin of many languages on earth, it may be inferred that:

1. Humanity was created with superior powers of reason and imagination.
2. After the Great Flood the descendants of Noah attempted to build a great city and a great tower with the selfish motive to make a great name for themselves.
3. God confused their language so they could not understand each other to stop their rebellion and

challenges to His authority, and He scattered them over the face of the earth.

According to the Timeline of Outstanding Historical Biblical Events, this confrontation over the building of the Tower of Babel occurred after 2239 B.C.E. Therefore, prior to 2239 B.C.E, all of the people on earth probably spoke the same language and occupied the same general area of the earth, emanating from the location of the Garden of Eden where humanity was created.

6. What happened to Satan and the other fallen angels after sin?

According to Genesis 6:1-4, God had more than one son, and some of His sons saw the beauty of the daughters of humanity and married them and had children by them, who became mighty men of renown on earth, and God determined that the life span of humanity should be limited to 120 years: "And it came to pass, when men began to multiply on the face of the earth, and daughters were born unto them, That the sons of God saw the daughters of men that they were fair; and they took them wives of all which they chose. And the Lord said, My spirit shall not always strive with man, for that he also is flesh: yet his days shall be an hundred and twenty years. There were giants in the earth in those days; and also after that, when the sons of God came in unto the daughters of men, and they bare children to them, the same became mighty men which were of old, men of renown" (Gen. 6:1-4).

Logical Conclusion: From the scriptures about the sons of God in Genesis 6:1-4, it may be inferred that:

1. The sons of God that took wives of the daughters of men were likely Satan and the other fallen angels who were

cast out of the family of God and were now residing on earth and in the spiritual universe.

2. Since Satan had the power to appear on earth in the form of a serpent, he and his followers also likely had, at that time, the power to appear on earth in the form of men, but still have the attributes of a spirit.

3. The offspring born to the union of Satan and the other fallen angels and the daughters of men would probably have had some supernatural powers, but would still be mortal, as Jesus was.

4. Because of their supernatural powers, the offspring of Satan and the other fallen angels would be powerful witnesses for their spiritual and evil fathers among normal individuals.

5. Consequently, it is very possible that Satan and the other fallen angels are the idol gods that are mentioned by name throughout the Bible.

6. It is probable that, because of the influence of Satan and the other fallen angels on the populations of the world, God reduced the lifespan of humanity from an average of about 850 years to a limit of 120 years.

7. Before sin, all of the spiritual universe was the family of God. After sin, Satan and his followers were driven out of the family of God, at the same time Adam and Eve were driven out of the Garden of Eden. Consequently, Satan no resides in the family of God, but he still resides in the spiritual universe. God uses Satan to test the free will of humanity, but not beyond humanity's capacity to resist Satan's temptations. The Book of Job describes God's relationship to Satan, because just as God allowed Satan to test Job, He also allowed Satan to test Jesus.

According to the Timeline of Outstanding Historical Biblical Events, these events occurred between the time Adam and Eve began to have children and the great flood in 2370 B.C.E.

Exhibit 1 – The Names of Animals in the Bible

EXHIBIT 1

NAMES OF ANIMALS IN THE BIBLE		
NAME	**BIBLICAL CLASSIFICATION AND DESCRIPTION (Where Available)**	**REFERENCE**
Antelope	Animal that parteth the hoof, is clovenfooted and cheweth the cud.	Deut. 14:5
Ape	Animal that walks upright on two feet.	1 Kin. 10:22
Asp	Animal that goes on the belly.	Is. 11:8
Ass	Animal that cheweth not the cud and divideth not the hoof.	Gen. 22:3
Badger	Creeping thing that creeps on the earth.	Ex. 25:5
Bats	Fowl with wings but no feathers.	Deut. 14:18
Bear	Animal with paws and go on all four feet.	1 Sam. 17:34
Boar	Animal that parteth the hoof, is clovenfooted but cheweth not the cud. Male swine.	Ps. 80:13
Bulls	Animal that parteth the hoof, is clovenfooted and cheweth the cud. Male cow.	Jer. 52:20
Calf	Animal that parteth the hoof, is clovenfooted and cheweth the cud.	Gen 18:7
Camel	Animal that cheweth the cud but divideth not the hoof.	Gen. 12:16
Cattle	Animal that parteth the hoof, is clovenfooted and cheweth the cud.	Gen. 1:25
Chameleon	Creeping thing that creeps on the earth. In the lizard family.	Lev. 11:30
Chamois	Animal that parteth the hoof, is clovenfooted and cheweth the cud. In the deer family.	Deut. 14:5
Cockatrice (Adder)	Animal that goes on the belly.	Is. 11:8
Colt	Animal that cheweth not the cud and divideth not the hoof.	Zech. 9:9
Coney (Rock Badger)	Animal that cheweth the cud but divideth not the hoof.	Lev. 11:5
Cow	Animal that parteth the hoof, is clovenfooted and cheweth the cud.	Gen. 32:15, 41:2
Deer	Animal that parteth the hoof, is clovenfooted and cheweth the cud.	Deut. 14:5
Dog	Animal with paws and go on all four feet.	Deut. 23:18
Elephant ("Ivory")	Referred to indirectly by the ivory that comes from it. Large mammal.	1 Kin. 10:22
Ewe Lambs	Animal that parteth the hoof, is clovenfooted and cheweth the cud.	Gen. 21:30
Ferret	Creeping thing that creeps on the earth.	Lev. 11:30
Fish	Water animal with fins and scales. Water animal with fins and no scales.	Deut.4:15-18
Great Fish (Whale)	Water animal with fins and no scales.	Jon. 1:17
Fox	Animal with paws and go on all four feet.	Judg. 15:4
Frogs	Creeping thing that creeps on the earth.	Ex. 8:2-14
Gazelle	Animal that parteth the hoof, is clovenfooted and cheweth the cud.	Deut. 12:15
Goat	Animal that parteth the hoof, is clovenfooted and cheweth the cud.	Gen 27:9
Greyhound	Animal with paws and go on all four feet.	Prov. 30:31
Hare	Animal that cheweth the cud but divideth not the hoof.	Deut. 14:7
Hart (Male Deer)	Animal that parteth the hoof, is clovenfooted and cheweth the cud.	Ps. 42:1
Heifer	Animal that parteth the hoof, is clovenfooted and cheweth the cud.	Gen. 15:9
Hind	Animal that parteth the hoof, is clovenfooted and cheweth the cud. A female red deer.	Hab. 3:19
Horse	Animal that cheweth not the cud and divideth not the hoof.	Gen. 47:17
Jackal ("Dragons"?)	Animal with paws and go on all four feet.	Is. 13:22
Kine (Cattle)	Animal that parteth the hoof, is clovenfooted and cheweth the cud.	Gen. 32:15
Lamb	Animal that parteth the hoof, is clovenfooted and cheweth the cud.	Ex. 29:39
Leopard	Animal with paws and go on all four feet.	Rev. 13:2
Lion	Animal with paws and go on all four feet.	1 Sam. 13:29
Lizard	Creeping thing that creeps on the earth.	Lev. 11:29-30
Mole	Creeping thing that creeps on the earth.	Is. 2:20
Mouse	Creeping thing that creeps on the earth.	Lev. 11:29
Mule	Animal that cheweth not the cud and divideth not the hoof.	2 Sam. 13:29
Ox	Animal that parteth the hoof, is clovenfooted and cheweth the cud.	Ex. 21:28
Pygarg	Animal that parteth the hoof, is clovenfooted and cheweth the cud. In the deer family.	Deut. 14:5
Ram	Animal that parteth the hoof, is clovenfooted and cheweth the cud.	Gen. 15:9
Roebuck	Animal that parteth the hoof, is clovenfooted and cheweth the cud.	Deut. 14:5
Serpents	Animal that goes on the belly.	Matt. 10:16
Sheep	Animal that parteth the hoof, is clovenfooted and cheweth the cud.	Gen. 4:2
Snail	Animal that goes on the belly.	Lev. 11:30
Swine	Animal that parteth the hoof, is clovenfooted but cheweth not the cud.	Is. 65:2-4
Tortoise	Creeping thing that creeps on the earth.	Lev. 11:11:29

NAMES OF ANIMALS IN THE BIBLE		
NAME	**BIBLICAL CLASSIFICATION AND DESCRIPTION (Where Available)**	**REFERENCE**
Unicorn	This animal does not exist today.	Num. 23:22
Weasel	Creeping thing that creeps on the earth.	Lev. 11:29
Whale (Sea Monster)	Water animal with fins and no scales.	Gen. 1:21
Wolf	Animal with paws and go on all four feet.	Is. 11:6
Bittern	Fowl with feathers and wings.	Is. 14:22
Cock	Fowl with feathers and wings. A male chicken (Rooster).	Matt. 26:34, 74
Cormorant	Fowl with feathers and wings. Large marine diving bird with webbed feet and hooked bill.	Lev. 11:17
Crane	Fowl with feathers and wings.	Jer. 8:7
Cuckow	Fowl with feathers and wings.	Lev. 11:16
Dove	Fowl with feathers and wings.	Gen. 8:8
Eagle	Fowl with feathers and wings.	Job 39:27
Gier Eagle	Fowl with feathers and wings.	Lev. 11:18
Glede	Fowl with feathers and wings.	Deut. 14:13
Hawk	Fowl with feathers and wings.	Lev. 11:16
Night Hawk	Fowl with feathers and wings.	Lev. 11:16
Hen	Fowl with feathers and wings.	Matt. 23:37
Heron	Fowl with feathers and wings.	Lev. 11:19
Kite	Fowl with feathers and wings.	Deut. 14:13
Lapwing	Fowl with feathers and wings.	Lev. 11:19
Ospray	Fowl with feathers and wings.	Lev. 11:13
Ossifrage	Fowl with feathers and wings.	Lev. 11:13
Ostrich	Fowl with feathers and wings.	Lev. 11:16
Owls	Fowl with feathers and wings.	Job 30:29
Desert Owl	Fowl with feathers and wings.	Ps. 102:6
Great Owl	Fowl with feathers and wings.	Lev. 11:17
Little Owl	Fowl with feathers and wings.	Lev. 11:17
Partridge	Fowl with feathers and wings.	1 Sam. 26:20
Peacock	Fowl with feathers and wings.	1 Kin. 10:22
Pelican	Fowl with feathers and wings.	Ps. 102:6
Pigeon	Fowl with feathers and wings.	Lev. 12:6
Quail	Fowl with feathers and wings.	Num. 11:31-32
Raven	Fowl with feathers and wings.	Job 38:41
Sparrow	Fowl with feathers and wings.	Matt. 10:29-31
Stork	Fowl with feathers and wings.	Ps. 104:17
Swan	Fowl with feathers and wings.	Lev. 11:18
Swallow	Fowl with feathers and wings.	Ps. 84:3
Turtledove	Fowl with feathers and wings.	Song 2:12
Vulture	Fowl with feathers and wings.	Lev. 11:13
Ant	Creeping thing that creeps on the earth.	Prov. 6:6-8, 30:24
Scorpion	Creeping thing that creeps on the earth.	Deut. 8:15
Spider	Creeping thing that creeps on the earth.	Prov. 30:28
Bald Locust	Fowl that creeps on four or more legs.	Lev. 11:22
Bee	Fowl that creeps on four or more legs.	Judg. 14:8
Beetle	Creeping thing that creeps on the earth.	Lev:11:22
Caterpiller	Creeping thing that hath more feet among creeping things.	Is. 33:4
Flies	Fowl that creeps on four or more legs.	Ex. 8:21-31
Grasshopper	Fowl that creeps on four or more legs.	Lev. 11:22
Satyr (Butterfly)	Fowl that creeps on four or more legs.	Is. 13:21
Locust	Fowl that creeps on four or more legs.	Ex. 10:12-19
Moth	Fowl that creeps on four or more legs.	Job 13:28

CHAPTER 4
How Old is the Universe?
(Biblical Historical Timelines)

The commentary in this chapter about historical biblical dates comes from the following source: (Watch Tower Bible and Tract Society of Pennsylvania (1963), *"All Scripture is Inspired of God and Beneficial,"* First Edition, Brooklyn: Watchtower Bible and Tract Society of New York, Inc., International Bible Students Association, Pages 277-297). The information presented below comes from two studies from this book: Study Two, entitled "Time and the Holy Scriptures" and Study Three, entitled "Measuring Events in the Stream of Time."

The historical information in this book was chosen because it documents the process that was used to develop the "Chart of Outstanding Historical Dates" and "Main Events of Jesus' Earthly Sojourn" from the Biblical record and provides some explanations of why historical dates of events may differ slightly when they come from various sources or different calendars.

The historical information from the "Chart of Outstanding Historical Dates" and "Main Events of Jesus' Earthly Sojourn" has been used to determine the approximate dates of all Biblical events in this book. We are also utilizing the information from "The Year of the Israelites" and "Table of the Books of the Bible," which come from the same pages of this source. This information comes from Items 4a to 4i of our Book References at the back of this book.

A. Time and the Holy Scriptures (Source: Item 4b, Pages 277-283)

In the book entitled, *All Scripture is Inspired of God and Beneficial,* in the chapter intitled, "Time and the Holy Scriptures," the authors discuss how time impacts the lives of humanity, as reflected in Ecclesiastes 3:1-4: "To every thing there is a season, and a time to every purpose under the heaven: A time to be born, and a time to die; a time to plant, and a time to pluck up that which is planted; A time to kill, and a time to heal; a time to break down, and a time to build up; A time to weep, and a time to laugh." Our lives on this earth are fleeting so we should ask God to teach us how to use our limited number of days to seek wisdom as revealed in Psalm 90:10,12:

"The days of our years are threescore years and ten; and if by reason of strength they be fourscore years, yet is their strength labour and sorrow; for it is soon cut off, and we fly away. So teach us to number our days, that we may apply our hearts unto wisdom." And God has made everything in the world beautiful in his time such that no one can completely understand his judgments and his works, as revealed in Ecclesiastes 3:11: "He hath made every thing beautiful in his time: also he hath set the world in their heart, so that no man can find out the work that God maketh from the beginning to the end."

This study reveals that although time is universal, no man can say exactly what it is, but it does have characteristics that can be understood. The rate of flow of time can be measured, it moves in only one direction, the present is continually flowing into the past, the past is gone forever and can never be repeated, and the future is always flowing toward us. And God has provided enormous natural time indicators which are set in motion by the earth spinning on its axis, the moon revolving around the earth, and the earth revolving around the sun.

These giant indicators are illuminated by light from the sun such that humanity may be accurately advised of the time, and they are able to make divisions between day and night and they serve as signs for seasons and for days and for years. These heavenly bodies (indicators) have interlocking purposes and they move in perfect cycles which unendingly and unerringly measure the one-directional movement of time.

Day. According to the study, in the Bible, the word "day" has several different meanings, just as it has a variety of modern applications. When the earth makes one complete revolution on its axis, it measures one twenty-four-hour day. In this first meaning of day, *day* is made up of daytime and nighttime, a total of twenty-four hours. A second meaning of day is that the daylight period of about twelve hours is also called *day*. "And God called the light *Day*, and the darkness he called *Night*." (Gen. 1:5) This gives rise to the time term *night*, the period of about twelve hours of darkness. A third meaning of *day(s)* is the period of time associated with an important person, such as, the *days* of Noah. A fourth meaning of day is where one *day* with God is spoken of as being like a thousand years. A fifth meaning of *day* is the creative *day*, which for some people might mean a very long period of time. In the Bible, the scriptural context indicates how the word "day" is being applied.

Hour. The study reveals that the twenty-four-hour day is divided into subdivisions of sixty minutes and sixty seconds, which was an innovation of post-Flood times. The early Babylonian (Chaldean) and Egyptian civilizations used the duodecimal system based on twelves and sixties instead of the decimal system that is now in use. Our modern-day hours, minutes, and seconds are based on the duodecimal system. In the Christian Greek Scriptures, there is frequent mention of the word "hour," and it appears that this measure of time was about the same length as it is today. Hours were counted from sunrise, or about 6:00 AM. The "third hour" would be about 9:00 AM. The "sixth hour" would be about 12:00 Noon. The "ninth hour" would be about 3:00 PM.

Week. It reveals that humanity began counting days in cycles of seven from early in history. This follows the example of God who created the physical universe in seven days. Noah counted days in cycles of seven. In the Hebrew language, the word "week" literally means "sevened," or a cycle of seven.

Lunar Months. It reveals that the word "month" is derived from "moon," which is *luna* in the Latin language. A "lunar month" is a month that is actually determined by the new moon. There are four phases of the moon which encompass a period of slightly more than twenty-nine and one-half days (29.5 days). A person can look at the shape of the moon and tell approximately the day of the lunar month. Modern months are not lunar months, because they are determined by twelve arbitrary divisions of the solar year.

Noah appears to have recorded events by months of thirty days each, judging from the log kept by Noah on the ark. We understand that the Flood waters overflowed the earth for a period of five months, or "a hundred and fifty days." It took the earth twelve months and ten days to dry off, so that the passengers on the ark could go out. Consequently, the time of those epoch-making events were accurately recorded.

Seasons. According to the study, as the earth revolves around the sun, it is tilted at an angle of 23.5 degrees to the plane of its travel around the sun. As a result, the Southern Hemisphere of the earth is first tilted toward the sun and then the Northern Hemisphere is tilted toward the sun creating the seasons of the year. The times for planting and harvesting are controlled by the change of the seasons. God's word assures us that the change and contrast of the seasons throughout the year will continue as long as the earth exists. In Genesis 8:22 God makes the following promise: "While the earth remaineth, seedtime and harvest, and cold and heat, and summer and winter, and day and night shall not cease."

In Palestine, the year can generally be divided into the rainy season that runs from October to April, and the dry season that runs from May to September. The rainy season can be further divided into the early "autumn rain" (October-November), the heavy winter rains and colder weather (December-February), and the late "spring rain" (March-April). (Deut. 11:14; Joel 2:23) The seasons overlap due to variations in climate in different parts of the country, so these divisions are approximate. October-November was "plowing time" and time for the "sowing of seed," because the early rain softened up the dry ground. (Ex. 34:21; Lev. 26.5) During the heavy winter rains from December to February snow might fall and the temperature might drop below freezing at higher elevations during January and February.

March and April (the approximate Hebrew months of Nisan and Ziv) were the months of the "spring rain." (Zech. 10:1) This *late* rain was needed to make the grain planted in autumn swell and produce a good harvest. (Hos. 6:3; Jas. 5:7) God commanded Israel to offer the firstfruits of this harvest on Nisan 16, because this was the season of the early harvest. Although the month of May was the beginning of the dry season, an abundance of dew sustained the summer crops, especially on the western slopes of the mountains and on the coastal plains. (Deut. 33.28)

All of the grain was harvested during the month of May, and the Feast of Weeks (Pentecost) was celebrated at the end of May or the beginning of June. (Lev. 23:15-21) After the month of May the weather became warmer and the ground drier, and the grapes ripened on the vines and were harvested, followed by other summer fruits like olives, dates, and figs. (2 Sam. 16:1) At about the beginning of October when the dry season was ending and all of the produce of the land had been harvested, the Feast of Tabernacles was held. (Ex. 23:16; Lev. 23:39-43)

Year. The study reveals that there has been mention of the *year* from the very beginning of the history of humanity. (Gen. 1:14) The Hebrew word for "year" is *shanah*, which literally means "repetition." Since the cycle of seasons was repeated each year, this word was appropriate. A year is the time it takes for the earth to make one complete revolution around the sun. From our perspective here on earth, it takes the earth 365 days, 5 hours, 48 minutes, and 46 seconds to make one complete trip around the sun or about 365.25 days. This is called the solar year ("sun" in Latin is *sol*).

Bible Years. It reveals that the year ran from autumn to autumn according to ancient Biblical reckoning. This was particularly suited to an agricultural lifestyle in which the year begins with plowing and sowing in October and ends with the gathering of the harvest in September. The year was counted by Noah as beginning in the autumn. He recorded that the Flood began "in the second month," which would correspond to the latter half of October and the first half of November. (Gen. 7:11) Even today many people start their new year in the autumn of the year. God decreed that Abib (Nisan) would become "the start of the months" for the Jews at the time of the exodus from Egypt in 1513 BCE. The Jews now had a "sacred year" that ran from spring to spring, but they still observed a secular or civil year that begins in the autumn with Tishri being the first month.

Lunisolar Year. The study revealed that most nations used lunar years for counting time and used various methods for adjusting the lunar year to coincide more or less with the solar year up until the time of Christ. The common lunar year of twelve lunar months has

354 days, with the months having twenty-nine or thirty days based on the appearance of each new moon. Consequently, the lunar year is about eleven days short of the true solar year of 365.25 days. The Hebrews followed the lunar year, but the Bible does not explain how they adjusted their lunar year to coincide with the solar year. However, they must have added additional (*intercalary*) months when needed. The intercalary months were later systematized in the fifth century BCE into a cycle known as the Metonic cycle. This cycle allowed for the intercalary month to be added seven times in every nineteen years. The intercalary month was added to the Jewish calendar after the twelfth month Adar and was called V Adar, or "second Adar." As the Jewish lunar calendar is adjusted to the sun, the years that contain the thirteenth intercalary month are called "bound years" or "lunisolar years."

Julian and Gregorian Calendars. It revealed that a calendar is a system of determining the beginning, length, and divisions of the secular or civil year and arranging these divisions in the proper order. The Julian Calendar was established by Julius Caesar in 46 BCE to replace the Roman lunar year with a solar year time arrangement. The Julian Calendar contains 365 days in a year, except that on each fourth year ("leap year") one day is added to make 366 days in the year. Over time it was determined that the Julian Calendar lost one day in each 128 years. This happened because the Julian Calendar is 11 minutes longer than the true solar year.

In 1582, Pope Gregory XIII developed a slight revision to the Julian Calendar which is now called the Gregorian Calendar. The Gregorian Calendar provided that centuries not divisible by 400 are not to be considered leap years. For example, in the year 1900 no extra day was added to make it a leap year, but it is planned to add a leap-year day in the year 2000, because it is divisible by 400. The calendar now in general use in Western countries is the Gregorian Calendar. Historians usually use the Julian Calendar for dating events prior to AD 1600, and the Gregorian Calendar for dating events after AD 1600.

A Bible "Time." The study revealed that, in the Bible, a prophetic "time," whether literal or symbolic, is always taken as a year of twelve months, with each month having thirty days, for a total of 360 days. For example, one Biblical authority noted when commenting on Ezekiel 4:5 and Daniel 12:11: "We must suppose that Ezekiel knew a year of 360 days." The "prophetic year" is neither a true solar year nor a lunar year, it is an "average" year in which each month has thirty days. The 1290 days in Daniel 12:11 must be interpreted as 3.5 times 360 days plus 30 days of an intercalary month.

No Zero Year. It revealed that ancient peoples, including the Greeks, the Romans, and the Jews of Jesus' day, had no concept of the number *zero*. This is why the Christian era began with AD 1 and not *zero*. This is also the reason for the ordinal arrangement of numbers, such as first, second, third, tenth, hundredth, and so forth. In modern mathematics, which was designed primarily by the Arabs, everything is conceived as starting from *zero*, or nothing. The zero was invented by the Hindus in about AD 150, and then the Arabs introduced it into Europe some centuries later. Whenever *ordinal* numbers are used, the number *one* must always be subtracted to get the full number. For example, we live in the twenty-first century, but it does not mean that there have been twenty-one full centuries. It means twenty centuries plus some additional years. To express full numbers, the Bible, as well as modern mathematics, uses *cardinal* numbers or "whole numbers," such as 1, 2, 3, 10, 100, and so forth.

Since the Christian era did not begin with the year zero, but began with AD 1, and the calendar for the years before the Christian era did not count back from a zero year, but began with 1 BCE, the number given for the year in any date is in reality an ordinal number. That is, AD 2018 really represents 2017 full years since the beginning of the Christian era plus some additional months. The same principle applies to BCE dates. To determine how many years elapsed between October 1, 607 BCE and October 1, AD 1914, add 606 years (plus the last three months of the previous year) to 1913 (plus the first nine months of the next year), and the result is 2519 (plus twelve months), or 2520 years.

To determine what date would be 2520 years after October 1, 607 BCE, remember that 607 is an ordinal number; it really represents 606 full years, and since we are not counting from December 31, 607 BCE, but from October 1, 607 BCE, we must add the three months at the end of 607 BCE to 606. Now subtract 606 years (plus three months) from 2520 years. The remainder is 1913 years (plus nine months). That means that 2520 years from October 1, 607 BCE take us to 1913 years (plus nine months) into the Christian era. Nineteen hundred and thirteen (1913) full years take us to the beginning of AD 1914; the additional nine months take us to October 1, AD 1914.

Absolute Dates. According to the study, *absolute dates* provide the basis for reliable Biblical chronology. An *absolute date* is a calendar date that has been proven by secular history to be the actual date of an event recorded in the Bible. It can then become the starting point from which a series of Biblical events can be accurately located on the calendar. Once this *absolute date* has been determined, calculations forward or backward from this date can be made from accurate Biblical records, such as the stated lifespans of people or the duration of the reigns of kings. Also, starting from an absolute date, the reliable internal chronology of the Bible itself can be used in dating many Biblical events.

Absolute Date for the Hebrew Scriptures . It reveals that an important event that was recorded in the Bible and in pagan secular history is the overthrow of the city of Babylon by the Medes and Persians under Cyrus. The event was recorded in the Bible in Daniel

5:30. The pagan record of the event was made by King Nabonidus, and it has been dated by him in what is known as the Nabonidus Chronicle, which was discovered in 1879 and now preserved in the British Museum in London. Modern authorities have set the absolute date for the fall of Babylon as October 11-12, 539 BCE, according to the Julian Calendar, or October 5-6 by the Gregorian Calendar. The Hebrew day and the Babylonian day began at 6 p.m.

In Daniel 5:31, the Bible shows that Darius the Mede took over the kingdom. And since Daniel refers to "the first year of Darius," the inference is that he was king for at least one full year. (Dan. 9:1) But apparently by late in 538 BCE, Cyrus became king, and during his first year, at least before the spring of 537 BCE, he issued his famous edict, or decree, permitting the Jews to return to Jerusalem to rebuild the house of God. This would give ample opportunity for the Jews to resettle in their homeland, and to come up to Jerusalem to restore the worship of God in "the seventh month," or about October 1, 537 BCE. (Ezra 1:1-3; 3:1-6)

Absolute Date for the Christian Greek Scriptures. It reveals that an absolute date for the Christian Greek Scriptures can be determined by Tiberius Caesar's succession to Emperor Augustus. According to the Julian Calendar, this took place on August 19, AD 14. In Luke 3:1, 3, the Bible states that John the Baptist began his ministry in the fifteenth year of Tiberius' reign. From this absolute date we can therefore calculate the fifteenth year of Tiberius' actual rule to have extended from August 19, AD 28, to August 18, AD 29. Shortly after this date, Jesus, who was about six months younger than John the Baptist, came to be baptized by John the Baptist when he was "about thirty years old." (Luke 3:2, 21-23; 1:34-38)

This agrees with the fact that, according to Daniel 9:25, sixty-nine prophetic "weeks" of seven years each (thus totaling 483 years) would elapse from the time the decree was issued for the rebuilding of Jerusalem until the appearance of the Messiah. That decree was issued by Artaxerxes I in the latter part of the year 455 BCE. And 483 years later, in the latter part of AD 29, Jesus was baptized by John the Baptist and was also anointed by the Holy Spirit from God, thus becoming the Messiah or Anointed One.

The fact that Jesus was baptized and began his ministry in the latter part of AD 29 also agrees with the fact that he was to be cut off "at the half of the week" (or after three and a half years). (Dan: 9:27) Since he died in the spring, his ministry of three and a half years must have begun toward the fall of AD 29. These two lines of evidence also prove that Jesus was born in the autumn of 2 BCE, and not, as some commentators say, several years before that, since Luke 3:23 shows that Jesus was about thirty years of age when he began his ministry.

Logical Conclusion: From the analysis of the section about "Time and the Holy Scriptures," it may be inferred that:

1. **Time has characteristics that can be understood: the rate of flow of time can be measured, it moves in only one direction, the present is continually flowing into the past, the past is gone forever and can never be repeated, and the future is always flowing toward us.**
2. **God has provided enormous natural time indicators which are set in motion by the earth spinning on its axis, the moon revolving around the earth, and the earth revolving around the sun, which accurately divides time between day and night, days of the month, months of the year, and seasons of the year.**
3. **In the Bible the word *day* has several meanings: *day* is made up of daytime and nighttime, a total of twenty-four hours; *day* is also the daylight period of about twelve hours; *day(s)* is the period of time associated with an important person, such as, the *days* of Noah; *day* is where one *day* with God is spoken of as being like a thousand years; and *day* is the**

creative *day*, which for some people might mean a very long period of time. The scriptural context indicates how the word "day" is being applied in the Bible.

4. The *day* is divided into twenty-four *hours,* and each *hour* is divided into sixty minutes and sixty seconds. In Christian Greek Scriptures, *hours* were counted from sunrise, or about 6:00 AM. The "third hour" would be about 9:00 AM. The "sixth hour" would be about 12:00 Noon. The "ninth hour" would be about 3:00 PM.

5. The *week* has been counted in cycles of seven *days* from early history.

6. The *lunar month* is a month that is actually determined by the new moon. There are four phases of the moon which encompass a period of slightly more than twenty-nine and one-half days (29.5 days).

7. The *seasons* of the year are determined as follows: as the earth revolves around the sun, it is tilted at an angle of 23.5 degrees to the plane of its travel around the sun, which causes the Southern Hemisphere of the earth to first be tilted toward the sun and then the Northern Hemisphere to be tilted toward the sun creating the *seasons* of the year.

8. The *year* has been mentioned by humanity from the very beginning of history. A *solar year* is the time it takes for the earth to make one complete revolution around the sun, and, from our perspective here on earth, it takes the earth 365 days, 5 hours, 48 minutes, and 46 seconds to make one complete trip around the sun or about 365.25 days.

9. Prior to the exodus from Egypt, the biblical year ran from autumn to autumn. God decreed that Abib (Nisan) would become "the start of the months" for the Jews at the time of the exodus from Egypt in 1513 BCE, which caused the Jews to now have a "sacred year" that runs from spring to spring, but they still observe a secular or civil year that begins in the autumn with Tishri being the first month.

10. Most nations used *lunar years* consisting of twelve lunar months for counting time and used various methods for adjusting the lunar year to coincide more or less with the *solar year* up until the time of Christ. The *lunar year* has 354 days, with the months having twenty-nine or thirty days based on the appearance of each new moon. Consequently, the *lunar year* is about eleven days short of the true *solar year* of 365.25 days.

11. Additional months, called *intercalary* months, were systematized in the fifth century BCE into a cycle known as the Metonic cycle in which an *intercalary* month was added seven times in every nineteen years to the Jewish calendar. The *intercalary* month was added after the twelfth month Adar and was called V Adar, or "second Adar."

12. The *Julian Calendar* was established by Julius Caesar in 46 BCE to replace the Roman *lunar year* with a *solar year* time arrangement. The *Julian Calendar* contains 365 days in a year, except that on each fourth year ("leap year") one day is added to make 366 days in the year. Over time it was determined that the *Julian Calendar* lost one day in each 128 years. This happened because the *Julian Calendar* is 11 minutes longer than the true solar year.

13. In 1582, Pope Gregory XIII developed a slight revision to the *Julian Calendar* which is now called the *Gregorian Calendar*. The *Gregorian Calendar* provides that centuries not divisible by 400 are not to be considered leap years. For example, in the year 1900 no extra day was added to make it a leap year, but it is planned to add a leap-year day in the year 2000, because it is divisible by 400. The calendar now in general use in Western countries is the *Gregorian Calendar*. Historians usually use the *Julian Calendar* for dating events prior to AD 1600, and the *Gregorian Calendar* for dating events after AD 1600.

14. In the Bible, a prophetic "time," whether literal or symbolic, is always taken as a year of twelve months, with each month

having thirty days, for a total of 360 days. The "prophetic year" is neither a true *solar year* nor a *lunar year*, it is an "average" year in which each month has thirty days. The 1290 days in Daniel 12:11 must be interpreted as 3.5 times 360 days plus 30 days of an intercalary month.

15. Ancient peoples, including the Greeks, the Romans, and the Jews of Jesus' day, had no concept of the number *zero*. This is why the Christian era began with AD 1 and not *zero*. This is also the reason for the *ordinal* arrangement of numbers, such as first, second, third, tenth, hundredth, and so forth. In modern mathematics, which was designed primarily by the Arabs, everything is conceived as starting from zero, or nothing. To express full numbers, the Bible, as well as modern mathematics, uses *cardinal* numbers or "whole numbers," such as 1, 2, 3, 10, 100, and so forth.

16. Since the Christian era did not begin with the year *zero*, but began with AD 1, and the calendar for the years before the Christian era did not count back from a *zero* year, but began with 1 BCE, the number given for the year in any date is in reality an ordinal number. That is, AD 2018 really represents 2017 full years since the beginning of the Christian era plus some additional months.

17. *Absolute dates* provide the basis for reliable Biblical chronology. An *absolute date* is a calendar date that has been proven by secular history to be the actual date of an event recorded in the Bible. It can then become the starting point from which a series of Biblical events can be accurately located on the calendar. Once this *absolute date* has been determined, calculations forward or backward from this date can be made from accurate Biblical records, such as the stated lifespans of people or the duration of the reigns of kings.

B. Measuring Events in the Stream of Time (Source: Item 4c, Pages 283-286)

In Study Three of the subject book entitled "Measuring Events in the Stream of Time," the authors give examples of scriptures that indicate that God is an accurate timekeeper who accomplishes his purposes exactly on time, which include Daniel 11:27, 29, 35; Luke 21:24; and 1 Thessalonians 5:1-2. God has provided "guideposts" in his Word the Bible, that help us locate important events in the stream of time. A great deal of progress has been made in the understanding of Bible chronology in recent years. Archaeology and other research continue to reveal answers to various problems, which help us to calculate the timing of key Biblical events.

Ordinal and Cardinal Numbers. This study begins: earlier we learned that there is a difference between cardinal numbers and ordinal numbers. We will now apply this understanding to the interpretation of Jeremiah 52:31. This scripture speaks of "the thirty-seventh year of the exile of Jehoiachin the king of Judah." Note that "thirty-seventh" is an *ordinal* number which denotes thirty-six full years plus some months. Jehoiachin was exiled early in the year 617 BCE. The thirty-seventh year did not begin after thirty-seven years had passed, but after thirty-six full years had gone by, or early in the year 581. However, the scripture states that the event spoken of in this verse occurred "in the twelfth month, on the twenty-fifth day of the month," or almost a full year after the start of the thirty-seventh year. Since the thirty-seventh year started early in 581, the twelfth month would carry us over into the early part of 580 BCE (Thirty-six is used as a *cardinal* number in contrast to the ordinal number thirty-seventh. It does not end with "th," and so it signifies a full thirty-six years.)

Regnal and Accession Years. According to this study, the Bible makes references to the state records of the governments of Judah and Israel, as well as to the state affairs of Babylon and Persia. In all four of these countries, the state chronology was accurately calculated according to the rulerships of the kings, and the same system of calculation has been carried over into the Bible. The Bible will usually provide the name of the document quoted, as, for example, "the book of the affairs of Solomon." (1 Ki. 11:41) In the state records, the reign of a king would cover part of an accession year, followed by a complete number of regnal years. In all these countries, the official years in the kingship were the *regnal* years, and were normally calculated from Nisan to Nisan, or from spring to spring. When a king succeeded to the throne, the remaining months until the next spring month of Nisan were denoted as his *accession* year, during which he filled out the *regnal* term of rulership for his predecessor. However, his own official *regnal* term was reckoned as starting on the next Nisan 1.

For example, while David was still living, it appears that Solomon had an *accession* year beginning sometime before the month of Nisan in 1037 BCE. A short time later David died. (1 Ki. 1:39, 40; 2:10) However, the last regnal year of the reign of David continued until the spring of 1037 BCE, and was calculated as part of his administration of forty years. The accession year of Solomon lasted until the spring of 1037 BCE, which could not be counted as a regnal year, because he was still filling out the administrative term of his father. Therefore, Solomon's first full regnal year did not start until the month of Nisan in 1037 BCE. (1 Ki. 2:12). Ultimately, forty full regnal years were credited to the reign of Solomon as king. (1 Ki. 11:42) It is possible to calculate Bible chronology accurately by keeping the *regnal* years separated from *accession* years in this way.

Counting Back to Adam's Creation

Starting from the Absolute Date. The study reveals that the overthrow of the Babylonian Empire by Darius (the Mede) and Cyrus (the Persian) in 539 BCE is the absolute date for this calculation. Cyrus issued his proclamation of deliverance for the Jews during the first year of his reign, before the spring of 537 BCE. Ezra 3:1 reports that the children of Israel were back in Jerusalem by the seventh month, or the early autumn, and began making sacrifices to the Lord on an altar. So the autumn of 537 BCE is calculated for the date of the restoration of God's worship in Jerusalem and it marked the end of a prophetic period.

The prophetic period was the "seventy years" during which the Promised Land "must become a devastated place," and concerning which God also said, "after seventy years be accomplished at Babylon I will visit you, and perform my good word toward you, in causing you to return to this place." (Jer. 25:11, 12; 29:10) Daniel was very much aware of this prophecy and acted in accordance with it as the "seventy years" came to an end. (Dan. 9:1-3)

If the "seventy years" period ended in the autumn of the year 537 BCE, then it must have begun in the autumn of 607 BCE. This is supported by facts. Jeremiah 52:7-14 describes how the Babylonians broke through and the captured King Zedekiah in 607 BCE, and "in the fifth month, on the tenth day," the temple and the city were burned by the Babylonians. However, this was not yet the beginning of the "seventy years," because, as recorded in 2 Kings 25:22-26, the king of Babylon appointed Gedaliah as governor of the remaining Jewish settlements. Gedaliah and others were assassinated "in the seventh month" by Jewish conspirators, and the remaining Jews fled in fear to Egypt. It was only then, in early autumn, 607 BCE, that the land of Judah became a completely desolate place to fulfill the "seventy years" prophecy.

From 607 to 997 BCE. For this period, the study reveals that the reckoning of the period back from the desolation of Jerusalem and the kingdom of Judah in 607 BCE to the time when the unified kingdom was divided after the death of Solomon presents many problems. However, by comparing the reigns of the kings of Israel and of Judah as recorded in First and Second Kings, it can be determined that this time period covers 390 years. The prophecy of Ezekiel 4:1-13 is strong evidence that this time period is correct. This prophecy points to the time when Jerusalem would be surrounded and its occupants taken captive, which occurred in 607 BCE.

The forty years spoken of in the case of Judah in Ezekiel 4:6 terminated with the destruction of Jerusalem. The 390 years spoken of in the case of Israel in Ezekiel 4:5 did not end with the destruction of Samaria, because that occurred long before the time that Ezekiel prophesied, and the prophecy clearly states that it is directed toward the siege and destruction of Jerusalem. So the prophecy concerning Israel also terminated in 607 BCE.

Calculating back from this date, we see that the "iniquity of the house of Israel" began in 997 BCE when, after the death of Solomon, the Lord God "rent Israel from the house of David; and they made Jeroboam the son of Nebat king: and Jeroboam drave Israel from following the Lord, and made them sin a great sin," 2 Kings 17:21.

From 997 to 1513 BCE. For this period, the study reveals that Solomon's forty full regnal years ended in the spring of 997 BCE, therefore his first regnal year must have started in the spring of the year 1037 BCE. (1 Ki. 11:42) According to the Bible record, Solomon began to build the temple in Jerusalem in the second month of the fourth year of his reign. This means that he started building the temple three full years and one complete month from the beginning of his reign, which brings us to April-May, 1034 BCE.

However, 1 Kings 6:1 also states that he began building the temple in the four hundred and eightieth year after the children of Israel came out of the land of Egypt. Since 480th is an *ordinal* number, denoting 479 complete years, then 479 years must be added to 1034 BCE, to give the date of 1513 BCE as the year that the children of Israel came out of Egypt. The paragraph in the earlier section about "Bible years" explains how that from the time of the exodus in 1513 BCE, the spring month of Abib (Nisan) was to become "the first month of the year" for Israel (Ex. 12:2), instead of the autumn month of Tishri, which was previously the first month of the year.

The New Schaff-Herzog Encyclopedia of Religious Knowledge, 1957, Vol. 12, page 474, comments: "The reckoning of the regnal years of the kings is based upon the year which began in the spring, and is parallel to the Babylonian method in which this prevailed." As a consequence of this change in the Jewish calendar, from starting the year from autumn to starting the year from spring, being applied to periods of time in the Bible, a gain or loss of six months must be accounted for somewhere in the reckoning of time.

From 1513 to 1943 BCE. For this period, the study reveals that Moses records in Exodus 12:40- 41 that "the sojourning of the children of Israel, who dwelt in Egypt, was four hundred and thirty years." From the phrasing of the above scripture, it is clear that not all this "dwelling" was in Egypt. This time period started when Abraham departed from Haran for Canaan, which is the same time that God's covenant with Abraham went into effect. The first 215 years of this "dwelling" was in Canaan after Abraham left Haran at age 75, which is confirmed by the birth of Isaac, 25 years later when Abraham was 100 years old, the birth of Jacob 60 years later when Isaac was 60 years old, and the entry of Jacob and his family into Egypt when he was 130 years old. (Gen. 12:4; 21:5; 25:26; 47:9)

The remaining 215 of the 430 years of "sojourning" were spent in Egypt, until Israel became completely liberated by God, through Moses, of all Egyptian dominance and dependence in 1513 BCE. Galatians 3:17 also mentions the 430-year period, and confirms that this period started with the making of the covenant with Abraham when he followed God's instructions and moved from Haran to Canaan. This event occurred in 1943 BCE, when Abraham was seventy-five years old. (Gen.12:4). There is other evidence that supports the above computation: mention is made in Acts 7:6 of the seed of Abraham being afflicted for four hundred years. Since God eliminated the affliction by Egypt in 1513 BCE, the start of the affliction must have been in 1913 BCE, which was five years after the birth of Isaac. This agrees with Abraham's son Ishmael mocking Isaac at the time of his weaning. (Gen. 15:13; 21:8, 9).

From 1943 to 2370 BCE. For this period, the study reveals that since Abraham was seventy-five years old when his father Terah died and he left Haran and entered Canaan in 1943 BCE, it is now possible to move back in time to the days of Noah. Genesis 11:10 to 12:4 provides the time periods between the time of Abraham and the time of Noah and the Great Flood, which added up to a total of 427 years as follows:

From the beginning of the Flood to Arpachshad's birth	2 years
Then to the birth of Shelah	35 years
To the birth of Eber	30 years
To the birth of Peleg	34 years
To the birth of Reu	30 years
To the birth of Serug	32 years
To the birth of Nahor	30 years
To the birth of Terah	29 years
To the death of Terah, when Abraham was 75 years old	205 years
Total	427 years

By adding 427 years to 1943 BCE, the year Abraham left Haran for Caanan, we can determine that the Great Flood began in 2370 BCE.

From 2370 to 4026 BCE. For this final period, the study reveals that Genesis 5:3-29 and 7:11 take us back from the beginning of the Great Flood to the creation of Adam, the first human being, which spanned a total of 1,656 years as summarized below:

From Adam's creation to the birth of Seth	130 years
Then to the birth of Enosh	105 years
To the birth of Kenan	90 years
To the birth of Mahalalel	70 years
To the birth of Jared	65 years
To the birth of Enoch	162 years
To the birth of Methuselah	65 years
To the birth of Lamech	187 years
To the birth of Noah	182 years
To the Flood	600 years
Total	1,656 years

Adding 1,656 years to the previous date of 2370 BCE, the year that the Great Flood began, we arrive at 4026 BCE for the creation of Adam.

The authors of this discourse remind us that the creation of Adam does not correspond with the beginning of the "seventh" day, in which God rested. It does not mean that by the current year AD 2018 a total of 6043 full years have passed since God began resting on the "seventh" day. God accomplished other things after he created Adam and before the end of the "sixth" creative day, such as the creation of Eve and the naming of the animals by Adam, which would take some additional time.

Any time that passed between the creation of Adam and the end of the "sixth" creative day must be subtracted from the 6043 full years to determine the actual length of time from the beginning of the "seventh day" to the present time. It should also be noted that the previous "five" creative days and hours before the creation of Adam must be added to the 6043 full years to determine the actual beginning of the creation of the universe.

Note: This may lead the scientific community and others to speculate that each "creative day" consisted of many thousands or millions of years. However, the author of this book believes that God used the omnipotent power of his spoken words and his spiritual universe to create the physical universe in six days, each of which consisted of twenty-four hours, as defined and recorded in the Bible.

The study goes on to state that the modern scientific community makes claims that man has been on this earth for millions of years, but none of these claims about the origin of the earth have been substantiated by written records as has the Bible. The incredible dates attributed to "prehistoric man" are based on erroneous assumptions, which have been pointed out by reliable scientific evidence. Since these more reasonable conclusions are not considered sensational, they are often only reported in scientific journals and not to the public.

The fact is that the chronology of reliable secular history only goes back a few thousand years. But since its creation, the earth has experienced many changes and upheavals, such as the Great Flood, which have had enormous impacts on rock strata and fossil deposits, causing any pseudoscientific assertions of dates prior to the Flood extremely speculative. In stark contrast to these contradictory hypotheses and theories of humanity, the Bible appeals to reason by its precise and harmonious account of the origins of humanity and its carefully documented history of God's chosen people.

Our study of the Bible and our contemplation of the great accomplishments of our God, the great Timekeeper, should make us all feel very humble. We should realize that humanity is indeed very small in comparison to the Omnipotent God who performed the astounding act of creation many millenniums ago, which is so simply proclaimed in Scripture: "In the beginning God created the heaven and the earth." (Gen. 1:1)

Jesus' Earthly Residence (Source: Item 4e, Pages 286-290)

According to this study, the first four books of the New Testament provide inspirational accounts of the earthly life of Jesus and appear to have been written in this order: Matthew (c. AD 41), Luke (c. AD 56-58), Mark (c. AD 60-65) and John (c. AD 98). Luke 3:1-3 provides the absolute date of AD 14 for the start of Tiberius Caesar's reign (which is supported by secular history), and John the Baptist began his ministry in the fifteenth year of his reign, which establishes AD 29 as the year for Jesus' baptism by John and the beginning of his incredible ministry on this earth.

In the book of Matthew, events do not always follow in a chronological sequence, but, in most cases, the other three books appear to follow the actual order of the important events in the life of Jesus. The account by John was written more than thirty years after the other three writers and fills in important gaps in the history that are not covered by the other three. What is particularly notable is that John's account refers to the four Passovers of the earthly ministry of Jesus, which confirms his ministry of threeand-a-half years, ending in AD 33. (John 2:13; 5:1; 6:4; 12:1 and 13:1)

It reveals that the death of Jesus in AD 33 is also confirmed by astronomy.

The day of Nisan 15 was always a special sabbath, according to the law of Moses, regardless of the day of the week that it fell. If it occurred on the same day as an ordinary sabbath, then the day was called a "great" sabbath. John 19:31 indicates that such a sabbath followed the day that Jesus died, which was on a Friday. A review of astronomical tables for AD 28 to AD 33 reveal that the full moon of Nisan 14 occurred on Friday in AD 30 and AD 33. Since AD 30 would only allow for an earthly ministry of only six months, it is ruled out. Therefore, Nisan 14, the date of Jesus' death, must have occurred on Friday in AD 33, which is confirmed by astronomical evidence.

The "Seventieth Week," AD 29 to AD 36. For this period, the study reveals that Daniel 9:24-27 foretells the passage of sixty-nine weeks of years (483 years) from the going forth of the decree to restore and to rebuild Jerusalem until the coming of the Messiah. This decree went forth, as the result of a petition by Nehemiah, "in the twentieth year of Artaxerxes," king of Persia, according to Nehemiah 2:1-8. When did the reign of Artaxerxes begin? According to Thucydides, a Greek historian of Artaxerxes' time, the Athenian general Themistocles fled to Persia when Artaxerxes had "lately come to the throne." This timeframe is also supported by Plutarch, a Greek biographer of the first century AD and by Nepos, a Roman historian of the first century BCE.

Diodorus Siculus, another Greek historian of the first century AD, recorded the date of the death of Themistocles as 471 BCE. Themistocles had requested, after fleeing his country for Persia, the permission of Artaxerxes to study the Persian language for one year before appearing before him, which was granted. From this it might be reasonably reckoned that Themistocles' flight to Persia occurred in about 473 BCE and that Artaxerxes began his reign in about 474 BCE (**Note:** Secular history shows the beginning of Artaxerxes' reign as 465 BCE, but if Themistocles died in 471 BCE, then Artaxerxes' reign would had to have been before 471 BCE, if the above events occurred).

Based on the above analysis, "the twentieth year of Artaxerxes" would be 455 BCE. Calculating 483 years (the "sixty-nine weeks" of years) from this date, and considering that there was no "zero" year in crossing into the Common Era, we come to the year AD 29 for the arrival of the Messiah. Jesus became the Messiah when he was baptized by John the Baptist and anointed by the Holy Spirit in the autumn of AD 29.

Daniel 9:27 also provides that "at the half of the [seventieth] week he will cause sacrifice and gift offering to cease. This happened when the traditional Jewish sacrifices lost their legitimacy, due to the sacrifice of Jesus of himself. "The half" of this "week" of years takes us forward from the fall of AD 29 three-and-a-half years to the spring of AD 33, when Jesus was crucified.

According to Daniel 9:24, "Seventy weeks are determined upon thy people and upon thy holy city, to finish the transgression, and to make an end of sins." This indicates the continuation of God's special relationship with the children of Israel during the seven years from AD 29 to AD 36. After this period, the way was opened for uncircumcised Gentiles to receive the Holy Spirit, as revealed by the conversion of Cornelius in AD 36. (Acts 10:30.33, 44.48; 11:1)

Counting the Years in Apostolic Times (Source: Item 4e, Pages 290-292)

Between AD 33 and AD 49. For this period, the study reveals that a significant date that may be acknowledged for this period is the year AD 44. According to Josephus the Roman historian, his works, *Jewish Wars* and *Antiquities*, are in agreement that Herod Agrippa I reigned for three years after the accession of Emperor Claudius of Rome in AD 41. Historical and archaeological evidence reveals that this Herod died following the month Nisan in AD 44.

According to the Biblical record, just prior to Herod's death Agabus, the prophet, prophesied "through the spirit" about a great famine to come; Herod put the apostle James, the brother of John, to death; and Peter was put in prison by Herod at Passover time and was miraculously freed by an angel. The dates of all these events were during AD 44. (Acts 11:27, 28; 12:1-11, 20-23)

It reveals that the reign of Herod Agrippa, as revealed by secular history, was followed by Roman procurators, Cuspius Fadus and

Tiberius Alexander, and that it was during the rule of Tiberius Alexander that the famine foretold by Agabus occurred in about AD 46. According to Acts 12:25, Paul and Barnabas "returned from Jerusalem, when they had fulfilled their ministry," which must have been during the time of the famine.

After Paul and Barnabas returned to Syrian Antioch, they were inspired by the Holy Spirit to make their first missionary journey, which included Cyprus and many cities and districts of Asia Minor. This timeframe would probably have covered the period from the spring of AD 47 to the autumn of AD 48, with one winter being spent in Asia Minor. Based on Acts 14:26-28, it appears Paul returned back to Syrian Antioch and spent the following winter there, which takes us to the spring of AD 49. (Acts 13:1-14:28)

It further reveals that Chapters 1 and 2 of Galatians appear to confirm the above chronology from the Book of Acts. In Galatians 1:17-18 and 2:1, Paul talks about making two other specific visits to Jerusalem after his conversion, the one "after three years," and the other "fourteen years after." If the conversion of Paul was relatively soon after the resurrection of Jesus, as the record seems to show, and if these two periods of time are considered ordinals, which was the custom of the day, then we may calculate the three years and the fourteen years consecutively as AD 34-36 and AD 36-49.

Titus, who accompanied Paul on his second trip to Jerusalem, is said not to have been required to be circumcised, so this second Jerusalem visit mentioned in Galatians 2:1-10 seems to have been concerned with the circumcision issue. Therefore, this second visit appears to correspond with the visit described in Acts 15:1-35 to obtain a ruling on circumcision, and AD 49 fits between Paul's first and second missionary tours.

Paul's Second Missionary Journey, A.D. 49 to 52. For this period, the study reveals that according to Acts 15:35-36, after his return from his second visit to Jerusalem, Paul spent time in Syrian Antioch, and it must have been later in the summer of AD 49 that he left Antioch on his second missionary journey. This second journey was much more extensive than the first journey, and would require him to spend the winter in Asia Minor. It was probably in the spring of AD 50 that Paul responded to the invitation of the Macedonians and crossed over into Europe.

After entering Europe, he preached and organized new congregations in Philippi, Thessalonica, Beroea and Athens. After having made a journey of about 1,300 miles, mostly on foot, he would have arrived in Corinth, in the province of Achaia, in the autumn of AD 50. (Acts 16:9, 11, 12; 17:1, 2, 10, 11, 15, 16; 18:1) Paul spent eighteen months in Corinth, as recorded in Acts 18:11, which takes us to early AD 52. With the ending of winter, Paul could set sail for Caesarea, via Ephesus. Paul arrived back at his home base of Syrian Antioch, after going up to visit the congregation, apparently in Jerusalem, probably in the summer of AD 52. (Acts 18:12-22)

It further reveals that archaeological evidence supports AD 50-52 as the dates of Paul's first visit in Corinth. This evidence is a fragment of a rescript from Emperor Claudius to the Delphians of Greece which contains the words "in Gallio's proconsulship ... Claudius being Imperator for the 26th time." Other inscriptions reveal that Claudius was emperor for the twenty-third time after January 25, AD 51, and for the twenty-seventh time before August 1, AD 52. The term in office of the proconsuls was for one year, starting with the beginning of summer.

Therefore, the one-year term in office of Gallio as proconsul of Achaia must have run from the summer of AD 51 to the summer of AD 52. Acts 18:12 records the following: "And when Gallio was the deputy of Achaia, the Jews made insurrection with one accord against Paul, and brought him to the judgment seat." After Paul was acquitted by Gallio, the apostle stayed "a good while," and then sailed to Syria. (Acts 18:18)

This all seems to confirm that the spring of AD 52 was the end of Paul's eighteenmonth sojourn in Corinth. Acts 18:2 is another time marker because when Paul arrived in Corinth, he "found a Jew named Aquila, born in Pontus, lately come from Italy, with his wife Priscilla; (because that Claudius had commanded all Jews to depart from Rome)." According to Paulus Orosius, a historian of the early fifth century, this expulsion order was given by Claudius in his ninth year in office, on January 25, AD 50. Since Paul lived with them during his stay in Corinth, Aquila and Priscilla could have arrived in Corinth some time before the autumn of that year, which would allow for Paul's sojourn there from the autumn of AD 50 to the spring of AD 52.

Paul's Third Missionary Journey, AD 52 to 56. For this period, the study reveals that according to Acts 18:22-23 and 19:1, Paul spent some time in Syrian Antioch, went into Asia Minor again, and it is likely that he arrived in Ephesus by the winter of AD 52-53. While in Ephesus, Paul first spent "three months" teaching in the synagogue, but due to the disbelief of the people in the synagogue, he departed from the synagogue and began teaching in the school of Tyrannus for "two years," and after this period of time, he left for Macedonia. (Acts 19:8-10) Although Paul later reminded the leaders from Ephesus in Acts 20:31 that he had served among them "for three years," this is probably a round figure, because the actual time he spent there was about two-and-a-half years.

According to 1 Corinthians 16:8, it appears that Paul departed from Ephesus after "the festival of Pentecost" early in AD 55 and then traveled all the way to Corinth, Greece, in time to spend the three winter months there. (Acts 20:1-3) He then traveled north as far as Philippi and arrived there by the time of Passover in AD 56. (Acts 20:6) From there he sailed to Caesarea by way of Troas and Miletus. (Acts 20:15-16; 21:8). After spending a few days in Caesarea, he traveled up to Jerusalem, arriving by Pentecost of AD 56. (Acts 21:15-17)

The Closing Years, AD 56 to 100. For this final period, the study reveals that Paul was arrested shortly after he arrived in Jerusalem. After his arrest, Paul was relocated to Caesarea and remained in custody there for two years until Felix was replaced by Festus as governor. (Acts 21:33; 23:23.35; 24:27) Based on this scripture, the replacement of Felix by Festus appears to have occurred in AD 58. According to the *Encyclopedia Britannica,* two schools of thought argue AD 55 and AD 60-61 for the arrival of Festus, but adds: "It can be said confidently that the truth is between these two extremes, for the arguments urged in each case appear less to prove one extreme than to disprove its opposite." We will use AD 58 as the date of the arrival of Festus, and of Paul's trial and subsequent departure for Rome as a result of his appeal to Caesar. After being shipwrecked and wintering in Malta, the journey to Rome was over in the spring of AD 59. The record reveals that Paul continued preaching and teaching, while in captivity in Rome, for a period of two years, or until AD 61. (Acts 27:1; 28:1, 11, 16, 30, 31)

According to the study, although the historical record of Acts ends here, there are indications that Paul was released from prison and resumed his missionary journeying, possibly going to Spain in the west, and visiting Crete, Greece and Macedonia. It is reasonable to allocate three years for this ministry, which takes us to AD 64-65 for the final imprisonment and execution of Paul in Rome. According to secular history, July, AD 64, was the date of the great fire in Rome, after which Nero began his persecution of the Christians. The imprisonment and subsequent execution of Paul fit logically into this time period. (2 Tim. 1:16; 4:6, 7)

It further reveals that the time period covered by the five books written by the apostle John occurs at the end of a time of persecution by Emperor Domitian. It is said that Domitian acted like a madman during the last three years of his reign, which covered AD 81-96. It was about AD 96, while in exile on the isle of Patmos, that John wrote the Book of Revelation. He later wrote his Gospel and three letters from Ephesus or its vicinity after his release from exile, and John, the last of the apostles, died in about AD 100.

Comparing the events of secular history with the internal chronology and prophecy of the Bible helps us to more clearly understand Biblical events in the stream of time, and the harmony of Biblical chronology enhances our confidence in the Holy Scriptures as the Word of God.

From this review of historical biblical timelines, the following exhibits at the end of this chapter were developed for future reference throughout the remainder of this book: **Exhibit 2a** – Timeline of Outstanding Historical Biblical Events; **Exhibit 2b** – The Israelite Sacred and Secular Year; **Exhibit 2c** – The Origins and Authors of the Books of the Bible; and **Exhibit 3** – Modern Palestinian Regional History Timeline After AD 100.

Logical Conclusion: From the analysis of the section about "Measuring Events in the Stream of Time," it may be inferred that:

1. **The Bible makes references to the state records of the governments of Judah and Israel, as well as to the state affairs of Babylon and Persia. In all four of these countries, the state chronology was accurately calculated according to the rulerships of the kings, and the same system of calculation has been carried over into the Bible. In all these countries, the official years in the kingship were the *regnal* years, and were normally calculated from Nisan to Nisan, or from spring to spring. When a king succeeded to the throne, the remaining months until the next spring month**

of Nisan were denoted as his *accession* year, during which he filled out the *regnal* term of rulership for his predecessor. However, his own official *regnal* term was reckoned as starting on the next Nisan 1.

2. In order to count back to the creation of Adam, the overthrow of the Babylonian Empire by Darius (the Mede) and Cyrus (the Persian) in 539 BCE is the *absolute date* for this calculation. Cyrus issued his proclamation of deliverance for the Jews during the first year of his reign, before the spring of 537 BCE. Ezra 3:1 reports that the children of Israel were back in Jerusalem by the seventh month, or the early autumn, and began making sacrifices to the Lord on an altar. So the autumn of 537 BCE is calculated for the date of the restoration of God's worship in Jerusalem and it marked the end of a prophetic period. If the "seventy years" period ended in the autumn of the year 537 BCE, then it must have begun in the autumn of 607 BCE.

3. The reckoning of the period back from the desolation of Jerusalem and the kingdom of Judah in 607 BCE to the time when the unified kingdom was divided after the death of Solomon presents many problems. However, by comparing the reigns of the kings of Israel and of Judah as recorded in First and Second Kings, it can be determined that this time period covers 390 years. Calculating back from this date, we see that the "iniquity of the house of Israel" began in 997 BCE when, after the death of Solomon, the Lord God "rent Israel from the house of David; and they made Jeroboam the son of Nebat king: and Jeroboam drave Israel from following the Lord, and made them sin a great sin," 2 Kings 17:21.

4. Solomon's forty full regnal years ended in the spring of 997 BCE, therefore his first regnal year must have started in the spring of the year 1037 BCE. (1 Ki. 11:42) According to the Bible record, Solomon began to build the temple in Jerusalem in the second month of the fourth year of his

reign. This means that he started building the temple three full years and one complete month from the beginning of his reign, which brings us to April-May, 1034 BCE. However, 1 Kings 6:1 also states that he began building the temple in the four hundred and eightieth year after the children of Israel came out of the land of Egypt. Since 480th is an *ordinal* number, denoting 479 complete years, then 479 years must be added to 1034 BCE, to give the date of 1513 BCE as the year that the children of Israel came out of Egypt.

5. Moses records in Exodus 12:40, 41 that " the sojourning of the children of Israel, who dwelt in Egypt, was four hundred and thirty years." From the phrasing of the above scripture, it is clear that not all this "dwelling" was in Egypt. This time period started when Abraham departed from Haran for Canaan, which is the same time that God's covenant with Abraham went into effect. The first 215 years of this "dwelling" was in Canaan after Abraham left Haran at age 75, which is confirmed by the birth of Isaac, 25 years later when Abraham was 100 years old, the birth of Jacob 60 years later when Isaac was 60 years old, and the entry of Jacob and his family into Egypt when he was 130 years old. (Gen. 12:4; 21:5; 25:26; 47:9)

The remaining 215 of the 430 years of "sojourning" were spent in Egypt, until Israel became completely liberated by God, through Moses, of all Egyptian dominance and dependence in 1513 BCE. Galatians 3:17 also mentions the 430-year period, and confirms that this period started with the making of the covenant with Abraham when he followed God's instructions and moved from Haran to Canaan. This event occurred in 1943 BCE, when Abraham was seventy-five years old. (Gen.12:4).

6. Since Abraham was seventy-five years old when his father Terah died and he left Haran and entered Canaan in 1943 BCE, it is now possible to move back in time to the days of Noah. Genesis 11:10 to 12:4 provides the time periods between the time of Abraham and the time of Noah and the Great Flood, which added up to a total of 427 years. By adding 427 years to 1943 BCE, the year Abraham left Haran for Caanan, we can determine that the Great Flood began in 2370 BCE.

7. Genesis 5:3-29 and 7:11 take us back from the beginning of the Great Flood to the creation of Adam, the first human being, which spanned a total of 1,656 years. Adding 1,656 years to the previous date of 2370 BCE, the year that the Great Flood began, we arrive at 4026 BCE for the creation of Adam.

8. To determine the dates of the ministry of Jesus Christ on earth, we must look at the first four books of the New Testament. The first four books of the New Testament provide inspirational accounts of the earthly life of Jesus and appear to have been written in this order: Matthew (c. AD 41), Luke (c. AD 56-58), Mark (c. AD 60-65) and John (c. AD 98). Luke 3:1-3 provides the absolute date of AD 14 for the start of Tiberius Caesar's reign (which is supported by secular history), and John the Baptist began his ministry in the fifteenth year of his reign, which establishes AD 29 as the year for Jesus' baptism by John and the beginning of his incredible ministry on this earth.

9. John's account refers to the four Passovers of the earthly ministry of Jesus, which confirms his ministry of three-and-a-half years, ending in AD 33. (John 2:13; 5:1; 6:4; 12:1 and 13:1). The death of Jesus in AD 33 is also confirmed by astronomy. The day of Nisan 15 was always a special sabbath, according to the law of Moses, regardless of the day of the week that it fell. If it occurred on the same day as an ordinary sabbath, then the day was called a "great"

sabbath. John 19:31 indicates that such a sabbath followed the day that Jesus died, which was on a Friday.

10. Daniel 9:24-27 foretells the passage of sixty-nine weeks of years (483 years) from the going forth of the decree to restore and to rebuild Jerusalem until the coming of the Messiah. This decree went forth, as the result of a petition by Nehemiah, "in the twentieth year of Artaxerxes," king of Persia, according to Nehemiah 2:1-8. When did the reign of Artaxerxes begin? According to Thucydides, a Greek historian of Artaxerxes' time, the Athenian general Themistocles fled to Persia when Artaxerxes had "lately come to the throne."

Diodorus Siculus, another Greek historian of the first century AD, recorded the date of the death of Themistocles as 471 BCE. Themistocles had requested, after fleeing his country for Persia, the permission of Artaxerxes to study the Persian language for one year before appearing before him, which was granted. From this it might be reasonably reckoned that Themistocles' flight to Persia occurred in about 473 BCE and that Artaxerxes began his reign in about 474 BCE.

11. Based on the above analysis, "the twentieth year of Artaxerxes" would be 455 BCE. Calculating 483 years (the "sixty-nine weeks" of years) from this date, and considering that there was no "zero" year in crossing into the Common Era, we come to the year AD 29 for the arrival of the Messiah. Jesus became the Messiah when he was baptized by John the Baptist and anointed by the Holy Spirit in the autumn of AD 29.

12. Daniel 9:27 also provides that "at the half of the [seventieth] week he will cause sacrifice and gift offering to cease. This happened when the traditional Jewish sacrifices lost their legitimacy, due to the sacrifice of Jesus of himself. "The

half" of this "week" of years takes us forward from the fall of AD 29 three-and-a-half years to the spring of AD 33, when Jesus was crucified.

13. According to Daniel 9:24, "Seventy weeks are determined upon thy people and upon thy holy city, to finish the transgression, and to make an end of sins." This indicates the continuation of God's special relationship with the children of Israel during the seven years from AD 29 to AD 36. After this period, the way was opened for uncircumcised Gentiles to receive the Holy Spirit, as revealed by the conversion of Cornelius in AD 36. (Acts 10:30-33, 44-48; 11:1)

Exhibit 2a – Timeline of Outstanding Historical Biblical Events

EXHIBIT 2a

TIMELINE OF OUTSTANDING HISTORICAL BIBLICAL EVENTS

Note: Many of the following dates are firmly established, but in the case of some, approximate dates are provided, based on the available evidence. The purpose of the chart is to help Bible scholars to locate events in the stream of time and see their relationship to one another. Symbols are as follows: "a" for "after"; "b" for "before"; and "c" for "circa or about." **Source**: Watch Tower Bible and Tract Society of Pennsylvania (1963), "All Scripture is Inspired of God and Beneficial," First Edition, Brooklyn: Watchtower Bible and Tract Society of New York, Inc., International Bible Students Association, Pages 292-296.

DATE	EVENT	REFERENCE
4026 BCE	Adam's creation	Gen. 2:7
a. 4026 BCE	Edenic covenant made, first prophecy	Gen. 3:15
b. 3896 BCE	Cain slays Abel	Gen. 4:8
3896 BCE	Birth of Seth	Gen. 5:3
3404 BCE	Birth of righteous Enoch	Gen. 5:18
3339 BCE	Birth of Methuselah	Gen. 5:21
3152 BCE	Birth of Lamech	Gen. 5:25
3096 BCE	Death of Adam	Gen. 5:5
3039 BCE	Transference of Enoch; ends his period of prophesying	Gen. 5:23, 24; Jude 14
2970 BCE	Birth of Noah	Gen. 5:28, 29
2490 BCE	God's pronouncement as to humanity	Gen. 6:3
2470 BCE	Birth of Japheth	Gen. 5:32; 9:24;10:21
2468 BCE	Birth of Shem	Gen. 7:11; 11:10
2370 BCE	Death of Methuselah	Gen. 5:27
	Flood waters fall (in November)	Gen. 7:6, 11
2369 BCE	Making of the covenant after the Flood	Gen. 8:13; 9:16
2368 BCE	Birth of Arpachshad	Gen. 11: 10
a. 2239 BCE	Building of the Tower of Babel	Gen. 11:4
2020 BCE	Death of Noah	Gen. 9:28, 29
2018 BCE	Birth of Abraham	Gen. 11: 26, 32; 12:4
1943 BCE	Abraham enters Canaan; Abrahamic covenant; beginning of the	Gen. 12:4,7;
	430-year period to law covenant	Ex. 12:40; Gal. 3:17
b. 1933 BCE	Lot rescued; Abraham visits Melchizedek	Gen. 14:16, 18;16:3
1932 BCE	Ishmael born	Gen. 16: 15,16
1919 BCE	Covenant of circumcision made with Abraham	Gen. 17:1, 10, 24
	Judgment of Sodom and Gomorrah	Gen. 19:24
1918 BCE	Birth of Isaac the true heir; beginning of the "about 450 years"	Gen. 21:2, 5; Acts 13:17·20
1913 BCE	Weaning of Isaac; Ishmael sent away; beginning of the	Gen. 21:8; 15:13;
	400-year affliction	Acts 7:6
1881 BCE	Death of Sarah	Gen. 17:17; 23:1
1878 BCE	Marriage of Isaac and Rebekah	Gen. 25:20
1868 BCE	Death of Shem	Gen. 11:11
1858 BCE	Birth of Esau and Jacob	Gen. 25:26
1843 BCE	Death of Abraham	Gen. 25:7
1818 BCE	Esau marries first two wives	Gen. 26:34
1795 BCE	Death of Ishmael	Gen. 25:17
1781 BCE	Jacob flees to Haran; his vision at Bethel	Gen. 28:2, 13, 19
1774 BCE	Jacob marries Leah and Rachel	Gen. 29:23-30
1767 BCE	Birth of Joseph	Gen. 30:23, 24
1761 BCE	Jacob returns to Canaan from Haran	Gen. 31:18, 41
c. 1761 BCE	Jacob wrestles angel; is named Israel	Gen. 32:24-28
1750 BCE	Joseph sold as a slave by his brothers	Gen. 37:2, 28
1738 BCE	Death of Isaac	Gen. 35:28, 29
1737 BCE	Joseph made prime minister of Egypt	Gen. 41:40, 46
1728 BCE	Jacob with his whole family enters Egypt	Gen. 45:6; 46:26; 47:9

DATE	EVENT	REFERENCE
1711 BCE	Death of Jacob	Gen. 47:28
1657 BCE	Death of Joseph	Gen. 50:26
b. 1613 BCE	Job's trial	Job 1:8; 42:16
a. 1600 BCE	Egypt attains prominence as First World Power	Ex. 1:8
1593 BCE	Birth of Moses	Ex. 2:2, 10
1553 BCE	Moses offers himself as deliverer; flees to Midian	Ex. 2:11, 14, 15; Acts 7:23
c. 1514 BCE	Moses at the burning thornbush	Ex. 3:2
1513 BCE	Passover; Israelites leave Egypt; Red Sea, Deliverance;	Ex. 12:12; 14:27, 29, 30;
	Egypt's power shaken; end of 400-year period of affliction	Gen. 15:13, 14
	Law covenant made at Mt. Sinai (Horeb)	Ex. 24:6-8
	End of the 430-year period from Abrahamic Covenant	Gal. 3:17; Ex. 12:40
	Moses compiles Genesis in wilderness; Bible writing begins	John 5:46
1512 BCE	Tabernacle construction completed	Ex. 40:17
	Consecration of the Aaronic priesthood	Lev. 8:34-36
	Moses completes Exodus and Leviticus	Lev. 27:34; Num. 1:1
c. 1473 BCE	Moses completes the book of Job	Job 42:16, 17
1473 BCE	Moses completes Numbers on Moab plains	Num. 35:1; 36:13
	Covenant of the Repeated Law in Moab	Deut. 29:1
	Moses writes Deuteronomy	Deut. 1:1, 3
	Moses dies on Nebo in Moab	Deut. 34:5, 7
	Israel inters Canaan under Joshua	Josh. 4:19
1467 BCE	End of Joshua's war operations in Canaan;	Josh. 11:23; 14:7, 10-15
	end of the "about 450 years" of Acts 13:17-20	
c. 1433 BCE	Book of Joshua completed	Josh. 1:1; 24:26
	Death of Joshua	Josh. 24:29
1117 BCE	Samuel anoints Saul as king of Israel	1 Sam. 10:24; Acts 13:21
1107 BCE	Birth of David at Bethlehem	1 Sam. 16:1; 2 Sam. 5:4
c. 1100 BCE	Samuel completes the book of Judges	Judg. 21:25
c. 1090 BCE	Samuel completes the book of Ruth	Ruth 4:18-22
c. 1077 BCE	Book of 1 Samuel completed	1 Sam. 31:6
1077 BCE	David becomes king of Judah at Hebron	2 Sam. 2:4
1070 BCE	David becomes king of all Israel; takes Jerusalem; Makes it capital	2 Sam. 5:3-7
a. 1070 BCE	The Ark brought into Jerusalem; Kingdom covenant made with David	2 Sam. 6:15; 7:12-16
c. 1040 BCE	Gad and Nathan complete 2 Samuel	2 Sam. 24:18
1037 BCE	Solomon succeeds David as king of Israel	1 Ki. 1:39; 2:12
1034 BCE	Construction of Solomon's temple begun	1 Ki. 6:1
1027 BCE	Solomon's temple in Jerusalem completed	1 Ki. 6:38
c. 1020 BCE	Solomon completes the Song of Solomon	Song of Sol. 1:1
c. 1000 BCE	Solomon completes the book of Ecclesiastes	Eccl. 1:1
997 BCE	Rehoboam succeeds Solomon, kingdom split;	1 Ki. 11:43; 12:19, 20
	Jeroboam begins reign as king of Israel	
993 BCE	Shishak assaults Jerusalem and takes treasures from temple	1 Ki. 14:25, 26
980 BCE	Abijam succeeds Rehoboam as king of Judah	1 Ki. 15:1, 2
978 BCE	Asa succeeds Abijam as king of Judah	1 Ki. 15:9, 10
977 BCE	Nadab succeeds Jeroboam as king of Israel	1 Ki. 14:20
976 BCE	Baasha succeeds Nadab as king of Israel	1 Ki. 15:33
953 BCE	Elah succeeds Baasha as king of Israel	1 Ki. 16:8
952 BCE	Zimri succeeds Elah as king of Israel	1 Ki. 16:15
	Tibni and Omri succeed Zimri as kings of Israel	1 Ki. 16:21
948 BCE	Omri rules as king of Israel alone	1 Ki. 16:22, 23
941 BCE	Ahab succeeds Omri as king of Israel	1 Ki. 16:29
938 BCE	Jehoshaphat succeeds Asa as king of Judah	1 Ki. 22:41, 42
922 BCE	Ahaziah succeeds Ahab as king of Israel	1 Ki. 22:51, 52

DATE	EVENT	REFERENCE
921 BCE	Jehoram of Israel succeeds Ahaziah as king	2 Ki. 3:1
917 BCE	Jehoram of Judah succeeds Jehoshaphat as king	2 Ki. 8:16, 17
910 BCE	Ahaziah succeeds Jehoram as king of Judah	2 Ki. 8:25, 26
909 BCE	Queen Athaliah usurps throne of Judah	2 Ki. 11:1-3
	Jehu succeeds Jehoram as king of Israel	2 Ki. 9:24, 27; 10:36
903 BCE	Jehoash succeeds Ahaziah as king of Judah	2 Ki. 12:1
881 BCE	Jehoahaz succeeds Jehu as king of Israel	2 Ki. 13:1
867 BCE	Jehoash succeeds Jehoahaz as king of Israel	2 Ki. 13:10
866 BCE	Amaziah succeeds Jehoash as king of Judah	2 Ki. 14:1, 2
852 BCE	Jeroboam II succeeds Jehoash as king of Israel	2 Ki. 14:23
c. 852 BCE	Jonah completes the book of Jonah	Jonah 1:1, 2
826 BCE	Uzziah (Azariah) succeeds Amaziah, king of Judah	2 Ki. 15:1, 2
c. 820 BCE	Joel completes the book of Joel	Joel 1:1
c. 811 BCE	Amos completes the book of Amos	Amos 1:1
789 BCE	Zechariah succeeds Jeroboam II as king of Israel	2 Ki. 15:8
788 BCE	Shallum succeeds Zechariah as king of Israel	2 Ki. 15:13, 17
	Menahem succeeds Shallum as king of Israel	
777 BCE	Pekahiah succeeds Menahem as king of Israel	2 Ki. 15:23
775 BCE	Pekah succeeds Pekahiah as king of Israel	2 Ki. 15:27
c. 775 BCE	Isaiah begins to prophesy	Isa. 1:1; 6:1
774 BCE	Jotham succeeds Uzziah (Azariah), king of Judah	2 Ki. 15:32, 33
759 BCE	Ahaz succeeds Jotham as king of Judah	2 Ki. 16:1,2
748 BCE	Hoshea succeeds Pekah as king of Israel	2 Ki. 17:1
745 BCE	Hezekiah succeeds Ahaz as king of Judah	2 Ki. 18:1, 2
a. 745 BCE	Hosea completes the book of Hosea	Hos. 1:1
740 BCE	Assyria, 2nd World Power, subjugates Israel, takes Samaria	2 Ki. 17:6, 13, 18
732 BCE	Sennacherib invades Judah	2 Ki. 18:13
a. 732 BCE	Isaiah completes the book of Isaiah	Isa. 1:1
b. 716 BCE	Micah completes the book of Micah	Mic. 1:1
c. 716 BCE	Compiling of Proverbs completed	Prov. 25:1
716 BCE	Manasseh succeeds Hezekiah as king of Judah	2 Ki. 21:1
661 BCE	Amon succeeds Manasseh as king of Judah	2 Ki. 21:19
659 BCE	Josiah succeeds Amon as king of Judah	2 Ki. 22:1
b. 648 BCE	Zephaniah completes the book of Zephaniah	Zeph. 1:1
647 BCE	Jeremiah begins preaching	Jer. 1:1, 2
b. 633 BCE	Nahum completes the book of Nahum	Nah. 1:1
c. 633 BCE	Nineveh falls to Chaldeans and Medes	Nah. 3:7
	Babylon now in line to become 3rd World Power	
628 BCE	Jehoahaz succeeds Josiah as king of Judah	2 Ki. 23:31
	Jehoiakim succeeds Jehoahaz as king of Judah	2 Ki. 23:36
c. 628 BCE	Habakkuk completes the book of Habakkuk	Hab. 1:1
625 BCE	Nebuchadnezzar rules as king of Babylon	Jer. 25:1
620 BCE	Nebuchadnezzar makes Jehoiakim tributary king	2 Ki. 24:1
618 BCE	Jehoiachin succeeds Jehoiakim as king of Judah	2 Ki. 24:6, 8
617 BCE	Nebuchadnezzar takes first Jewish captives to	Dan. 1:1-4; 2 Ki. 24:12-18
	Babylon Zedekiah is made king of Judah	
613 BCE	Ezekiel begins prophesying	Ezek. 1:1-3
609 BCE	Nebuchadnezzar attacks Judah third time; begins siege of Jerusalem	2 Ki. 25:1, 2
607 BCE	Fifth Month (Ab 7-10), temple razed and Jerusalem destroyed	2 Ki. 25:8-10; Jer. 52:12-14
	Seventh month, Jews abandon Judah; 7 gentile times begin count	2 Ki. 25:25, 26
	Jeremiah writes Lamentations	Lam., preamble LXX
c. 607 BCE	Obadiah completes the book of Obadiah	Obad. 1

DATE	EVENT	REFERENCE
591 BCE	Ezekiel completes the book of Ezekiel	Ezek. 40:1; 29:17
c. 580 BCE	Books of 1 and 2 Kings and Jeremiah completed	Jer. 52:31; 2 Ki. 25:27
539 BCE	Babylon falls to the Medes and Persians:	Dan. 5:30, 31
	Medo-Persia becomes the 4th World Power	
537 BCE	Decree of Cyrus the Persian, permitting Jews to return to Jerusalem,	2 Chron. 36:22, 23;
	takes effect; Jerusalem's 70-year desolation ends	Jer. 25:12; 29:10
536 BCE	Daniel completes the book of Daniel	Dan. 10:1
	Foundation of temple laid by Zerubbabel	Ezra 3:8-10
522 BCE	Ban put on temple-building work	Ezra 4:23, 24
521 BCE	Haggai completes the book of Haggai	Hag. 1:1
519 BCE	Zachariah completes the book of Zechariah	Zech. 1:1
516 BCE	Zerubbabel completes second temple	Ezra 6:14, 15
c. 474 BCE	Mordecai completes the book of Ester	Esther 3:7; 9:32
468 BCE	Ezra and priests return to Jerusalem	Ezra 7:7
c. 460 BCE	Ezra completes the books of 1 and 2 Chronicles	Ezra 1:1
	and Ezra; final compilation of Psalms	2 Chron. 36:22; Ps. 137
455 BCE	Jerusalem's walls rebuilt by Nehemiah;	Neh. 1:1; 2:1, 11; 6:15;
	prophecy of 70 weeks begins fulfillment	Dan. 9:24
a. 443 BCE	Nehemiah completes the book of Nehemiah	Neh. 5:14
	Malachi completes the book of Malachi	Mal. 1:1
406 BCE	Jerusalem fully rebuilt to ancient glory	Dan. 9:25
332 BCE	Greece, 5th World Power, rules Judea	Dan. 8:21
c. 280 BCE	The Greek Septuagint translation begun	
165 BCE	Renewal of temple after desecration by Greek	John 10:22
	Idolatry; Festival of Dedication	
63 BCE	Rome, 6th World Power, rules Jerusalem	John 19:15; Rev. 17:10
37 BCE	Herod (appointed king by Rome) takes Jerusalem by storm	
17 BCE	Herod begins rebuilding the temple in Jerusalem	John 2:20
2 BCE	Birth of John the Baptist and of Jesus	Luke 1:60; 2:7
AD 29	John the Baptist and Jesus begin their ministries	Luke 3:1, 2, 23
AD 33	Nisan 14, Jesus is crucified	Luke 22:20; 23:33
	Nisan 16, the resurrection of Jesus	Matt. 28:1-10
	Sivan 6, Pentecost; outpouring of spirit; Peter opens the way for	Acts 2:1-17; Matt. 16:19;
	Jews to Christian congregation; uses first key	Acts 2:38
AD 36	End of the 70 weeks of years; Peter uses second key, uncircumcised	Dan. 9:24-27
	people of the nations enter the Christian congregation	Acts 10:1, 45
c. AD 41	Matthew writes the Gospel entitled "Matthew"	
c. AD 47-48	Paul's first missionary tour	Acts 13:1-14:28
c. AD 49	Governing Body rules against Gentile circumcision for the believers	Acts 15:28, 29
	from the nations	
c. AD 49-52	Paul's second missionary tour	Acts 15:36-18:22
c. AD 50	Paul writes 1 Thessalonians from Corinth	1 Thess. 1:1
c. AD 50-52	Paul writes Galatians from Corinth or Syrian Antioch	Gal. 1:1
c. AD 51	Paul writes 2 Thessalonians from Corinth	2 Thess. 1:1
c. AD 52-56	Paul's third missionary tour	Acts 18:23-21:17
c. AD 55	Paul writes 1 Corinthians from Ephesus and 2 Corinthians	1 Cor. 15:32;
	from Macedonia	2 Cor. 2:12, 13
c. AD 56	Paul writes the letter to the Romans from Corinth	Rom. 16:1
c. AD 56-58	Luke writes the Gospel entitled "Luke"	Luke 1:1, 2
c. AD 60-61	From Rome Paul writes: Ephesians	Eph. 3:1
	Philippians	Phil. 4:22
	Colossians	Col. 4:18

DATE	EVENT	REFERENCE
	Philemon	Philem. 1
c. AD 60-65	Mark writes the Gospel entitled "Mark"	
c. AD 61	Paul writes letter to the Hebrews from Rome	Heb. 13:24; 10:34
	Luke completes the book of Acts in Rome	
c. AD 61-64	Paul writes 1 Timothy from Macedonia	1 Tim. 1:3
	Paul writes Titus from Macedonia (?)	Titus 1:5
b. AD 62	James, Jesus' brother, writes "James" from Jerusalem	Jas. 1:1
c. AD 62-64	Peter writes 1 Peter from Babylon	1 Pet. 1:1; 5:13
c. AD 64	Peter writes 2 Peter from Babylon (?)	2 Pet. 1:1
c. AD 65	Paul writes 2 Timothy from Rome	2 Tim. 4:16-18
	Jude, Jesus' brother, writes "Jude"	Jude 1, 17, 18
AD 70	Jerusalem and its temple destroyed by Romans and Jews dispersed	Dan. 9:27; Matt. 23:37, 38;
	to Armenia, Iraq, Persia, Arabia, Egypt, Italy, Spain and Greece.	Luke 19:42-44
c. AD 96	John, on Patmos, writes Revelation	Rev. 1:9
c. AD 98	John writes the Gospel entitled "John" and his	John 21:22, 23
	letters 1, 2, and 3 John; Bible writing completed	
c. AD 100	John, the last of the apostles, dies	2 Thess. 2:7

Exhibit 2b – The Israelite Sacred and Secular Year

EXHIBIT 2b

THE SACRED AND SECULAR YEAR OF THE ISRAELITES

Name of the Month	Corresponds to:	Sacred Year	Secular Year	Citations	Festivals/Comments
Abib or Nisan	March-April	1st Month	7th Month	Ex. 13:4; Neb. 2:1	Nisan 14 Passover Nisan 15-21 Festival of unfermented cakes Nisan 16 Offering of firstfruits
Ziv or Iyyar	April-May	2nd Month	8th Month	1 Ki. 6:1	
Sivan	May-June	3rd Month	9th Month	Ester 8:9	Sivan 6 Feast of weeks (Pentecost)
Tammuz	June-July	4th Month	10th Month	Jer. 52:6	
Ab	July-August	5th Month	11th Month	Ezra 7:8	
Elul	August-September	6th Month	12th Month	Neh. 6:15	
Ethanim or Tishri	September-October	7th Month	1st Month	1 Ki. 8:2	Ethanim 1 Day of the trumpet blast Ethanim 10 Day of atonement Ethanim 15-21 Festival of booths Ethanim 22 Solemn assembly
Bul or Heshvan	October-November	8th Month	2nd Month	1 Ki. 6:38	
Chislev	November-December	9th Month	3rd Month	Neh. 1:1	
Tebeth	December-January	10th Month	4th Month	Ester 2:16	
Shebat	January-February	11th Month	5th Month	Zech. 1:7	
Adar	February-March	12th Month	6th Month	Ester 3:7	
V Adar or "2nd Adar"	Intercalary month (was added 7 times each 19 years to convert lunar year to solar year)	13th Month			The Hebrews followed the lunar year of 354 days with months of 29 or 30 days. After 5th century BCE, lunar year was converted to solar year of about 365.25 days using V Adar.

Note: In 46 BCE the Julian Calendar was introduced, which consisted of 365 days in a year, with the exception that on each fourth year ("leap year") one day was added, to make it 366 days. However, it was found that the Julian Calendar year was about 11 minutes longer than the true solar year. In 1582, the Gregorian Calendar was introduced, which revised the Julian Calendar such that centuries not divisible by 400 would not be considered leap years. The Gregorian Calendar is now the one in general use in Western countries. **Source:** Watch Tower Bible and Tract Society of Pennsylvania (1963), "All Scripture is Inspired of God and Beneficial," First Edition, Brooklyn: Watchtower Bible and Tract Society of New York, Inc., International Bible Students Association, Page 280.

Exhibit 2c – The Origins and Authors of the Books of the Bible

EXHIBIT 2c

TABLE OF THE BOOKS OF THE BIBLE

Note: The names of the writers of some books and the places where they were written are uncertain. Many dates are only approximate, with the symbol a. meaning "after," b. meaning "before" and c. meaning "circa" or "about." **Source:** Watch Tower Bible and Tract Society of Pennsylvania (1963), "All Scripture is Inspired of God and Beneficial," First Edition, Brooklyn: Watchtower Bible and Tract Society of New York, Inc., International Bible Students Association, Page 297.

Books of the Hebrew Scriptures Written before the Common or Christian Era				
Name of Book	The Writer	Place Written	Writing Completed (BCE)	Time Covered (BCE)
Genesis	Moses	Wilderness	1513	4026 - 1657
Exodus	Moses	Wilderness	1512	1657 - 1512
Leviticus	Moses	Wilderness	1512	1 Month (1512)
Numbers	Moses	Plains of Moab	1473	1512 - 1473
Deuteronomy	Moses	Plains of Moab	1473	2 Months (1473)
Joshua	Joshua	Canaan	c. 1433	1473 - c. 1433
Judges	Samuel	Israel	c. 1100	c. 1433 - 1190
Ruth	Samuel	Israel	c. 1090	11 Years of judges' rule
1 Samuel	Samuel, Gad, Nathan	Israel	c. 1077	c. 1190 - 1077
2 Samuel	Gad, Nathan	Israel	c. 1040	1077 - c. 1040
1 Kings	Jeremiah	Jerusalem, Israel, and	1 roll c. 580	c. 1040 - 917
2 Kings	Jeremiah	Egypt		922 - c. 580
1 Chronicles	Ezra	Jerusalem (?)	1 roll c. 460	1077 - 1037
2 Chronicles	Ezra	Jerusalem (?)		1037 - 537
Ezra	Ezra	Jerusalem	c. 460	537 - 467
Nehemiah	Nehemiah	Jerusalem	a. 443	456 - a. 443
Esther	Mordecai	Shushan, Elam	c. 474	c. 484 - 474
Job	Moses	Wilderness	c. 1473	Between 1657 - 1473
Psalms	David and others		c. 460	
Proverbs	Solomon, Agur, Lemuel		c. 716	
Ecclesiastes	Solomon	Jerusalem	c. 1000	
The Song of Solomon	Solomon	Jerusalem	c. 1020	
Isaiah	Isaiah	Jerusalem	c. 732	c. 775 - 732
Jeremiah	Jeremiah	Jerusalem, Egypt	c. 580	647 - c. 580
Lamentations	Jeremiah	Near Jerusalem	607	
Ezekiel	Ezekiel	Babylon	591	613 - 591
Daniel	Daniel	Babylon	536	618 - 536
Hosea	Hosea	Samaria (District)	a. 745	b. 811 - a. 745
Joel	Joel	Judah	c. 820 (?)	
Amos	Amos	Judah	c. 811	
Obadiah	Obadiah		c. 607	
Jonah	Jonah		c. 852	
Micah	Micah	Judah	b. 716	c. 774 - 716
Nahum	Nahum	Judah	b. 633	
Habakkuk	Habakkuk	Judah	c. 628	
Zephaniah	Zephaniah	Judah	b. 648	
Haggai	Haggai	Jerusalem rebuilt	521	112 Days (521)
Zechariah	Zechariah	Jerusalem rebuilt	519	521 - 519
Malachi	Malachi	Jerusalem rebuilt	a. 443	

Books of the Greek Scriptures Written During the Common or Christian Era				
Name of Book	The Writer	Place Written	Writing Completed (AD)	Time Covered (AD)
Matthew	Matthew	Palestine	c. 41	2 BCE - AD 33
Mark	Mark	Rome	c. 60-65	29 - 33
Luke	Luke	Caesarea	c. 56-58	3 BCE - AD 33
John	John	Ephesus, or near	c. 98	After Prologue, 29 - 33
Acts	Luke	Rome	c. 61	33 - c. 61
Romans	Paul	Corinth	c. 56	
1 Corinthians	Paul	Ephesus	c. 55	
2 Corinthians	Paul	Macedonia	c. 55	
Galatians	Paul	Corinth or Syrian Antioch	c. 50 - 52	
Ephesians	Paul	Rome	c. 60 - 61	
Philippians	Paul	Rome	c. 60 - 61	
Colossians	Paul	Rome	c. 60 - 61	
1 Thessalonians	Paul	Corinth	c. 50	
2 Thessalonians	Paul	Corinth	c. 51	
1 Timothy	Paul	Macedonia	c. 61 - 64	
2 Timothy	Paul	Rome	c. 65	
Titus	Paul	Macedonia (?)	c. 61 - 64	
Philemon	Paul	Rome	c. 60 - 61	
Hebrews	Paul	Rome	c. 61	
James	James (Jesus' brother)	Jerusalem	b. 62	
1 Peter	Peter	Babylon	c. 62 - 64	
2 Peter	Peter	Babylon (?)	c. 64	
1 John	John	Ephesus, or near	c. 98	
2 John	John	Ephesus, or near	c. 98	
3 John	John	Ephesus, or near	c. 98	
Jude	Jude (Jesus' brother)	Palestine (?)	c. 65	
Revelation	John	Patmos	c. 96	

Exhibit 3 – Modern Palestinian Regional
History Timeline After AD 100

EXHIBIT 3

PALESTINIAN REGIONAL HISTORY TIMELINE AFTER AD 100		
DATE	EVENT	REFERENCE
c. AD 100	John, the last of the apostles, dies.	2 Thess. 2:7
AD 130	Roman emperor Hadrian builds a Roman city he called "Colonies Aelia Capitolina" on the ruins if Jerusalem.	
AD 132-135	The Bar Kokhba revolt takes place, the third major rebellion by the Jews of Judaea Province against the rule of the Roman Empire. After the rebellion failed emperor Hadrian changed the name of the province from Judaea to "Syria Palaestina" to complete the dissociation between the Jewish rebels to the region.	https://en.wikipedia.org/wiki/Timeline_of_the_history_of_the_region_of_Palestine
AD 324	Emperor of the Eastern Roman Empire Constantine the Great, having defeated Emperor Maximian, Caesar of the Western Roman Empire at the Battle of the Milvian Bridge becomes the sole ruler of the re-united Roman Empire with its capital at Byzantium and declares Christianity as the official religion of the empire.	
AD 326-333	Concurrent construction of the world's first 4 church buildings under Queen Helena's tutelage: The Church of the Nativity is built in Bethlehem, marking the site where Jesus was born; "Eleona" on the Mount of Olives in Jerusalem marking the site where Jesus ascended to heaven; The Church of The Holy Sepulchre, on hill of Golgotha where Jesus was crucified, buried and resurrected; and Mamre, near Hebron.	
AD 351-352	Jewish revolt against Emperor Constantius Gallus in the Palestine region, which was quickly subdued by Gallus' general Ursicinus.	https://en.wikipedia.org/wiki/Timeline_of_the_history_of_the_region_of_Palestine
AD 362	Roman emperor Julian the Apostate ordered Alypius of Antioch to rebuild the Jewish Temple.	
AD 363	The severe Galilee earthquake of 363 occurred, which halted the temple construction. Plan was scrapped after death of emperor Julian in 363.	
AD 425	The Sanhedrin is disbanded by the Byzantine Roman Empire.	
AD. 614	The Persian Empire under general Shahrbaraz captures and sacks Jerusalem; the Church of the Holy Sepulchre is damaged by fire and the True Cross is captured.	
AD 629	Byzantine Emperor Heraclius retakes Jerusalem, after the decisive defeat of the Sassanid Empire at the Battle of Nineveh (627). Heraclius personally returns the True Cross to the city.	
AD 638	The conquest of Jerusalem by the armies of the Rashidun Caliphate (Islamic Empire) under Caliph Umar Ibn el-Khatab. Jews are permitted to return to the city after 568 years of Roman and Byzantine rule.	https://en.wikipedia.org/wiki/Timeline_of_the_history_of_the_region_of_Palestine
AD 661	The beginning of the Umayyad Caliphate rule from Demascus following the assassination of the Caliph Ali ibn Abi Talib.	
AD 687-691	The caliph Abd al-Malik ibn Marwan of the Umayyad dynasty establishes the Muslim shrine Dome of the Rock on the Temple Mount in Jerusalem at the site of the First and Second Jewish Temples, a site which according to Muslim tradition was the place where Muhammad ascended to heaven.	

PALESTINIAN REGIONAL HISTORY TIMELINE AFTER AD 100		
DATE	EVENT	REFERENCE
AD 749	The Seventh Earthquake: Another powerful earthquake is recorded in the Jordan Rift Valley. The cities of Tiberias, Beit She'an, Hippos and Pella were largely destroyed and many others were damaged. The earthquake reportedly claimed tens of thousands of victims.	https://en.wikipedia.org/wiki/Timeline_of_the_history_of_the_region_of_Palestine
AD 750	The Abbasids overthrew the Umayyad Caliphate.	
AD 878	The Tulunids occupied most of the former Byzantine Diocese of the East, enabling them to defend Egypt against Abbasid attack.	
AD 905	The Abbasids reconquered the region.	
AD 970	The Fatimids, a self-proclaimed Shia caliphate, took control and appointed a Jewish governor.	
AD 1009	(Oct. 18) The Church of the Holy Sepulchre is destroyed by Caliph al-Hakim bi-Amr Allah.	
AD 1071	The Seljuk Turks invaded large portions of West Asia, including Asia Minor and the Eastern Mediterranean.	
AD 1095	(Nov. 27) Pope Urban II launches the First Crusade at the Council of Clermont with the principal objective - the Catholic reconquest of the sacred city of Jerusalem and the Holy Land and freeing the Eastern Christians from Islamic rule.	https://en.wikipedia.org/wiki/Timeline_of_the_history_of_the_region_of_Palestine
AD 1096-1099	First Crusade and the establishment of the Catholic Kingdom of Jerusalem in Outremer.	
AD 1099	(Jul. 15) Catholic soldiers under Godfrey of Bouillon, Robert II of Flanders, Raymond IV of Toulouse and Tancred take Jerusalem after a difficult siege, killing nearly every inhabitant. (Aug. 12) The Crusaders defeat the Fatimids at the Battle of Ascalon.	
AD 1177	(Nov. 25) Battle of Montgisard: Baldwin IV of Jerusalem and Raynald of Chatillon defeat Saladin.	
AD 1187	(May 1) Battle of Cresson: Saladin defeats the Crusaders. (Jul.4) Battle of Hattin: Saladin defeats Guy of Lusignan, King of Jerusalem. (Oct. 2) Saladin captured Jerusalem from the Crusaders.	
AD 1189-1192	Third Crusade led by the armies of Richard the Lionhearted. The Siege of Acre took place during the Third Crusade (Aug. 1189-July 1191).	
AD 1191	(Aug. 20) Richard the Lionhearted had 2,700 of the Muslim prisoners from the garrison of Acre decapitated. (Sep. 7) Richard I of England defeats Saladin at the Battle of Arsuf during the Third Crusade.	https://en.wikipedia.org/wiki/Timeline_of_the_history_of_the_region_of_Palestine
AD 1260	Battle of Ain Jalut between the Egyptian Mamluks and the Mongols which took place in the Jazreel Valley.	
AD 1265	The Mamluk Bahri dynasty of Egypt captures several cities and towns from Crusader states in the Middle East, including the cities of Haifa, Arsuf, and Caesarea Maritima.	
AD 1291	(May 18) Fall of Acre: Al-Ashraf Khalil of Egypt captures Acre, thus exterminating the Crusader Kingdom of Jerusalem (the final Catholic landholding remaining from the Crusades), and ending the Ninth Crusade and effectively all Crusades, by eliminating the possibility of further attacks on the Holy Land.	

PALESTINIAN REGIONAL HISTORY TIMELINE AFTER AD 100		
DATE	EVENT	REFERENCE
AD 1517	Conquest of the Levant by the armies of the Turkish Sultan Selim I. 1517 Hebron pogrom.	https://en.wikipedia.org/wiki/Timeline_of_the_history_of_the_region_of_Palestine
AD 1538-1535	Suleiman the Magnificent restores the Dome of the Rock in Jerusalem and the Jerusalem city walls (which are the current walls of the Old City of Jerusalem).	
AD 1541	Ottoman Sultan Suleiman I sealed off the Golden Gate to prevent the Jewish Messiah's entrance.	
AD 1546	(Jan. 14) A devastating earthquake shook the Jordan Rift Valley region. The epicenter of the earthquake was in the Jordan River in a location between the Dead Sea and the Sea of Galilee. The cities of Jerusalem, Hebron, Nablus, Gaza and Damascus were heavily damaged.	
AD 1660	The towns of Safed and nearby Tiberias, with substantial Jewish communities, were destroyed in the turmoil, following the 1658 death of Mulhim Ma'n, with only Safed being repopulated shortly after the destruction. Some sources place the destruction of Safed in 1662.	https://en.wikipedia.org/wiki/Timeline_of_the_history_of_the_region_of_Palestine
AD 1664	First Protectorate of missions agreed under the Capitulations of the Ottoman Empire, in which Ahmad I agreed that the subjects of Henry IV of France were free to visit the Holy Places of Jerusalem. French missionaries begin to travel to Jerusalem and other major Ottoman cities.	
AD 1663-1665	Sabbatai Zevi, founder of the Sabbateans, preaches in Jerusalem before travelling back to his native Smyrna where he proclaimed himself the Messiah.	
AD 1700	Judah the Pious with 1,000 followers settle in Jerusalem.	
AD 1759	(Oct. 30) Another devastating earthquake shook the Jordan Rift Valley region. The epicenter of the earthquake was again in the Jordan River, in a location between the Sea of Galilee and the Hula Valley. The cities of Safed, Tiberias, Acre, Sidon were heavily damaged.	
AD 1798	Napoleon Bonaparte leads the French Campaign in Egypt and Syria.	
AD 1799	(Mar. 3-7) Napoleonic Wars: Siege of Jaffa - Napoleon captures the city of Jaffa. (Mar. 20-May 21) Siege of Acre - An unsuccessful attempt by Napoleon to capture the city of Acre. (Apr. 8) Battle of Nazareth. (Apr. 11) Battle of Cana. (Apr. 16) The Battle of Mount Tabor - Napoleon drives Ottoman Turks across the River Jordan near Acre.	https://en.wikipedia.org/wiki/Timeline_of_the_history_of_the_region_of_Palestine
AD 1832	(May 10) Mohammed Ali leading Egyptian forces, and aided by local Maronites, seize Acre from the Ottoman Empire after a 7-month siege.	
AD 1834	Arab revolt in Israel.	
AD 1837	(Jan. 1) Galilee earthquake of 1837 - A devastating earthquake that shook the Galilee region, killing thousands of people.	

PALESTINIAN REGIONAL HISTORY TIMELINE AFTER AD 100		
DATE	EVENT	REFERENCE
AD 1840	(Jul. 15) The Austrian Empire, the United Kingdom of Great Britain and Ireland, the Kingdom of Prussia, and the Russian Empire sign the Convention of London with the ruler of the Ottoman Empire. The signatories offered to Muhammad Ali and his heirs permanent control over Egypt and the Acre Sanjak (roughly what is now Israel), provided that these territories would remain part of the Ottoman Empire and that he agreed within ten days to withdraw from the rest of Syria and returned to Sultan Abdulmecid I the Ottoman fleet which had defected to Alexandria. Muhammad Ali was also to immediately withdraw its forces from Arabia, the Holy Cities, Crete, the district of Adana, and all of the Ottoman Empire.	https://en.wikipedia.org/wiki/ Timeline_of_the_history_of_t he_region_of_Palestine
AD 1860	The first Jewish neighborhood (Mishkenot Sha'ananim) is built outside the walls of the Old City of Jerusalem.	
AD 1874	Jerusalem becomes a Mutesarrifiyyet gaining a special administrative status.	
AD 1882-1903	The First Aliyah took place in which 25,000-35,000 Jew immigrants immigrated to Ottoman Syria.	
AD 1887-1888	Ottoman Syria was divided into Jerusalem Sanjak, Nablus Sanjak, and Acre Sanjak.	
AD 1897	(Aug. 29-31) The First Zionist Congress is held in Basel, Switzerland, in which the World Zionist Organization was founded and the Basel Declaration was approved which determined that the Zionist movement ultimate aim is to establish and secure under public law a homeland for the Jewish people. It is to be located in the Biblical region daubed variously "The Holy Land" or "Palestine" by the European Christians during the Catholic and later secular Enlightenment.	https://en.wikipedia.org/wiki/ Timeline_of_the_history_of_t he_region_of_Palestine
AD 1898	German Kaiser Wilhelm visits Jerusalem to dedicate the Lutheran Church of the Redeemer. He meets Theodore Herzl outside city walls.	
AD 1901	The Jewish National Fund was founded at the Fifth Zionist Congress in Basel with the aim of buying and developing land in the southern region of Ottoman Syria for Jewish settlement.	
AD 1909	(Apr. 11) Tel Aviv was founded on the outskirts of the ancient port city of Jaffa.	
AD 1915	(Jan. 26-Feb. 4) German led Ottoman Army advanced from Southern Palestine, conducted a Raid on the Suez Canal in an attempt to stop traffic through the canal.	
AD 1915	(Mar. -Oct.) The 1915 locust plague spreads out in the Eastern Mediterranean coastal region.	
AD 1916-1918	The Arab Revolt.	
AD 1916	(May 16) Britain and France conclude the secret Sykes-Picot Agreement, which defines their respective spheres of influence and control in Western Asia after the expected demise of the Ottoman Empire at the end of World War I. It was largely a trade agreement with a large area set aside for indirect control through an Arab state or a confederation of Arab states.	https://en.wikipedia.org/wiki/ Timeline_of_the_history_of_t he_region_of_Palestine
AD 1916	(Aug. 3-5) German led Ottoman Army attack British Empire forces defending the Suez Canal at the Battle of Romani.	

PALESTINIAN REGIONAL HISTORY TIMELINE AFTER AD 100		
DATE	**EVENT**	**REFERENCE**
AD 1916	(Dec. 23) Anzac Mounted Division occupy El Arish and capture Ottoman garrison during the Battle of Magdhaba.	
AD 1917	(Jan. 9) Sinai and Palestine Campaign: Battle of Rafa - British Empire forces defeat the Ottoman Empire garrison at Rafah after re-capturing the Egyptian Sinai Peninsula by the Egyptian Expeditionary Force.	
AD 1917	(Mar. 26) Sinai and Palestine Campaign: First Battle of Gaza - British attack strong Ottoman defenses at Gaza, failed after 17,000 German led Ottoman troops block their advance in the Southern Coastal Plain.	https://en.wikipedia.org/wiki/ Timeline_of_the_history_of_t he_region_of_Palestine
AD 1917	(Apr. 6) Sinai and Palestine Campaign: The Tel Aviv and Jaffa deportation - The Ottoman authorities deport the entire civilian population of Jaffa and Tel Aviv pursuant to the order from Ahmed Jamal Pasha, the military governor of Ottoman Syria during First World War. Although the Muslim evacuees are allowed to return before long, the Jewish evacuees were not able to return until after the British conquest of Palestine.	
AD 1917	(Apr. 19) Sinai and Palestine Campaign: Second Battle of Gaza - Ottoman defenders repels the second British assault on Gaza.	
AD 1917	(Oct. 31) Sinai and Palestine Campaign: Battle of Beersheba - XX Corps infantry and Desert Mounted Corps mounted infantry attack and capture Beersheba on the Gaza to Beersheba defensive line on the northern edge of the Negev Desert, from the Ottoman Empire.	
AD 1917	(Oct. 31-Nov. 7) Sinai and Palestine Campaign: Third Battle of Gaza - British forces capture Gaza.	
AD 1917	(Nov. 2) The Balfour Declaration is published in which the British Government declares its support for the establishment of a Jewish national home in what is to become Mandate Palestine.	https://en.wikipedia.org/wiki/ Timeline_of_the_history_of_t he_region_of_Palestine
AD 1917	(Nov. 15) Sinai and Palestine Campaign: Australian and New Zealand troops capture Jaffa after the Battle of Mughar Ridge fought on November 13.	
AD 1917	(Nov. 17-Dec. 30) Sinai and Palestine Campaign: Battle of Jerusalem - The Ottoman Empire is defeated by the British Empire forces at the Battle of Jerusalem. The British Army's General Allenby enters Jerusalem on foot, in a reference to the entrance of Caliph Umar in 637.	
AD 1918	(Feb. 21) Sinai and Palestine Campaign: Capture of Jericho - begins Egyptian Expeditionary Force occupation of the Jordan Valley.	
AD 1918	(Mar. 8-12) Sinai and Palestine Campaign: Battle of Tell 'Asur - series of attacks along the Jaffa to Jerusalem line which pushed the front line a few miles north.	
AD 1918	(Mar. 21-Apr. 2) Sinai and Palestine Campaign: First Transjordan attack on Amman including the First Battle of Amman - an infantry and a mounted division invaded Ottoman Empire territory only to be forced by superior Ottoman forces to retreat back to the Jordan Valley	

DATE	EVENT	REFERENCE
	PALESTINIAN REGIONAL HISTORY TIMELINE AFTER AD 100	
AD 1918	(Apr. 30-May 4) Sinai and Palestine Campaign: Second Transjordan attack on Shunet Nimrin and Es Salt - second attempt to capture Ottoman Empire territory east of the Jordan River when three divisions were again forced back to the Jordan Valley by superior Ottoman defenders.	https://en.wikipedia.org/wiki/Timeline_of_the_history_of_t he_region_of_Palestine
AD 1918	(Jun.) First meeting between the Zionist leader Chaim Weizmann and the son of the Sharif of Mecca Hashemite Prince Faisal, who led the Arab forces in the Arab Revolt against the Ottoman Empire during the First World War, which takes place in Faisal's headquarters in Aqaba in an attempt to establish favorable relations between Arabs and Jews in the Middle East.	
AD 1918	(Jul. 14) Sinai and Palestine Campaign: Battle of Abu Tellul.	
AD 1918	(Sep. 19-25) Sinai and Palestine Campaign: In several battles the Egyptian Expeditionary Force attacked and captured large numbers of Ottoman and German soldiers and Ottoman territory. These battles included the capture of Amman, Arara, Afulah, Beisan, Haifa, Jenin, Nablus, Samakh, Tabsor, and Tiberias Tulkarm, including a series of air raids in the Judean Hills when bombs were dropped on retreating German and Ottoman columns.	https://en.wikipedia.org/wiki/Timeline_of_the_history_of_t he_region_of_Palestine
AD 1918	(Sep. 26-Oct. 1) Sinai and Palestine Campaign: Capture of Damascus - continuing the Egyptian Expeditionary Force attacks and captures of almost two Ottoman armies and territory extending into Syria. During this advance Irbid, Jisr Benat Yakub, Kaukab, and Kiswe were captured. The British Empire offensive continued into Syria with the Charge at Khan Ayash and the Pursuit to Haritan including the Battle of Aleppo to end with the Charge at Haritan on October 26.	
AD 1918	(Oct. 30) Sinai and Palestine Campaign: The British Sinai and Palestine Campaign officially ends with the signing of the Armistice of Mudros and, shortly thereafter, the Ottoman Empire is dissolved.	
AD 1927	(Jul. 11) 1927 Jericho earthquake - A powerful earthquake occurs in the Jordan Rift Valley region.	
AD 1929	The outbreak of the 1929 Palestine riots.	https://en.wikipedia.org/wiki/Timeline_of_the_history_of_t he_region_of_Palestine
AD 1936-1939	The Great Arab Revolt.	
AD 1947	(Nov. 29) UN General Assembly proposes to divide Mandate Palestine into an Arab and Jewish state.	
AD 1948	(May 14) Israeli Declaration of Independence: the Jewish leadership in the region of Palestine announces the establishment of the independent and sovereign State of Israel.	
AD 1948	(May 14-Jan. 7, 1949) The 1948 Arab-Israeli War: a large-scale war between Israel and five Arab countries and the Palestinian-Arabs. The war resulted in an Israeli victory, with Israel annexing territory beyond the borders of the proposed Jewish state and into the borders of the proposed Arab state and West Jerusalem. Jordan, Syria, Lebanon, and Egypt signed the 1949 Armistice Agreements with Israel. The Gaza Strip and the West Bank, were occupied by Egypt and Transjordan, respectively until 1967. In 1951, the UN Conciliation Commission for Palestine estimated that some 711,000 Palestinian refugees were displaced by the war.	https://en.wikipedia.org/wiki/Timeline_of_the_history_of_t he_region_of_Palestine

PALESTINIAN REGIONAL HISTORY TIMELINE AFTER AD 100		
DATE	**EVENT**	**REFERENCE**
AD 1956	(Oct. 29-Nov. 5) The Sinai Campaign was held. This war, followed Egypt's decision of July 26, 1956 to nationalize the Suez Canal. The war was initiated by United Kingdom and France, and conducted in cooperation with Israel, aimed at occupying the Sinai Peninsula, with the Europeans regaining control over the Suez Canal. Although the Israeli occupation of the Sinai was successful, the US and USSR forced it to abandon this conquest. However, Israel managed to re-open the Straits of Tiran and secured its southern border.	he_region_of_Palestine
AD 1967	(Jun. 5-10) The Six-Day War took place and was fought between Israel and all of its neighboring countries: Egypt, Jordan, Syria and Lebanon, which were aided by other Arab countries. The war lasted six days and concluded with Israel expanding its territory significantly - Gaza Strip and Sinai from Egypt, the West Bank and Jerusalem from Jordan and the Golan Heights from Syria.	
AD 1973	(Oct. 6-24) The Yom Kippur War was fought. The war began with a surprise joint attack on two fronts by the armies of Syria (in the Golan Heights) and Egypt (in the Suez Canal), deliberately initiated during the Jewish holiday of Yom Kippur. The Egyptian Army got back Sinai that was occupied by the Israeli armies for almost 7 years.	https://en.wikipedia.org/wiki/ Timeline_of_the_history_of_t he_region_of_Palestine
AD 1974	The PLO is allowed to represent the Palestinian Arab refugees in the UN as their sole political representative organization.	
AD 1978	(Sep. 18) Israel and Egypt sign a comprehensive peace agreement at Camp David which included a condition of Israel's withdrawal from the Rest of Sinai.	
AD 1979	(Mar. 26) The peace treaty with Egypt was signed by the Israeli Prime Minister Menachem Begin, the Egyptian President Anwar Sadat and U.S. President Jimmy Carter.	
AD 1982	(Jun.-Dec.) The First Lebanon War took place during which Israel invaded southern Lebanon due to the constant terror attacks on northern Israel by the Palestinian guerrilla organizations resident there. The war resulted in the expulsion of the PLO from Lebanon, and created an Israeli Security Zone in southern Lebanon.	https://en.wikipedia.org/wiki/ Timeline_of_the_history_of_t he_region_of_Palestine
AD 1984	Nov. 21-Jan.5, 1985) Operation Moses: IDF forces conduct a secret operation in which approximately 8,000 Ethiopian Jews were brought to Israel from Sudan.	
AD 1988	(Nov. 15) Palestinian Declaration of Independence (1988) - The Palestinian National Council, the legislative body of the Palestinian Liberation Organization (PLO), in Algiers unilaterally proclaimed the establishment of a new independent state called the "State of Palestine."	
AD 1987-1991	The First Intifada: The first Palestinian uprising took place in the Gaza Strip and the West Bank against the Israeli occupation of the Palestinian Territories.	
AD 1991	(May 24-25) Operation Solomon: IDF forces conduct a secret operation in which approximately 14,400 Ethiopian Jews were brought to Israel within 34 hours in 30 IAF and El Al aircraft.	https://en.wikipedia.org/wiki/ Timeline_of_the_history_of_t

PALESTINIAN REGIONAL HISTORY TIMELINE AFTER AD 100		
DATE	**EVENT**	**REFERENCE**
AD 1993	(Sep. 13) The first Oslo Accords are signed at an official ceremony in Washington in the presence of Yitzhak Rabin if Israel, Yasser Arafat for PLO and Bill Clinton for the United States.	~~Timeline of the history of t~~ he_region_of_Palestine
AD 1994	(Oct. 26) The peace agreement between Israel and Jordan is signed.	
AD 1995	(Nov. 4) Israeli Prime Minister Yitzhak Rabin was assassinated by right-wing Israeli radical Yigal Amir.	
AD 2000-2005	The Second Intifada: The second Palestinian uprising took place in the Gaza Strip and the West Bank against the Israeli occupation of the Palestinian Territories. The uprising which began as massive protests carried out by Palestinians in the Palestinian Territories, soon turned into a violent Palestinian guerrilla campaign which included numerous suicide attacks carried out against Israeli civilians within the state of Israel.	
AD 2002	(Jun.) As a result of the significant increase of suicide bombing attacks within Israeli population centers during the first years of the Second Intifada, Israel began the construction of the West Bank Fence along the Green Line border arguing that the barrier was necessary to protect Israeli civilians from Palestinian terrorism. The significantly reduced number of incidents of suicide bombings from 2002 to 2005 has been partly attributed to the barrier. The barrier's construction, which has been highly controversial, became a major issue of contention between the two sides.	https://en.wikipedia.org/wiki/ Timeline_of_the_history_of_t he_region_of_Palestine
AD 2005	(Aug. 23) Israel's unilateral disengagement plan: The evacuation of 25 Jewish settlements in the Gaza Strip and West Bank is completed.	
AD 2006	(July 12-Aug. 14) The Second Lebanon War took place, which began as a military operation in response to the abduction of two Israeli reserve soldiers by the Hezbollah, and gradually grew to a wider conflict. 1,191 Lebanese were killed, 4,409 were injured.	
AD 2008	(Dec. 27-Jan. 18, 2009) Operation Cast Lead: IDF forces conducted a large scale military operation in the Gaza Strip during which dozens of targets were attacked in the Gaza Strip in response to ongoing rocket fire on the western Negev. 1,291 Palestinians were killed.	https://en.wikipedia.org/wiki/ Timeline_of_the_history_of_t he_region_of_Palestine
AD 2012	(Nov. 14-21) Operation Pillar of Cloud: IDF forces launches a large-scale military operation in the Gaza Strip in response to Palestinian militants firing over a hundred rockets from the Gaza Strip into southern Israel beginning on November 10, with the aims of restoring quiet to southern Israel and to strike at what it considers terror organizations. The operation officially began with the assassination of Ahmed Jabari, chief of the Gaza military wing of Hamas. 158 Palestinians were killed.	
AD 2012	(Nov. 29) United Nations General Assembly resolution 67/19: Upgrading of Palestine to non-member observer state status in the United Nations.	

Chapter 5
How Old is the Universe? (Secular Timelines/Archaeological Evidence)

A. How do major historical events in the Bible compare to Ancient World Power timelines?

Based on the questions that have already been answered about the Bible and the spiritual and physical universes, the following inferences will be used to compare major historical Biblical events with recorded secular history to test the feasibility of the Biblical record:

1. According to the Bible record, the physical universe was created in about 4026 BCE.
2. The Garden of Eden was located near the ancient lands of Ethiopia in northern Africa and Assyria in the country of Iraq, and near the Tigris and Euphrates Rivers.
3. Early civilizations would have emanated from the area near the Garden of Eden to other parts of the world.

4. All human beings lived in the same general area of the world prior to the Great Flood in about 2370 BCE, and they spoke the same language after the Flood and prior to the Tower of Babel.

5. There was a Great Flood that destroyed all human beings, except for Noah and his family, in about 2370 BCE, and after the flood the ark settled on Mount Ararat in eastern Turkey.

6. Over a period of 130 years Adam begat Cain, Abel, and Seth. After Seth Adam lived 800 years and begat other sons and daughters. So, it is probable that many family clans came from Adam, but only the clan of Seth walked with God and survived the Great Flood.

7. After the Flood in about 2239 BCE, humanity attempted to build a great city and the Tower of Babel in the country of Iraq in an effort to challenge the authority and sovereignty of God, but God confused their language so that they could not understand each other, and scattered them throughout the earth.

The following review of secular timelines will consider the feasibility of applying the above seven (7) inferences to each country timeline below. The Ancient World Power and Other Country Timelines can be investigated further by going to the adjacent website URL's for each country.

1. **Egypt – 1st World Power Timeline (3200 BCE):**
    https://www.cemml.colostate.edu/cultural/09476/egypt02-01enl.html (22). The timeline for Egypt starts in 4500 BCE, but there is no definitive evidence of human history until after 3200 BCE, which is within the 4026 BCE timeframe for the creation of the universe. It is logical that Egypt would be one of the first world powers because it is relatively close to the Garden of Eden. I could not find specific evidence that Egypt had a unique language from other human beings before 2239 BCE, but their writing or inscriptions could have been different from nations. After the Tower of Babel in about 2239 BCE,

its inhabitants and language could have been the result of the dispersion of people and languages by God at the Tower of Babel, and its original culture would have been buried under sedimentary rock from the Flood.

2. **Assyria – 2ⁿᵈ World Power Timeline (2750 BCE): http://timelines.ws/countries/ASSYRIA.HTML   (23b).** The timeline for Assyria starts in 9600 BCE, but there is no definitive evidence of human history until the period before 2750 BCE, which is within the 4026 BCE timeframe for the creation of the universe. It is logical that Assyria would be one of the first world powers because it is relatively close to the Garden of Eden and would have to defeat the existing world power. I could not find specific evidence that Assyria had a unique language from other human beings before 2239 BCE, but their writing or inscriptions could have been different from other nations. After the Tower of Babel in about 2239 BCE, its inhabitants and language could have been the result of the dispersion of people and languages by God at the Tower of Babel, and its original culture could have been buried under sedimentary rock from the Flood.

3. **Babylon – 3ʳᵈ World Power Timeline (2700 BCE): http://timelines.ws/countries/BABYLONIA.HTML (24b).** The timeline for Babylon starts in 3500 BCE, but there is no definitive evidence of human history until the period before 2700 BCE, which is within the 4026 BCE timeframe for the creation of the universe. It is logical that Babylon would be one of the first world powers because it is relatively close to the Garden of Eden and would have to defeat the existing world power. I could not find specific evidence that Babylon had a unique language from other human beings before 2239 BCE, but their writing or inscriptions could have been different from other nations. After the Tower of Babel in about 2239 BCE, its inhabitants and language could have been the result of the dispersion of people and languages by God at the Tower of Babel.

4. **Persia/Iran – 4th World Power Timeline (539 BCE): https://www.scaruffi.com/politics/persians.html (25b).** The timeline for Persia starts in 559 BCE, which is well within the 4026 BCE timeframe for the creation of the universe. It is logical that Persia/Iran would be one of the first world powers because it is relatively close to the Garden of Eden and would have to defeat the existing world power. Since Persia/Iran came into existence after 2239 BCE and is not in the same area as the Tower of Babel, its original inhabitants and language could have been the result of the dispersion of people and languages by God at the Tower of Babel.

5. **Greece – 5th World Power Timeline (3200 BCE): https://www.worldatlas.com/webimage/countrys/europe/ greece/grtimeln.htm (26b).** The timeline for Greece starts in 6000 BCE, but there is no definitive human history until 3200 BCE, which is within the 4026 BCE timeframe for the creation of the universe. It is logical that Greece would become a world power at a later time because it is a substantial distance from the Garden of Eden. It would probably need technological advancement to conquer the existing world power, because the size of their world was much greater than in earlier times. I could not find specific evidence that Babylon had a unique language from other human beings before 2239 BCE, but their writing or inscriptions could have been different from other nations. After the Tower of Babel in about 2239 BCE, its inhabitants and language could have been the result of the dispersion of people and languages by God at the Tower of Babel, and its original culture could have been buried under sedimentary rock from the Flood.

6. **Rome – 6th World Power Timeline (753 BCE): https://www.scaruffi.com/politics/romans.html (27a).** The timeline for Rome starts in 753 BCE, which is well within the 4026 BCE timeframe for the creation of the universe. It is logical that Rome would become a world power at a later time, because it is a substantial distance from the Garden of Eden

and they would need technological advancement to conquer the existing world power, and the world had become a much larger place numerically and culturally. Since Rome came into existence after 2239 BCE and is not in the same area as the Tower of Babel, its original inhabitants and language could have been the result of the dispersion of people and languages by God at the Tower of Babel.

B. How do major historical events in the Bible compare to Ancient Other Country timelines?

1. **Africa (3200 BCE): http://www.localhistories.org/aftime. html (30).** The timeline for Africa starts in 100,000 BCE, but there is no definitive evidence of human history until 3200 BCE, which is within the 4026 BCE timeframe for the creation of the universe. I could not find specific evidence that Babylon had a unique language from other human beings before 2239 BCE, but their writing or inscriptions could have been different from other nations. After the Tower of Babel in about 2239 BCE, its inhabitants and languages could have been the result of the dispersion of people and languages by God at the Tower of Babel, and its original cultures could have been buried under sedimentary rock from the Flood.

2. **Afghanistan (1500 BCE): http://www.ducksters.com/ geography/country/afghanistan history timeline.php (29).** The timeline for Afghanistan starts in 1500 BCE, which is within the 4026 BCE timeframe for the creation of the universe. Since Afghanistan came into existence after 2239 BCE and is a significant distance from the Tower of Babel, its original inhabitants and language could have been the result of the dispersion of people and languages by God at the Tower of Babel.

3. **Argentina (1000 BCE): http://www.ducksters.com/ geography/country/argentina history timeline.php (29).** The timeline for Argentina starts in 1000 BCE, which is

well within the 4026 BCE timeframe for the creation of the universe. Since Argentina probably came into existence after 2239 BCE and is a great distance from the Tower of Babel, its original inhabitants and language could have been the result of the dispersion of people and languages by God at the Tower of Babel.

4. **Australia (2000 BCE?): http://www.ducksters.com/geography/country/australia history timeline.php (29).** There is no definitive start date for the aborigine people who occupied Australia before the first European landed there in AD 1606, but it is estimated to be thousands of years, which could be within the 4026 BCE timeframe for the creation of the universe. Since Australia probably came into existence after 2239 BCE and is a great distance from the Tower of Babel, its original inhabitants and language could have been the result of the dispersion of people and languages by God at the Tower of Babel.

5. **Brazil (2000 BCE?): http://www.ducksters.com/geography/country/brazil history timeline.php (29).** Prior to the arrival of Europeans, Brazil was settled by thousands of small tribes and there is no recorded history about them. However, it is probable that they arrived within the 4026 BCE timeframe for the creation of the universe. These tribes did not develop writing or monumental architecture and little is known about them before 1500 BCE. Since Brazil probably came into existence after 2239 BCE and is a great distance from the Tower of Babel, its original inhabitants and language could have been the result of the dispersion of people and languages by God at the Tower of Babel.

6. **Canada (500 BCE): http://www.ducksters.com/geography/country/canada history timeline.php (29).** The timeline for Canada starts in 500 BCE, which is well within the 4026 BCE timeframe for the creation of the universe. Since Canada came into existence after 2239 BCE and is a great distance from the Tower of Babel, its original inhabitants and language could have

been the result of the dispersion of people and languages by God at the Tower of Babel.

7. **China: (2205 BCE?) https://www.ducksters.com/geography/ country/china_history_timeline.php (29).** The timeline for China starts in 2205 BCE with the Xia Dynasty, which is well within the 4026 BCE timeframe for the creation of the universe. Since China came into existence after 2239 BCE and is a substantial distance from the Tower of Babel, its original inhabitants and language could have been the result of the dispersion of people and languages by God at the Tower of Babel. However, since China's timeline begins with a dynasty, it is very likely that it existed much earlier than 2205 BCE and before the Great Flood occurred.

8. **Cuba (1000 BCE): https://www.ducksters.com/geography/ country/cuba_history_timeline.php (29).** The timeline for Cuba starts in 1000 BCE, which is well within the 4026 BCE timeframe for the creation of the universe. Since Cuba probably came into existence after 2239 BCE and is a great distance from the Tower of Babel, its original inhabitants and language could have been the result of the dispersion of people and languages by God at the Tower of Babel.

9. **France (600 BCE): http://www.ducksters.com/geography/ country/france_history_timeline.php (29).** The timeline for France starts in 600 BCE, which is well within the 4026 BCE timeframe for the creation of the universe. Since France came into existence after 2239 BCE and is a substantial distance from the Tower of Babel, its original inhabitants and language could have been the result of the dispersion of people and languages by God at the Tower of Babel.

10. **Germany (500 BCE): http://www.ducksters.com/geography/ country/germany_history_timeline.php (29).** The timeline for Germany starts in 500 BCE, which is well within the 4026 BCE timeframe for the creation of the universe. Since Germany probably came into existence after 2239 BCE and is a substantial distance from the Tower of Babel, its original inhabitants and

language could have been the result of the dispersion of people and languages by God at the Tower of Babel.

11. **India (3000 BCE): http://www.ducksters.com/geography/ country/india history timeline.php (29).** The timeline for India starts in 3000 BCE, which is within the 4026 BCE timeframe for the creation of the universe. I could not find specific evidence that India had a unique language from other human beings before 2239 BCE, but their writing or inscriptions could have been different from other nations. After the Tower of Babel in about 2239 BCE, its inhabitants and language could have been the result of the dispersion of people and languages by God at the Tower of Babel, and its original culture could have been buried under sedimentary rock from the Flood.

12. **Iraq (3500 BCE): http://www.ducksters.com/geography/ country/iraq history timeline.php (29).** The timeline for Iraq starts in 3500 BCE, which is within the 4026 BCE timeframe for the creation of the universe. I could not find specific evidence that Iraq had a unique language from other human beings before 2239 BCE, but their writing or inscriptions could have been different from other nations. After the Tower of Babel in about 2239 BCE, its inhabitants and language could have been the result of the dispersion of people and languages by God at the Tower of Babel, and its original culture could have been buried under sedimentary rock from the Flood.

13. **Ireland (2000 BCE): http://www.ducksters.com/geography/ country/ireland history timeline.php (29).** The timeline for Ireland starts in 2000 BCE, which is well within the 4026 BCE timeframe for the creation of the universe. Since Ireland probably came into existence after 2239 BCE and is a substantial distance from the Tower of Babel, its original inhabitants and language could have been the result of the dispersion of people and languages by God at the Tower of Babel.

14. **Japan (2500 BCE): http://www.ducksters.com/geography/ country/japan history timeline.php (29).** The timeline for Japan starts in 2500 BCE, but the specific times of human

settlements came after 2500 BCE, which is well within the 4026 BCE timeframe for the creation of the universe. I could not find specific evidence that Japan had a unique language from other human beings before 2239 BCE, but their writing or inscriptions could have been different from other nations. After the Tower of Babel in about 2239 BCE, its inhabitants and language could have been the result of the dispersion of people and languages by God at the Tower of Babel, and its original culture could have been buried under sedimentary rock from the Flood.

15. **Korea (3000 BCE): http://www.art-and-archaeology.com/ korea/history.html (31).** The timeline for Korea starts in 7000 BCE, but there is no definitive evidence of human history until 3000 BCE, which is within the 4026 BCE timeframe for the creation of the universe. I could not find specific evidence that Korea had a unique language from other human beings before 2239 BCE, but their writing or inscriptions could have been different from other nations. After the Tower of Babel in about 2239 BCE, its inhabitants and language could have been the result of the dispersion of people and languages by God at the Tower of Babel.

16. **Maya (2000 BCE): http://www.historymuseum.ca/cmc/ exhibitions/civil/maya/mmc09eng.shtml (32).** The timeline for Maya starts in 11000 BCE, but there is no definitive evidence of human history until 2000 BCE, which is within the 4026 BCE timeframe for the creation of the universe. Since Maya came into existence after 2239 BCE and is a great distance from the Tower of Babel, its original inhabitants and language could have been the result of the dispersion of people and languages by God at the Tower of Babel.

17. **Mexico (1400 BCE): http://www.ducksters.com/geography/ country/mexico_history_timeline.php (29).** The timeline for Mexico starts in 1400 BCE, which is within the 4026 BCE timeframe for the creation of the universe. Since Mexico came into existence after 2239 BCE and is a great distance from the

Tower of Babel, its original inhabitants and language could have been the result of the dispersion of people and languages by God at the Tower of Babel.

18. **Netherlands (2000 BCE): http://www.ducksters.com/ geography/country/netherlands history timeline.php (29).** The timeline for the Netherlands starts in 2000 BCE, which is within the 4026 BCE timeframe for the creation of the universe. Since the Netherlands came into existence after 2239 BCE and is a substantial distance from the Tower of Babel, its original inhabitants and language could have been the result of the dispersion of people and languages by God at the Tower of Babel.

19. **Pakistan (3000 BCE): http://www.ducksters.com/ geography/country/pakistan history timeline.php (29).** The timeline for Pakistan starts in 3000 BCE, which is within the 4026 BCE timeframe for the creation of the universe. I could not find specific evidence that Pakistan had a unique language from other human beings before 2239 BCE, but their writing or inscriptions could have been different from other nations. After the Tower of Babel in about 2239 BCE, its inhabitants and language could have been the result of the dispersion of people and languages by God at the Tower of Babel, and its original culture could probably have been buried under sedimentary rock from the Flood.

20. **Peru (1200 BCE): www.discover-peru.org/peru-history-timeline/ (33).** The timeline for Peru starts in 7500 BCE, but there is no definitive evidence of human history until 1200 BCE, which is within the 4026 BCE timeframe for the creation of the universe. Since Peru probably came into existence after 2239 BCE and is a great distance from the Tower of Babel, its original inhabitants and language could have been the result of the dispersion of people and languages by God at the Tower of Babel.

21. **Poland (700 BCE): (https://www.ducksters.com/geography/ country/italy history timeline.php) (29).** The timeline for

Poland starts in 2300 BCE, but there is no definitive evidence of human history until 700 BCE, which is within the 4026 BCE timeframe for the creation of the universe. Since Poland probably came into existence after 2239 BCE and is a substantial distance from the Tower of Babel, its original inhabitants and language could have been the result of the dispersion of people and languages by God at the Tower of Babel.

22. **Russia (1200 BCE): http://www.history-timelines.org.uk/places-timelines/36-russian-history-timeline.htm (34).** The timeline for the Russia starts in 1200 BCE, which is within the 4026 BCE timeframe for the creation of the universe. Since Russia probably came into existence after 2239 BCE and is a substantial distance from the Tower of Babel, its original inhabitants and language could have been the result of the dispersion of people and languages by God at the Tower of Babel.

23. **Spain (1800 BCE): http://www.ducksters.com/geography/country/spain_history_timeline.php (29).** The timeline for Spain starts in 1800 BCE, which is within the 4026 BCE timeframe for the creation of the universe. Since Spain probably came into existence after 2239 BCE and is a substantial distance from the Tower of Babel, its original inhabitants and language could have been the result of the dispersion of people and languages by God at the Tower of Babel.

24. **South Africa (1000 BCE): http://www.ducksters.com/geography/country/south_africa_history_timeline.php (29).** The timeline for South Africa starts in 1000 BCE, which is within the 4026 BCE timeframe for the creation of the universe. Since South Africa probably came into existence after 2239 BCE and is a substantial distance from the Tower of Babel, its original inhabitants and language could have been the result of the dispersion of people and languages by God at the Tower of Babel.

25. **Sweden (AD 800): http://www.ducksters.com/geography/country/sweden_history_timeline.php (29).** The timeline for

Sweden starts in 4000 BCE, but there is no definitive evidence of human history until AD 800, which is within the 4026 BCE timeframe for the creation of the universe. Since Sweden probably came into existence after 2239 BCE and is a substantial distance from the Tower of Babel, its original inhabitants and language could have been the result of the dispersion of people and languages by God at the Tower of Babel.

26. **Turkey (1600 BCE): http://www.ducksters.com/geography/ country/turkey_history_timeline.php (29).** The timeline for Turkey starts in 1600 BCE, which is within the 4026 BCE timeframe for the creation of the universe. Since Turkey probably came into existence after 2239 BCE, its original inhabitants and language could have been the result of the dispersion of people and languages by God at the Tower of Babel.

27. **United Kingdom (2200 BCE): http://www.ducksters.com/ geography/country/united_kingdom_history_timeline.php (29).** The timeline for the United Kingdom starts in 6000 BCE, but there is no definitive evidence of human history until the construction of Stonehenge in 2200 BCE, which is within the 4026 BCE timeframe for the creation of the universe. However, if Stonehenge was completed in 2200 BCE, then it must have been started before 2239 BCE and probably after the Great Flood in 2370 BCE, because the flood waters would probably have destroyed the formation. I could not find specific evidence that the United Kingdom had a unique language from other human beings before 2239 BCE, but their writing or inscriptions could have been different from other nations. After the Tower of Babel in about 2239 BCE, its inhabitants and language could have been the result of the dispersion of people and languages by God at the Tower of Babel.

28. **United States (1000 BCE): http://www.ducksters.com/ geography/country/united_states_history_timeline.php (29).** The timeline for the United States starts in 5000 BCE, but there is no definitive evidence of human history until 1000 BCE, which is within the 4026 BCE timeframe for the creation

of the universe. Since the United States is a great distance from the Tower of Babel, its original inhabitants and language could have been the result of the dispersion of people and languages by God at the Tower of Babel.

29. **Vietnam (2879 BCE): http://www.ducksters.com/ geography/country/vietnam_history_timeline.php (29).** The timeline for Vietnam starts in 2879 BCE with the Hong Bang Dynasty, which is within the 4026 BCE timeframe for the creation of the universe. I could not find specific evidence that Vietnam had a unique language from other human beings before 2239 BCE, but their writing or inscriptions could have been different from other nations. After the Tower of Babel in about 2239 BCE, its inhabitants and language could have been the result of the dispersion of people and languages by God at the Tower of Babel, and its original culture could have been buried under sedimentary rock from the Flood.

Based on this analysis, the original descendants from some of the above countries could have been in existence prior to the dispersion of people and languages by God at the Tower of Babel and some elements of their cultures prior to the Great Flood should be available for archaeological discovery and study. The countries with definitive timelines that show evidence of existence before the Great Flood are: Egypt, Assyria, Greece, Africa, China, India, Iraq, Japan, Pakistan, and Vietnam.

Logical Conclusion: From the comparison of biblical historical dates and secular historical dates it may be inferred that:

1. **There is no definitive evidence from secular historical timelines that the universe was not created in about 4026 BCE as recorded in the Bible.**

2. **There is solid evidence from secular historical timelines that the first four world powers (Egypt, Assyria, Babylon,**

and Persia), of the six world powers mentioned in the Bible, emanated from the area near the Garden of Eden.

3. There is no definitive evidence that all the people in the world did not speak the same language before the great flood in 2370 BCE, but their writing and inscriptions might have been different.

4. There is no mention of the Great Flood in any of the timelines of the major countries in the world.

5. There is evidence from secular timelines that many countries in various parts of the world could have been the result of the dispersion of people and languages by God at the Tower of Babel.

6. Some of the dates for historical biblical events from our Timeline of Outstanding Historical Biblical Events are different from the secular source. For example, the dates for Babylon's conquest of Judah are 617 BCE to 607 BCE versus 597 BCE to 587 BCE from the secular source. This may be the result of using different historical calendars to record these events.

C. Does archaeology support the Biblical record?

The commentary in this chapter about Biblical archaeology comes from the study Bible: (Boa, et al. (1985), *The Open Bible, Expanded Edition, KJV*, Nashville: Thomas Nelson Publishers), which has a section devoted to "The Greatest Archaeological Discoveries and Their Effects on the Bible," pages 1353 - 1374. This source is Item 5a of our reference list at the back of Volume 5 of this book.

1. Introduction (Source: Item 5b, Page 1353)

Definition and Importance of Biblical Archaeology. There has been the birth, growth, and phenomenal development of the science of biblical archaeology since the late 18th century. The background material provided by this new science has illustrated, illuminated, and in many cases authenticated the message and meaning of the Old and New Testament Scriptures.

The definition of Biblical archaeology involves the study of past records, based on their excavation, decipherment, and critical evaluation, to determine how they relate to the Bible. The general field of archaeology is fascinating, but the study of Biblical archaeology is much more captivating, because it deals with the Holy Scriptures, which is the reason for the growing enthusiasm for this field of study. This appeal comes from its utmost importance in authenticating the message and meaning of the Bible.

The Scriptures have always held a dominant place in the interests and affections of humanity, because they are generally recognized as the inspired Word of God, which meets the deepest needs of humanity. By illuminating the Bible in its historical setting and lifestyles, Biblical archaeology appeals to some of the same influences as the Bible itself. Therefore, this relatively new science has the worthwhile ministry of increasing Biblical knowledge for all of humanity.

There has been no greater challenge and promise in the field of research than that presented by biblical archaeology. Very little was known of ancient biblical times and biblical surroundings, except for the Old Testament record or the writings of classical antiquity, until the beginning of the 19th century. Although there was a considerable amount of secular information about the New Testament period, there was very little secular history to verify the Old Testament record, because Greek and Latin historians recorded very little information before the 5th century BCE. There was very little contemporary secular knowledge about the Old Testament period, except that which was recorded in the Bible.

Consequently, prior to the science of modern archaeology there was almost nothing to authenticate Old Testament history and literature. The enlightening archeological discoveries in Bible lands from the 1800's to the present time have stimulated great enthusiasm among serious biblical scholars. In fact, the beginning of modern archaeology may be said to have occurred in the year 1798, when Napoleon's Egyptian Expedition began the scientific study of the rich antiquities of the Nile Valley.

2. **Foundational Discoveries of the Nineteenth Century**
(Source: Item 5b, Pages 1353-1356)

The most prominent Old Testament biblical discoveries did not occur until the 20th century. However, some foundational discoveries were accomplished in the 19th century that prepared the way for the 20th century discoveries.

a. **The Rosetta Stone-Key to Egypt's Splendid Past**

An officer in Napoleon's Expedition to Egypt discovered a very important monument in 1798 at Rosetta (Rashid) near the westernmost mouth of the Nile River. It was a slab of black basalt inscribed in three languages, which made it possible to interpret the language and literature of ancient Egypt. This important discovery was the key that opened the modern period of scientific biblical archaeology.

The three languages inscribed on the monument were the Greek language of 200 BCE, an old version of Egyptian writing, and a later version of Egyptian writing. The older version contained a more complicated hieroglyphic script, and the later version contained a simplified and more popular demotic script, which was the common language of the people. The Greek script could be read immediately and provided the clues necessary to translate the other two ancient Egyptian scripts. Sylvester de Sacy of France and J. D. Akerblad of Sweden were able to decipher the later version of Egyptian script by recognizing the Greek personal names of Ptolemy, Arsinoe, and Berenike.

Thomas Young of England then used this information to find the name of Ptolemy in the older hieroglyphic script, where groups of characters enclosed in oval frames, called cartouches, had already been presumed to be royal names. After these discoveries, a young Frenchman by the name of Jean Francois Champollion, who lived from 1790-1832, was able to interpret the hieroglyphics of the monument, show the true nature of the hieroglyphic script, create a dictionary, formulate a grammar, and interpret many Egyptian texts, from the period of 1818 to 1832.

The achievements of Champollion formally began the science of Egyptology. From this time forward, scholars were able to read Egyptian monumental inscriptions and reliefs, and the literary treasures of the Nile Valley were opened to scholarly study. Many universities now provide chairs in the language and culture of ancient Egypt. These studies have provided knowledge of Egyptian history which was previously unknown, from about 2800 BCE to 63 BCE when Egypt was conquered by the Roman Empire. Most of the history of the Nile Valley can now be documented and traced.

Of course, the history of Egypt has an enormous bearing on the background of the Bible. Egypt has played a well-known role in the narratives of the Book of Exodus and throughout the Pentateuch. Consequently, the background story of Joseph and the dwelling of the children of Israel in Egypt, their liberation from Egyptian bondage under Moses, their wondering in the desert, and their later history in Canaan can now be established in the general context of Egyptian secular history.

The whole background of Old Testament history, from Abraham to Christ, is made considerably clearer because of the enormous advances in our knowledge of Egyptian secular history. Egypt also interacted with other great powers, such as the Assyrian and Babylonian empires on the Tigris and Euphrates Rivers and the Hittite power on the Halys River, across the tiny strip of land which was ancient Palestine.

b. **The Behistun Inscription-Gateway to Assyrian-Babylonian Antiquity**

The famous Behistun Inscription monument was the key to the languages of Assyria and Babylonia. It contained numerous columns of inscription on a large relief panel, which was boldly carved about 500 feet above the surrounding plain of Karmanshah on the face of a mountain on the old caravan route from Babylon to Ecbatana. It is comprised of about 1200 lines of inscription written in the wedge-shaped characters of ancient Assyria-Babylonia. The three languages inscribed on the monument were all written in cuneiform characters, consisting of Old Persian, Elamite, and Akkadian. The Akkadian language was the wedge-shaped language of ancient Assyria and Babylonia, which was inscribed on many thousands of clay tablets that were discovered in the Tigris-Euphrates region.

This strange wedge-shaped Babylonian-Akkadian writing appeared on a large volume of material in early excavations, and it was an unsolved mystery. Almost no progress was made toward the resolution of this mystery until in 1835 and the following years, Henry C. Rawlinson, a young

English officer in the Persian army, made the hazardous climb to the monument and made copies and plaster of paris impressions of it.

Since Rawlinson knew the modern Persian language, he was able to decipher the old Persian portion of the inscription. He finally succeeded in translating the five columns of nearly 400 lines of the old Persian portion of the Behistun Inscription, after a decade of labor. He sent his translation to Europe in 1845, and in 1847 the translation text and the commentary on it were published in the *Journal of the Royal Asiatic Society.*

A life-sized figure with numerous individuals bowing before it also appeared along with the literary portion of the monument. This person was determined to be Darius the Great (522-486 BCE), the Achemenid prince who prevented a rebellion from occurring in the Persian Empire. Rawlinson's translation of the Persian portion of the inscription shows that the scene depicts the king receiving the submission of the rebels.

The king is shown at the top of the relief with his foot placed upon the horizontal figure of a leading rebel and accompanied by two attendants. The king's right hand is lifted toward a winged disc representing Ahura-Mazda, the spirit of good, whom Darius worshiped, and his left hand holds a bow. A procession of rebel leaders roped together by their necks are standing behind the prostrate rebel. The three languages describing how Darius defended the throne and crushed the revolt appear beside and beneath the sculptured panel with the numerous columns of the inscriptions.

Scholars were soon able to read the second Elamite language by working on the theory that the other inscriptions told the same story as the old Persian inscriptions. Using this same supposition, scholars were eventually able to decipher the Akkadian or Assyro-Babylonian inscriptions, which was the most important discovery. This was a great discovery because this wedge-shaped writing is recorded on numerous literary remains from the Tigris-Euphrates Valley, which has opened up an enormous new field of biblical background knowledge.

Consequently, as in the case of the Rosetta Stone opening up the science of Egyptology, the Behistun Inscription has given birth to the science of Assyriology. The science of Egyptology and the science of Assyriology both provide great assistance in understanding biblical backgrounds and biblical history. The great discoveries of these two sciences cannot be ignored by any modern Bible dictionary, Bible handbook or Bible commentary.

c. **The Moabite Stone-A Sensational Literary Find**

Another example of a discovery of the 19th century that paved the way for the great finds of the 20th century is the *Moabite Stone*, which was discovered in 1868. The inscriptions on the monument date from about 850 BCE when it was erected by Mesha, king of Moab, and it is often called the *Mesha Stone*. The inscriptions tell about the wars between Mesha of Moab and Omri, king of Israel, and Omri's successors. They also tell about Mesha's wars with the Edomites. The historical record on the Moabite Stone corresponds to the biblical history that is recorded in Second Kings, chapters 1 and 3.

Many places mentioned in the Old Testament occur on the inscribed monument, which include: Arnon (Num. 21:13; Deut. 2:24), Ataroth (Num. 32:34), Baal-meon or Beth-baal meon (Josh. 13:17), Beth-bamoth or Bamoth-baal (Josh. 13:17), Beth-diblathaim (Jer. 48:22), Bezer (Josh. 20:8), Dibon (Num. 32:34), Jahaza (Josh. 13:18), Medeba (Josh. 13:9), and Nebo (Num. 32:38).

The Moabite Stone measures 3 feet 8-1/2 inches in height, 2 feet 3-1/2 inches in width, and one foot 1-3/4 inches in thickness, and its 34 lines of inscription represent the longest single literary inscription of secular history that deals with Palestine in the period from 900 BCE to 600 BCE. The inscriptions reveal that Moab had been defeated by Omri and his son Ahab but Mesha's god Chemosh set Moab free from the yoke of Israel. Chemosh, the deity, is depicted as directing King Mesha to go to war against Israel. According to 2 Kings 3:27, Mesha offered up his eldest son as a burnt offering upon the wall to appease Chemosh and to secure his favor.

The Moabite language is very similar to the Hebrew language at the time of Omri and Ahab, and the Moabite Stone inscriptions are written in the language of Moab. Therefore, the inscriptions have had immense value in tracing the growth of early Hebrew language through the centuries. The Moabite Stone was the longest and oldest Phoenician-Hebrew inscription in existence when it was discovered, and it was the only one.

The Gezer Calendar, which is a school boy's exercise written in perfect classical Hebrew, is now the oldest Phoenician-Hebrew inscription and it dates from about 925 BCE. This calendar is a small limestone tablet that was discovered at ancient Gezer, which provides insight into

Palestinian agriculture and ancient Hebrew writing. The Gezer Calendar and the Moabite Stone not only provide background information that supports the biblical record, but they also provide firsthand knowledge about the culture and history of the ancient people that lived outside the Nation of Israel.

3. **Great Discoveries of the Twentieth Century** (Source: Item 5b, Pages 1356-1374)

The Rosetta Stone, the Behistun Inscription, the Moabite Stone, and the Gezer Calendar were very important discoveries in the 19th century which provided the foundations for scientific archaeology. However, the 20th century produced the most exciting and exceptional archaeological finds. During the 20th century biblical archaeology became an advanced and accurate science, which added to the boundaries of biblical knowledge and made incredible contributions to the background, history, and culture of the ancient nations mentioned in the written Word of God.

a. **The Code of Hammurabi-Light on Mosaic Laws**

The Code of Hammurabi was inscribed on a slab of black diorite (a granite-textured crystalline rock) over 7 feet tall and 6 feet wide, which was discovered in 1901. The inscriptions on this monument contain almost 300 paragraphs of legal stipulations dealing with the commercial, social, domestic, and moral life of the Babylonians during the time of King Hammurabi (1728-1676 BCE). Jacques de Morgan discovered a copy of this code at Susa in Elam, where it had been transported from Babylon by the Elamites. The king is shown receiving the laws from the sun god Shamash, patron of law and justice, at the top of the inscribed monument. An Elamite conqueror carried away the monument to Susa at a time in history when Babylon was weak. This monument has been one of the most astounding legal discoveries in history.

The code is important in providing background material for comparison with other ancient laws, such as the biblical laws of Moses. The fact that the Code of Hammurabi is over three centuries older than the laws of Moses has dispelled some unsustainable theories of the critics that detailed codes of law like those recorded in the Pentateuch were not probable for such an early period in ancient history. The discoveries of Hammurabi's laws and much earlier codes in Mesopotamia have shattered this theory.

Discoveries like this illustrate how archaeology eliminates radical theories, such as the theory that placed the origin of many of the laws ascribed to Moses to much later times like the 9th, 8th, and 7th centuries BCE, or even later. These inaccurate theories had to be revised drastically or rejected entirely when the Code of Hammurabi was discovered. On the other hand, the discovery of this ancient code of secular laws has led many to embrace the equally flawed view that the Mosaic laws were simply a collection and revision of these Babylonian laws.

As the collection of laws from these two sources are studied, the only valid conclusion is that the Mosaic code is neither borrowed from, nor dependent upon, the Babylonian code. The Mosaic code is divinely inspired, as it claims to be, and unique to the chosen, theocratic Nation of Israel.

b. **The Elephantine Papyri-Light on the Ezra-Nehemiah Era**

The Elephantine Papyri, which were discovered in 1903 on the island of Elephantine at the First Cataract of the Nile in

Egypt, provide insight into one of the remote regions of the Persian Empire during the latter part of the 5th century BCE. These important documents, which come from a Jewish military colony which was established there, were inscribed in the Aramaic language. Aramaic was the language of diplomacy and trade all over western Asia during the period of the Persian Empire, and was slowly replacing Hebrew as the common language of the Jewish people.

The contents of the documents were diverse and ranged from a copy of the Behistun Inscription of Darius to a Jewish marriage contract. According to some of the letters, a Jewish temple at Elephantine was destroyed when the Jews were being persecuted in about 411 BCE. The worship of God, whom they referred to as Yahu, was practiced by the Jews at this colony.

The Brooklyn Museum has published other letters from Elephantine which have been discovered in recent years that reveal that the temple was rebuilt after its destruction. They mention the name of Yahu as "the god who dwells in Yeb, the fortress," which compares to Psalm 31:3. These two papyri discoveries reveal that Egypt was still under the authority of the Persian Empire during the early reign of Artaxerxes II (404-359 B.C.E.).

The time period reflected by the Elephantine Papyri therefore provides insight into the historical context of the Ezra-Nehemiah biblical period and the earlier period of the Persian empire. They show what life was like for the Jewish inhabitants of a remote frontier place such as Elephantine in Egypt. They also provide important knowledge of the Aramaic language during that period in history, and the many biblical customs and names that are disclosed by these papyri documents.

c. The Hittite Monuments from Boghaz-Keui - Mementos of an Imperial People

The Boghaz-Kenu site is located 90 miles east of Ankara in the great bend of the Halys River in Asia Minor, and excavations began there in 1906 by Professor Hugo Winkler of Berlin. It was determined that this was an ancient Hittite capital, and the large number of clay tablets discovered there were inscribed in six different languages. Many of these clay tablets were inscribed in the cuneiform characters of the Hittite language, which were eventually interpreted by three men, one of whom was the Czech scholar Friedrich Hrozny. Those tablets inscribed in the Hittite language were key to a significant amount of biblical background information.

The biblical references to the Hittites were generally considered as historically insignificant until the Boghaz-Keui tablets revealed them to be an ancient people. In Exodus 33:2, Deuteronomy 7:1, 20:17, and Joshua 3:10, 24:11, the Bible refers to the Hittites as inhabiting the land of Canaan and as being among those whom the Israelites would drive out of the land. None of these biblical references imply that the Hittites were either a powerful imperial people or a small local tribe.

Before the excavations at Boghaz-Keui, the "Hittites" meant little more to the Bible reader than the "Hivite" or the "Perizzite" does today. Although the Bible record reveals that Abraham had Hittites as neighbors (Gen. 49:10) and that David had a Hittite soldier in his army (2 Sam. 11:2-17), who would have expected this nation to be more prominent than the "Gadites" or the "Beerothites"?

It is now known that there were two great periods of Hittite power and influence: the first period goes back to about

1800 BCE and the second occurred from about 1400-1200 BCE. It was during the second period of supremacy that the powerful Hittite rulers reigned at Boghaz-Keui. The name of one of these powerful rulers was Subbiluliuma who extended the Hittite Empire to the borders of Syria-Palestine. The great Rameses II of Egypt collided with Hittite power in the famous battle of Kadesh. In the 21st year of the reign of Rameses II, a peace treaty with the Hittite nation was confirmed by a royal marriage.

The great Hittite Empire collapsed in about 1200 BCE, and the Hittite city of Boghaz-Keui was defeated. However; Hittite power continued for a time at Carchemish, Sengirli, Hamath, and other places in north Syria. The whole background of the ancient biblical world has been clarified as a result of the excavation and decoding of various Hittite monuments.

d. **d. The City of Ur - Abraham's Home**

Ur was located on the Euphrates River in lower Mesopotamia, present-day Iraq, and is a significant city of the ancient world. A prominent line of kings reigned in this very important city during the 2nd and 3rd dynasties of Ur, several centuries before Abraham lived there as a boy and grew up there as a young man. The city was suddenly destroyed in the period from about 1960-1830 BCE, when foreigners stormed down from the surrounding hills and took the reigning king, Ibi-Sin, captive and reduced the capital city of Ur to ruins.

The destruction of the city was so complete that it remained buried in obscurity for centuries until, like Nineveh, it was resurrected by the dedicated effort of modern archaeologists. Another example of how thoroughly was the destruction of the city, is that when it is referred to as the ancestral home of Abraham in Genesis 11:28-31 and 15:7, scribes later added the descriptive phrase, "of the Chaldeans," to the name of the city so readers would know where it was located.

The work of many archaeologists, particularly the work of Sir Leonard Woolley (1922-1934), have revived the history of the long-lost and buried city. The site of the ancient city was completely unknown until the year 1854, and the Arabs called the location Almuqayyer, "Mount of bitumen." It was a very unwelcoming place with a climate of tremendous heat and bordered by severe desolation. J. E. Taylor, an English archaeologist, with the assistance of others, made some initial excavations in 1854. Some of the cylinders were inscribed with cuneiform characters stating that King Nabonidus of Babylon (556-539 BCE) had restored the famous ziggurat (temple tower) of Ur-Nammu.

Campbell Thompson and H. R. Hall made some later investigations in 1918. But it was the momentous work of Sir Leonard Woolley, which began in 1922 as a joint expedition of the British Museum, the University of Pennsylvania, and the University Museum, that provided a complete history and description of the ancient city. The Woolley expedition accomplished twelve very effective archaeological campaigns to the site of the city, and by 1934 the forgotten and buried city of Ur had become one of the best-known locations in all the ancient Near East.

e. **The Religious Texts from Ras Shamra (Ugarit) - Canaanite Cults Exposed**

The recovery of hundreds of clay tablets in the city of **Ras Shamra (Ugarit)** in northern Syria was one of the most important discoveries of the 20th century. These tablets date between the 15th and 14th centuries BCE and were housed in a library located between two great temples, which were dedicated to Baal and Dagon. The inscriptions on the tablets are the earliest known alphabet written in wedge-shaped signs and were recognized by Professor H. Bower of the University of Halle as Semitic in origin. The decipherment of this new Semitic language was begun by several scholars who included E. Dhorme and Charles Virol-leaud.

The tablets were inscribed in a dialect that was very similar to biblical Hebrew and Phoenician and was religious and cultic in nature. This new writing, though Semitic in form, showed indications of Akkadian influence, because Mesopotamians wrote from left to right on clay tablets with wedge-shaped characters. Nothing was known about the ancient city of Ugarit until the spring of 1928 when a Syrian peasant found some artifacts while plowing in his field a little north of present-day Minet el-Beida.

Excavations began at Minet el-Beida on April 2, 1929, under the leadership of Claude F. Schaffer. After working for only one month at this site, the work was changed to nearby Ras Sharma, and on May 20, 1929 the first tablets were uncovered. Excavations were continued by Schaffer from 1929 to 1937, but the bulk of significant religious texts were discovered in the royal library between 1929 and 1933. The inscriptions on many of the tablets were in an early Canaanite dialect, which approximated the time period of Moses.

Religious Significance of the Ugaritic Inscriptions. The most important contributions of the religious texts from Ras Shamra (Ugarit) is that they give background material for the study of Old Testament religions. The Ugarit texts describe very clearly the **Canaanite pantheon**. The

Canaanite pantheon was headed up by the god El, the highest Canaanite deity. In the Old Testament, this is also a name by which God is known, and this name, El, often occurs in Old Testament poetry. It is also frequently used in prose in compound names, for example, El Elyon, the God Most High (Gen. 14:18); El Shaddai, Almighty God (Gen. 17:1); El Hai, the living God (Josh. 3:10).

This does not mean that the name, El, in the Old Testament has any connection with the Canaanite god. It is simply the common Semitic word for God. In the Ugaritic culture, El was a bloody, lustful oppressor. The description of him and other Canaanite gods by the Ugarit texts fully validates the testimony of the Old Testament concerning the wickedness and contaminating influence of the Canaanite religion.

Baal was the son of El, and he served as the active king of the other gods in the Canaanite pantheon and he dominated all the other gods. He was the god of the storm and the rain, and thunder was believed to be the echo of his voice in the heavens. An inscribed stone was discovered at Ras Shamra depicting Baal holding a stylized thunderbolt, and three Ugaritic poems about Baal. The worship of Baal was one of the most devastating and damaging influences which threatened the Hebrews in Palestine.

Baal was very prominent in the mythology of the Canaanites, because he was believed to be the giver of rain and all fertility. He has a fight with Mot, the god of death and drought, and Baal is killed in the battle, which results in the seasonal drought that occurs from June to late October in Ugarit. After the battle, Anath, the sister and lover of Baal, searches for him, discovers his dead body, and slays his enemy, Mot. Baal is then revived back to life, which ensures the restoration of vegetation for a seven-year period. This is an illustration of the central theme of Baal in Ugarit.

In addition to gods who were violent and wicked, the Phoenicians at Ugarit also had three goddesses who were prominent by the names of Anath, Astarte, and Asherah. They were patronesses of war and sex, and their characters were like that of El and Baal, since they portrayed war in its aspect of lustful tolerance of violence, murder and sex, which confirms the damaging effects of the Canaanite religion.

The Bible student is benefitted by this new knowledge of the Canaanite religion to more properly evaluate the testimony of the Old Testament concerning the divine command for God's chosen people to exterminate these Canaanite cults. Old Testament examples include the destruction of the city of Jericho, the extermination of the Amalekites by King Saul, and the general displacement of the Canaanites from their land.

These examples can be better understood when viewed in the light of the depravity of Canaanite religion. In Abraham's day the Lord acknowledged in Genesis 15:16 that, "the iniquity of the Amorites" was not yet "full." But in Joshua's day, 400 years later, archaeology reveals that the religious immorality of the Canaanites was complete and had to be destroyed.

f. **The Nuzi Tablets and the Biblical Horites**

The present-day site of the ancient city of Nuzi is located 150 miles north of Baghdad near southern Khurdistan. In ancient times Nuzi was located east of Asshur and a short distance west of Arrapkha. It was most prominent during the period from 2000-1400 BCE when it was occupied by the Hurrians, the biblical Horites.

Before the period of the Hurrians (Horites), the Nuzi site was settled by the Subarians, which was a different ethnic group, and the city was called by an earlier name of Gasur. However, the city of Nuzi has gained its current importance from its occupation during the period of the Hurrians (Horites) and from the cuneiform texts that have been discovered in it from that Hurrian period.

The city of Nuzi was excavated by the American School of Oriental Research in Baghdad and Harvard University during the period from 1925 to 1931. The thousands of cuneiform texts which have been discovered in Nuzi and the city of Arrapkha (modern Kirkuk), 9 miles to the east, have proved to be of enormous value in illustrating the prominence of the Hurrian people and their patriarchal customs.

The Nuzi Tablets and the Hurrians (Horites). The Horites are mentioned several times in the first five books of the Bible. In Genesis 14:4-6, the Horites who dwelt at Mount Seir are defeated by Chedorlaomer, king of Elam during the time of Abraham. In Genesis 36:20-30, the descendants and leaders of the Horites, who dwelt with Esau at Mount Seir, are described. Deuteronomy 2:12 and 22 documents that the descendants of Esau defeated the Horites at Mount Seir and took over their land.

Biblical historians once thought of the Horites as a local group of cave dwellers who got their name from the Hebrew word *hor*, which means "hole" or "cave." However, the discovery of the Nuzi Tablets reveals that the Horites were well-known people who occupied a prominent place in ancient history. This unknown group not only existed, but played an influential role in the cultural history of the Near East. Because of modern archaeology, the historical notion that these people were "cave dwellers" has been abandoned.

The Nuzi Tablets and the Patriarchs. The primary contribution of the Nuzi Tablets is that they reveal many of the customs that existed during the times of the biblical patriarchs. Although the Nuzi and Arrapkha Tablets are dated in the 15th and 14th centuries BCE, several centuries after the biblical patriarchal period of 2000-1800 BCE, they still illustrate the times and customs of the patriarchs. When Abraham came out of Ur and dwelt in Haran, he and his immediate descendants mingled with the western Hurrian society. The Tablets from Nuzi and Arrapkha reveal that both cities, east and west, had the same customs. Consequently, the Hurrian customs and influence should also be valid for the earlier centuries of 2000-1800 BCE.

Abraham petitions the Lord concerning his childless condition in Genesis 15:2 and the fact that Eliezer, his servant, was to become his heir. In Hurrian society it was customary for an older married couple who did not have a child to adopt a son to take care of his foster parents until they died, and in return become the heir to their property. But if a natural son were born, this agreement would be invalidated, and the natural son would become the primary heir, as was the case when Isaac was born to Abraham and Sarah.

The Hurrian marriage contract occasionally stipulated that a specific slave girl would be given to a new bride. This is exactly what happened in Jacob's marriage to Leah in Genesis 29:24 and his marriage to Rachel in Genesis 29:29. Other provisions of the marriage contract stipulated that an upper class wife who was childless would provide her husband with a slave girl as a concubine, and the wife was entitled to treat the offspring of the concubine as her own. This happened with Sarah and Abraham in Genesis 16:2-3, with Rachel and Jacob in Genesis 30:34, and with Leah and Jacob in Genesis 30:9.

Hurrian laws concerning marriage were primarily concerned with the bearing of children and not with companionship, and they provided various ways for families to produce and maintain offspring. If, in the case of an adopted son, a couple has a natural born son, that adopted son was not to be expelled from the family. In Genesis 21:9-14, it took a divine exemption to cause Abraham to violate this law and expel Hagar and her son from the family.

The Nuzi texts revealed that the birthright in Hurrian society was more a matter of parental decree than being the first born in the family. These parental decrees were more binding than other decrees when they were made from the deathbed and were introduced by the formula: "Behold now, I am old." This custom is illustrated in Genesis 27 when Jacob steals the family blessing from his older brother Esau. It is further illustrated in Genesis 48:9-22 when Jacob blesses Joseph's son Ephraim above his older brother Manasseh and Jacob took the birthright that would have normally been given to his firstborn son Reuben and gave it to Joseph's two sons.

Nuzi law also explained the significance of the teraphim, which were small household deities. The possession of these deities signified leadership of the family. If possessed by a daughter, they provided assurance that her husband would have the right to her father's property. In Genesis 31 when Jacob was fleeing from his father-in-law Laban, his wife

Rachel stole her father's deities, which would have given Jacob first rights to her father's property over her brothers. Laban chased after Jacob to retrieve the deities but never found them (Gen. 31:19,30,35).

In Genesis 12:10-20 and 20:2-6, Abraham introduces his wife Sarah as his sister when he goes into a strange land. In Genesis 26:1-11, Isaac does the same with his wife Rebekah. These appear to be cowardly acts on the part of these patriarchs. However, the Nuzi texts reveal that marriage was a very solemn oath among the Hurrians, and the wife could also have the legal status of sister, although the husband and wife might not have any blood ties. Consequently, under certain circumstance, the term "wife" and "sister" could officially be used interchangeably, and by resorting to the wife-sister relationship, Abraham and Isaac were taking advantage of the toughest protections that the existing law could provide.

Critical Value. The discovery of the Nuzi Tablets has provided a background of ancient customs and laws that help the students of ancient biblical history understand the influence that these laws and customs have had on the biblical record during the patriarchal period. By studying the social customs of the people of Mesopotamia that occupied the same area as the patriarchs and mingled with the patriarchs, we gain a better understanding of the biblical record of the patriarchs and the historical setting that influenced them.

g. **The Mari Letters-Light on the World of the Patriarchs**

The city of Mari (modern Tell el-Hariri) is located on the Middle Euphrates about 7 miles northwest of Abu-Kemal, which is a small town on the Syrian side of the Syro-Iraq border. This city was important in ancient time due to its location on caravan routes that crossed the Syrian desert and linked the city with Syria, the Mediterranean coast, and the Assyrian and Babylonian civilizations. The Mari excavation site was first identified by William Foxwell Albright in 1932.

Excavation began at the site in 1933 by Andre Parrot with the backing of the Musee du Louvre. An ancient imperial city of great importance and splendor was the result of the excavation. The excavations were interrupted by World War II in 1939 after six very successful campaigns. Excavations resumed in 1951 and four addition campaigns were completed by 1956, when work was discontinued due to a dispute over the Suez Canal.

Some of the most important discoveries at Mari included the great temple of Ishtar, the Babylonian goddess of propagation, and a temple tower (ziggurat). The courts of the temple were of the Sumerian type with columns and an inner room (cella). The temple tower was similar to the ones at Ur and other Mesopotamian sites. The popularity of the Ishtar fertility cult was illustrated by the statuettes of her that were uncovered. The fact that Mari's ruling monarch was believed to have received his staff and ring, the emblems of his authority, from Ishtar, is depicted by one of the murals in the palace.

The royal palace was another important discovery at Mari. This expansive building, which was built in the center of the mound, contained almost 300 rooms and was contemporary with the first dynasty of Babylon. Rare specimens of well-preserved wall paintings were found in the throne room. This enormous structure with its royal apartments, administrative offices, scribal school, and beautifully colored mural paintings is considered one of the best-preserved palaces in the Middle East. The palace was built by the Amorites who lived in a later period and worshipped the deities, Adad and Dagon. The excavations that took place after World War II were concerned primarily with older strata that went back to the time of the dynasty of Akkad during the pre-Sargonic period.

The Royal Archives. The excavation of the ***Mari Letters***, which consisted of about 20,000 clay tablets, have revolutionized the knowledge of the ancient biblical record. These documents date back to about 1700 BCE during the time of Hammurabi and were written in the Old Babylonian dialect. They consist of correspondence by the King and governors of the city-state of Mari. They cover the time period of the reign of King Yasmah-Adad, who began the construction of the palace, to the reign of King Zimri-Lim, who completed the construction of the palace.

Some of the Mari correspondence is between King Yasmah-Adad and his father, King Shamshi-Adad I of Assyria, the powerful empire builder, as well as with the representatives of the provinces that were a part of his kingdom. The correspondence of King Zimri-Lim included diplomatic exchanges with King Hammurabi of Babylon, the king of Aleppo, as well as his subordinates. Two letters from Aleppo to King Zimri-Lim deal with prophecies delivered in the name of the god Adad of Aleppo, which resemble biblical prophecies.

Biblical Value of the Mari Texts. These records have biblical important because they come from an area that was home to the Hebrew patriarchs during the period when Abraham migrated from Ur to the land of Canaan. Abraham left Ur during the 3rd dynasty of Ur when Mari was under the control of Ur, some 400 years prior to the time of King Zimri-Lim and the fall of Mari. However, a Mari prince by the name of Ishbi-Irra later conquered the city-state of Isin in about 2021 BCE and was involved in the overthrow of the city of Ur. The city of Nahor, which is mentioned in Genesis 24:10 as the home of Isaac's wife Rebekah, is also often mentioned in the Mari Letters.

As in the Nuzi texts, the term "Hebiru" is also found in the Mari Letters, which is very important because Abraham is the first person in the Bible to be called a "Hebrew" in Genesis 14:13. In both cases, the term apparently means "a wanderer," "one who crosses over" or "one who passes from one place to another." This description applies very well to Abraham and his early descendants, Isaac and Jacob.

The Mari Letters mention "sons of the right," which means, "sons of the south," because directions were obtained as one faced the east, and the southerly direction would be to the right. The "sons of the right" that the letters refer to were a fierce tribe of wanderers called Benjaminites, which have no connection to the "Benjamites" in the Bible. The name "Benjamin," "son of the south," which means, "southerner," was a term used in Mari, and the parallel term, "sons of the left," which means, "sons of the north," was also found in the Mari Letters.

In Genesis 35:16-19, Jacob's twelfth son was born after he returned form Mesopotamia, and he named him Benjamin. When Jacob gives his final blessings to his sons in Genesis 49:27, he describes Benjamin as a ravenous wolf. This description has a close resemblance to the Benjaminite tribe described in the Mari Letters. Also, when the word "chieftain" is translated with reference to the southern Benjaminite tribe, the Mari word "dawidum" is used, which means "leader." This provides insight into the etymology of the name, "David," king of Israel, which means "the leader."

Historical Value of the Mari Letters. The Mari Letters established that King Shamski-Adad I of Assyria, who reigned from about 1748-1716 BCE, and Hammurabi of Babylon, who reigned from about 1728-1676, were contemporaries. Biblical scholars no longer identify Hammurabi of Babylon with Amraphel, king of Shinar, in Genesis 14:1. The four kings named in Genesis 14:1 are still a mystery. Hammurabi, a strong military leader and administrator, was a member of the 1st dynasty of Babylon that reigned from 1830 to about 1550 BCE, and it reached greatest power during the reign of Hammurabi. He conquered Rim-Sin of Larsa and took control of all of the city-states of Lower Babylon, and his great military machine was able to destroy Mari.

The Babylonian story of creation was developed during the reign of Hammurabi, and the poem glorified Marduk, the patron god of Babylon, who was established by Hammurabi as the national god of Babylonia. During the reign of Hammurabi, the early Sumerian language declined and the Semitic-Babylonian language came into common usage.

The Mari Letters and the Amorites. In about 2000 BCE there was a Semitic-nomadic group of people known as "Westerners," and in the Old Testament as "Amorites," who lived along the edges of the Fertile Crescent. These Amorites invaded the areas of developed civilization, and established Amorite states all over Mesopotamia. The cities of Nahor, Haran, Mari, Qatna, and Ugarit were established with Amorite kings. Under Hammurabi, Babylon itself became the capital of an Amorite state.

These historical facts about the Amorites are clearly reflected in the Mari Letters. Archaeological discoveries such as these are continuing to provide a historical framework that complements and clarifies the biblical record concerning the patriarchs.

h. **The Lachish Letters - Jeremiah's Age Lives Again**

In the early excavations at Lachish in 1933, eighteen letters were found embedded in a layer of burnt charcoal and ashes. In 1938 three more letters were found. The vast majority of these letters were written by a person named Hoshiah to a person named Jaosh. Hoshiah was stationed at a military outpost, and Jaosh appears to have been a high-ranking officer in the garrison at Lachish. The letters were written in Hebrew using the ancient Phoenician script.

These letters were written during the period before the final destruction of Jerusalem by the Babylonians in 587 BCE, and were in the layer of ashes representing the final destruction of the city of Lachish. (**Note:** This 587 BCE date for the destruction of Jerusalem is 20 years later than the biblical date used in this book, which may be due to the use of different calendars.) These particular letters are dated from 588 BCE when Nebuchadnezzar was making his final siege of Jerusalem, Lachish and Azekah.

Identification of Lachish. The excavation site for Lachish is located about 30 miles southwest of Jerusalem, 20 miles from the Mediterranean coast, and 50 miles west of Hebron. The city of Lachish is mentioned in the Amarna Letters and in earlier sources from Egypt. It was of strategic importance because it was on the main route from Egypt to central Palestine. Its location overlooked the rich terrain which sloped down to the coastal lowland. This fortress city was one of the primary fortified cities of Judah and one that was captured by the Israelites in their conquest of Palestine (Josh. 10:31-35). It was an ideal barrier between the plains of the Philistines and the elevated Judaean country side.

Excavations at Lachish. Several other sites were first thought to be the city of Lachish. First the site of Umm-Lakis was thought to be the city. Sir Flinders Petrie, a pioneer archaeologist, thought Tell el-Hesy might be the city. William Foxwell Albright finally correctly identified the city as the large mound at Tell el-Duweir, and excavations were begun at Lachish by the Wellcome-Marston Archaeological Expedition in 1933 under the direction of J.L. Starkey.

The work was continued by Lankester Harding and Charles H. Inge in 1938 after Starkey was killed by Arab bandits. Lachish was captured by Nebuchadnezzar during the period from 588-586 BCE (Jer. 34:7). The excavation shows signs of a huge fire on the road leading up to the gate and on the adjacent wall, which indicates that the attackers relied on fire to capture the city and that felled olive trees, not yet harvested, were used to fuel the fire.

The Results of the Excavation at Lachish. The excavation at Lachish revealed that it had been occupied by the Hyksos from about 1720-1550 BCE when they overran Egypt. A typical Hyksos defense ditch (*fosse*) was discovered, which had a ramp made of clay and lime that apparently provided an area for their horses. Three Canaanite Egyptian temples built from 1450-1225 BCE were excavated in the defense ditch. A Persian temple was also discovered from a much later period. A huge quantity of pottery, jewelry, acarabs, and skeletal remains were found in the cemeteries at Lachish.

The remains of a huge engineering excavation for water storage, which was not completed, consisted of a 200-foot-deep well located inside the city. The shaft of the well terminated in a rectangular area 80 feet long by 70 feet wide by 80 feet deep. This water system would have been much larger than a similar one built by King Hezekiah for Jerusalem and comparable to similar systems at Gezer and Megiddo.

The excavations also produced a good quantity of inscribed materials. A bronze dagger from about 1700 BCE contains four pictographic signs from an earlier script. A picture and bowl show samples of the early writing found at Serabit el-Khadem. The name "Gedaliah" was discovered on a jar handle, which may be the name of the official that Nebuchadnezzar appointed to govern Judah after the fall of Jerusalem as described in Jeremiah Chapters 40 through 42.

Contents of the Lachish Letters. Of all the inscriptions and letters discovered at Lachish, the most important are the ones that describe the state of affairs as Judah was being invaded and conquered by Nebuchadnezzar's army. The content of the most important letters may be described briefly as follows: Letter 1 contained a list of names, and most of these names are in the Old Testament record. The contents of Letters 2 and 5 were mostly greetings. Letter 3 was the longest of the letters and contained the most information. It provides information about Jewish troop movements and makes an interesting note to an unknown prophet and his word of warning. Letter 4 makes note of the fact that Hoshiah can see the signals coming from Lachish, but he cannot see the signals coming from Azekah. This implies that Azekah may have already been captured, because the letter states, "We are watching for the signal station at Lachish according to all the signals you are giving, because we cannot see the signals of Azekah." The following biblical expression is found in Letter 6, "to weaken the hands of the people," which is also found in Jeremiah 38:4.

Historical Importance of the Lachish Letters. As Nebuchadnezzar launched his military campaign against Judah, the Lachish Letters provide an independent view of the conditions that existed in the last days before the fall of Jerusalem. Nebuchadnezzar invaded the city after an eighteen-month siege and destroyed the walls of the city, burned the houses and the temple, and carried the people away to exile in Babylon (2 Kin. 25:1-12).

This all happened during the ministry of Jeremiah the prophet and he makes reference to this event in the Old Testament as follows: "When the king of Babylon's army fought against Jerusalem, and against all the cities of Judah that were left, against Lachish, and against Azekah: for these defensed cities remained of the cities of Judah" (Jer. 34:7). A place in the Shephelah region of Palestine called Tell Zakariya has been identified as Azekah, and it was excavated in 1898 by Frederick K. Bliss of the Palestine Exploration Fund. It had a tough inner fortification strengthened with eight large towers, which verifies Jeremiah's account of it as one of the defensed cities of Judah.

As mentioned earlier, the Lachish Letters deal with the time just before the fall of Jerusalem and provide the same conditions of chaos and confusion that are presented in the Book of Jeremiah. Many of the place names that appear in the Bible are also found in the letters, as well as the personal names of individuals. The name "Hoshaiah" shows up in Jeremiah 42:1 and Nehemiah 12:32. The four-letter word YHWH refers to God, which are the consonants of the name "Yahweh" or "Jehovah." Although a prophet like

Jeremiah is referred to in the letters, there is no indication that this prophet is Jeremiah.

The destruction of the kingdom of Judah by the Babylonians was so complete that it took many centuries for it to recover. The coins of the Jewish state of Judah were stamped with the name "Yehud," which means, Judah, but it was not until after 300 BCE that substantial numbers of these coins show up in archaeological remains, and their number is still very small. This is one source of evidence that supports the fact that the destruction of Jewish power by the Babylonians lasted for many centuries.

i. **The Dead Sea Scrolls**

In 1947 a young Bedouin shepherd found a cave south of Jericho that contained a large number of leather scrolls with Hebrew and Aramaic writing and about 600 fragmentary inscriptions. New caves containing fragments of later scrolls written in Hebrew, Greek, and Aramaic were found in 1952. These discoveries were followed by additional manuscript discoveries in other caves in the Dead Sea area.

The Date of the Dead Sea Scrolls. Scholars have defined three time periods for the Dead Sea area manuscripts after extensive study: (1) The Archaic Period from about 200-150 BCE; (2) The Hasmonaean Period from about 150-30 BCE; and (3) The Herodian Period from about 30 BCE to AD 70. The vast majority of the manuscripts originated in the last half of the 2nd period and the last half of the 3rd period.

Attacks have been made against the antiquity and authenticity of these documents, but they have been authenticated by two lines of evidence. The radiocarbon scientific method of dating has placed the date of the linen in which the scrolls were wrapped in the time period of 175 BCE to AD 225. Scholars knowledgeable in the science of paleography have dated these documents according to the form of the letters and the way they are written when compared to the writing from other ancient time periods.

They have demonstrated that this script comes from the period between the 3rd century BCE and the middle of the 1st century AD. W. F. Albright, an American biblical archaeologist, makes the following observation, "All competent students of writing conversant with the available material and with paleographic method date the scrolls in the 250 years before AD 70."

The Contents of the Dead Sea Scrolls. The manuscripts obtained from the Dead Sea caves were partly biblical and partly nonbiblical. The biblical portion contained two scrolls of Isaiah, one of which was complete, most of the first two chapters of Habakkuk, and fragments of all the other books of the Old Testament except for Esther. A large number of partial manuscripts were recovered for the first five books of Moses, Isaiah, Psalms, Jeremiah, and Daniel.

The best known of the discoveries at the Qumran site has been the complete scroll of Isaiah, because it is 1000 years older than the oldest Hebrew text preserved in the Masoretic Hebrew Bible. All recent translations of the Bible are based on the Masoretic Hebrew Bible, and it does not go back any earlier than AD 900. The fact that the Hebrew text of Isaiah and the other manuscripts date back to 150-125 BCE establishes them as the greatest of modern discoveries, because they were the oldest Bible manuscripts in any language.

In the original group of scrolls that were discovered in 1947 there was a commentary on Habakkuk and a "Manual of Discipline" relating to a pre-Christian sect called the Essenes. Also included in the original group of scrolls was a later scroll of Isaiah that conformed to the traditional Hebrew language and a document called "The War Between the Children of Light and Darkness." This document was evidently concerned with the Maccabaean battles against Greek paganism in 158-137 BCE.

Excavations began at the original manuscript-bearing cave in the winter of 1949 by Pierre de Vaux and Lankester Harding, two well-known Palestinian archaeologists. They recovered fragments of Geneses, Deuteronomy, Judges, and a fragment of Leviticus in Old Hebrew script. Their nonbiblical discoveries included a fragment of the "Book of Jubilees," which was associated with Enoch literature, and some other unfamiliar material.

Other Manuscript-Yielding Sites. A cave was discovered at Murabbaat in another part of the desert in 1952. It contained manuscripts primarily from the 2nd century AD in Hebrew, Greek, and Aramaic, which included a few texts of Genesis, Exodus, Deuteronomy, and Isaiah. Also included were letters from the period of Bar Cocheba, who led the revolt against Rome in AD 132-135. There was one notable exception to the 2nd century dating of this material, which was an archaic Hebrew papyrus, a palimpsest (written on more than once), with a list of names and numbers dating from the 6th century BCE.

Other caves have been discovered in the same general area. One group of caves in Khirbet Mird, northeast of the monastery of Mar Saba, contained Arabic papyri, Greek and Christo-Palestinian-Syrian documents, with fragments of biblical manuscripts, all dating from the Byzantine and early Arabic periods. Another group of manuscripts dating from the 2nd century BCE contained primarily Murabbaat material. This material included a Greek version of the minor prophets and a large collection of Nabataean papyri, both of which are of great biblical and historical importance.

Excavations at Khirbet Qumran. Khirbet Qumran, which was an Essene community, was excavated from 1951 to 1954, and proved to be one of the richest manuscript-yielding sites in the Dead Sea area. The members of the Essenic community at Khirbet Qumran, which was 7 miles south of Jericho near the Dead Sea, copied these manuscripts and preserved them by hiding them in the caves. In sectarian Judaism, the Essenes were next in importance to the Pharisees and Sadducees. Because of the phenomenal manuscript discoveries in the cave-dotted cliffs in this area, this particular site has become one of the most publicized places in Palestine.

The excavations at Khirbet Qumran have resulted in the recovery of coins, pottery, and architectural remains which have fully authenticated it as the center of Essenic Judaism. This makes it possible for the story of the occupation of Qumran to be told. Four periods can be traced in the later history of the site.

Period 1 dates from its founding under the ruler, John Hyrcanus, in about 110 BCE to the seventh year of Herod in 31 BCE. A large number of coins of John Hyrcanus, as well as other Hasmonaean rulers, including Antigonus from 40-37 BCE, the last ruler of this line. Apparently at the time of the last ruler an earthquake leveled the site, and indications are that during Herod's reign the site was abandoned due to his antagonism against the Essenes.

Period 2 at Qumran dates from its rebuilding and expansion in about AD 1 to its destruction in June of AD 68 by the Romans. Qumran flourished during the lifetimes of Jesus, John the Baptist, and the early Christian apostles, and was influential in Judaism and the early Christian Church. Coins have been discovered at the site which date from the reign of Archelaus from AD 4-6, and from the period of the Roman procurators down to the second year of the first revolt by the Jews in AD 66-70. When the Roman army captured Jericho in June of AD 68, they evidently captured Qumran at the same time. A coin marked with an X, belonging to the Tenth Legion, was found at the site, and iron arrowheads were found in a layer of burned ash.

Period 3 marks the period of Roman occupation after the destruction of Jerusalem in AD 70. There were some coins found at the site that describe *Judaea Capta,* which date during the reign of Titus from AD 79-81, and mark this period as a time of Roman occupation. There is evidence that the structures at Qumran were converted to army barracks and that a Roman garrison was stationed there from AD 68 to about AD 100, when the site was apparently abandoned again.

Period 4 at Qumran is notable by the reoccupation of the site during the 2nd revolt of the Jews from AD 132-135. There are indications from the recovered coins that the Jews made their last stand at Qumran to drive the Romans out of their country, and after that the site sank into obscurity.

The architectural remains a Qumran reveal a main structure 100 feet by 120 feet that formed the communal center and hub of the complex. A huge defense tower with thick walls reinforced by stone embankments was located in the northwest corner of the complex. Some of the coins from the 2nd Jewish revolt reveal the use of this tower as a fortress against the Roman army.

The largest hall of the main building, which was located alongside the general meeting room, contained the scriptorium. Several inkwells of the Roman period indicate that the manuscripts had been copied by the community's scribes in this area. There were two carefully plastered cisterns (artificial reservoirs) in the complex and there were installations for bathing and baptisms. The bulk of the 40 cisterns and reservoirs discovered there must have been used for the storage of water in the dry, hot climate. The complex contained about 1000 burial places, many of which were excavated by De Vaux. He noted that they contained no jewelry and showed no evidence of luxury.

Khirbet Qumran and the Essenes. The fact that Khirbet Qumran was the headquarters of Essenic Judaism is not only demonstrated by the excavations at Khirbet Qumran, but also attested to by three authorities who were contemporary witnesses to the same fact. Those contemporaries were Pliny, Josephus, and Philo.

Pliny was Pliny the Elder (born Gaius Plinius Secundus, AD 23–79), a Roman author, naturalist, natural philosopher, and a naval and army commander of the early Roman Empire. Josephus was Titus Flavius Josephus, born Yosef ben Matityahu, (AD 37-100), a first-century Romano-Jewish scholar, historian and hagiographer, who was born in Jerusalem. Philo was Philo of Alexandria, also called Philo Judaeus, (AD 20-50), a Hellenistic Jewish philosopher who lived in Alexandria, in the Roman province of Egypt.

The location where Qumran is located was precisely designated by Pliny as "on the west side of the Dead Sea."

He also designated the town of En-gedi as being located "below the Essenes."

Josephus talked about the people at Qumran, their unselfish character, their industry, and their communal life style. He admired their love for common labor and wrote about how they dressed in white and described the three-year probationary period required before admission to the sect, as well as other phases of discipline. He commented on their various ceremonies, their celibacy, their piety, their convictions about immortality, and their belief that righteousness would be rewarded. They numbered about 4000.

Philo provided a similar description of the Essenes as Josephus. Their delight in the Bible and literature is reflected in the library at Qumran and the account given by Philo and Josephus. The Essenes carefully copied the Holy Scriptures and took pains to preserve them in the caves. Although there are some difficulties equating the sect described by Pliny, Josephus and Philo with the Essenes at Qumran, the similarities far outweigh the differences. The evidence these three individuals have provided seems to equate Qumran with the Essenes of the 1st century AD.

j. **Jerusalem**

The excavations done by Israeli institutions at the western and southern walls of the temple mountain in Jerusalem are probably the most important made so far. These excavations have uncovered the actual steps and entrances to Herod's temple and the tiny shops and narrow streets where the merchants must have sold their merchandise. The huge stone blocks thrown down into the streets from the top of the wall by Titus' troops in AD 70 were found where they fell.

In another part of the city, the grave of a Jew was found who had been crucified by the Romans, which was the first physical evidence of this method of execution ever found. The discoveries from these excavations were so extensive that it would take a generation to decipher and integrate them into the historical framework of the Roman Age.

k. **Ebla**

Ebla, which goes by the modern name Tell Mardikh, is a 140-acre mound in the northwest corner of Syria. Excavations began at this site in 1964 by archaeologists from the University of Rome, and an inscription was found in 1968 that identified the site as the ancient city of Ebla. Portions of impressive buildings from the period of the biblical patriarchs (1900-1700 BCE) were uncovered, and beneath these buildings' palaces and temples from the Early Bronze Age (2400-2250 BCE) were found. This was the discovery of a previously unknown advanced civilization from an earlier time period.

The excavations from 1974, 1975, and 1976 uncovered three rooms of one palace which generated almost 7,000 well-preserved clay tablets and about 13,000 fragments of other tablets containing cuneiform writing. This find was a very important archive of ancient Sumerian and Canaanite literature, which also included the economic, political, and legal records of Ebla.

These tablets provide biblical scholars with information that helps them understand the cultures of Israel's ancient neighbors, and aids in biblical interpretation. These ancient records show that Ebla was a merchant empire that controlled trade routes that reached the Mesopotamian Valley, the mountains of modern-day Turkey, and the edge of the Nile Valley.

Of more importance was the fact that some of these tablets contained the earliest known dictionaries that provided the meanings of words used in both the Sumerian and early Canaanite languages, which help archaeologists understand the cultures. Many of the Canaanite words found at Ugarit and Hebrew words in the Old Testament can be better understood because they also occur in these ancient tablets.

The continuous archaeological research in biblical lands should ensure that the thrilling story of biblical archaeology has not been completed, and that there is the promise of even greater contributions to biblical knowledge in the future. For example, since 1945 thirteen ancient Egyptian manuscripts from Nag Hammadi in Upper Egypt have almost matched the Dead Sea Scrolls in biblical importance. These manuscripts even include the apocryphal "Gospel of Thomas" and are of enormous importance in dating the literature of the New Testament.

The prospect of new and exciting discoveries about the Bible, coming from the study of secular history, linguistics, and archaeology, will enable us to achieve a more accurate understanding of the Bible's message and God's will for Humanity.

D. What is the potential for future archaeological discoveries about the Bible?

New archaeological discoveries have the potential to authenticate and provide additional background information about the above issues, which might include the following:

1. The discovery of the Ark of the Covenant would further authenticate the connection that Moses had with God as expressed by God in Numbers 12:1-16, and the history that Moses has presented in the first five books of the Bible from Creation in about 4026 BCE until his death in about 1473 BCE.

2. The discovery of Noah's Ark or portions of Noah's Ark would further authenticate that the Great Flood actually occurred.

3. The discovery of extinct species of animals buried in the ice at the North or South Poles would also reveal that the Great Flood occurred and that some animals were transported to the poles by ocean currents and frozen before they decayed or could be consumed by other animals.

4. According to Genesis 11:1, "the whole earth was of one language, and of one speech." Archaeological discoveries before the Tower of Babel in about 2,239 BCE and after the Great Flood in about 2,370 BCE should reflect the same verbal language. This would also have been true before the Flood, but the forms of writing or inscriptions from the different cultures would probably have been different.

5. The discovery of more ancient civilizations before the Great Flood and closer to creation might reveal new technologies about time, space, and motion that would make substantial contributions to modern science, because the technologies of advanced civilizations may have been lost during the Great Flood or when they were conquered by more primitive civilizations. It is also possible that some of the advanced ancient civilizations were buried in the oceans and seas by the Great Flood.

Logical Conclusion: From this review of archaeological evidence, it may be inferred that:

1. **Very little was known about ancient history and biblical history, except for the Old Testament record and classical antique writings, before the 19th century.**

2. Modern archaeology may be said to have had its beginning in 1798, when the Nile Valley was opened up to scientific study by Napoleon's Egyptian Expedition.

3. The foundational discoveries of the 19th century paved the way for major discoveries in the 20th century about ancient history.

4. The great discoveries of the 19th and 20th centuries have documented and authenticated Old Testament scriptures, personalities, and places, as well as the ancient laws and customs of secular nations.

5. Future archaeological discoveries have the potential to further authenticate biblical history and discover other ancient history that makes substantial contributions to modern technology.

CHAPTER 6
Who are our Ancestors (The Great Flood)?

A. Why did God send the Great Flood to destroy the earth?

God saw the wickedness of humanity, that the imagination of their thoughts was always of evil, and the earth was corrupt and filled with violence: "And God saw that the wickedness of man was great in the earth, and that every imagination of the thoughts of his heart was only evil continually. And it repented the Lord that he had made man on the earth, and it grieved him at his heart. And the Lord said, I will destroy man whom I have created from the face of the earth; both man, and beast, and the creeping thing, and the fowls of the air; for it repenteth me that I have made them. But Noah found grace in the eyes of the Lord. These are the generations of Noah: Noah was a just man and perfect in his generations, and Noah walked with God. And Noah begat three sons, Shem, Ham, and Japheth. The earth also was corrupt before God, and the earth was filled with violence. And God looked upon the earth, and, behold, it was corrupt; for all flesh had corrupted his way upon the earth. And God said unto Noah, The end of all flesh is come before me; for the earth is filled with violence through them; and, behold, I will destroy them with the earth" (Gen. 6:5-13).

Logical Conclusion: From these scriptures about why God sent the Great Flood, it may be inferred that:

1. The reasons that God sent the great flood to destroy all life on earth were humanity's wickedness, evil thoughts, violence, and corruption.
2. God saved the earth for the sake of one man, Noah, who was part of a lineage of generations who were faithful and walked with God.
3. God chose to replenish the earth with families of the same design as the original family of Adam and Eve, which is evidenced by the structure of Noah's family.
4. The offspring of Satan and the other fallen angels by the daughters of man would also have been destroyed by the flood, because they would have been mortal as Jesus was, and God would have the power to prevent Satan and the other fallen angels from having sexual intercourse with the daughters of men to produce offspring after the flood, but Satan and the other fallen angels would not have been destroyed by the flood because they were still a part of the spiritual universe.

B. What promises did God make after the Great Flood?

After the Great Flood, God promises not to curse the ground again, not to kill every living thing as He had done, and as long as the earth exists there will be seedtime and harvest time, cold and heat, summer and winter, and day and night will not end: "And Noah builded an altar unto the Lord; and took of every clean beast, and of every clean fowl, and offered burnt offering on the altar. And the Lord smelled a sweet savour; and the Lord said in his heart, I will not again curse the ground any more for man's sake;

for the imagination of man's heart is evil from his youth; neither will I again smite any more every thing living, as I have done. While the earth remaineth, seedtime and harvest, and cold and heat, and summer and winter, and day and night shall not cease" (Gen. 8:20-22).

Logical Conclusion: From the scriptures about the promises God made after the Great Flood, it may be inferred that:

1. God promises not to curse the ground any more for man's sake as he did when he drove Adam and Eve out of the Garden of Eden, because humanity's very nature is evil.
2. God promises not to destroy every living thing again as he did with the flood.
3. God promises that as long as the earth remains there will be a seedtime and a harvest, cold and heat, summer and winter, and day and night shall not cease.

C. **Is there evidence that the Great Flood occurred?**

The commentary in this section about the evidence that the Great Flood occurred comes from two sources: http://www.allaboutcreation. org/the-flood.htm (41) and http://www.allaboutcreation.org/the-flood-2.htm (42).

1. **What is the biblical story about the Great Flood?**

According to Genesis Chapters 6 through 9, God decided to destroy humanity, land animals, and the fowls of the air throughout the earth with a Great Flood, because of the wickedness, corruption, and violence of humanity. There was one man by the name of Noah who "found grace in the eyes of the Lord" (Gen. 6:8) that God chose to save, along with his family and a remnant from the animal kingdom, to replenish the earth after the Flood. God directed Noah to build a huge ark to house himself, his wife, his three sons, and their three wives, along with the remnant of the animal kingdom during the Flood. This worldwide Flood which devastated the whole earth occurred sometime between 2000-3000 BCE (2370 BCE according to the biblical account in this book)

2. Are there any universal traditions about the Flood event in other cultures?

After the Flood waters receded, the only human beings left on earth were Noah, his wife, his three sons, and his three son's wives (Gen. 8:18); eight persons. Since every culture of human beings that have lived on earth since the Flood are descendants of Noah and his family, traditions about this catastrophic Flood event should have been passed down from generation to generation through most of these cultures.

According to this article, literally hundreds of Flood traditions have been preserved throughout the world, including Europe, Asia, Africa, Australia, and the Americas, and collectively, they serve to corroborate the biblical account of the Flood. Two of the oldest accounts of the Flood that have survived the passage of time are: China's "Hihking Classic" and Babylon's "Epic of Gilgamesh." Both of these Flood traditions are unusually consistent, considering how isolated these cultures are, and the length of time since the Flood.

3. Are there physical evidences that a Great Flood has occurred on this earth?

The earth shows evidence that the Flood is not just a symbolic event meant to teach us about God's judgment of sin, but is an actual historical event. This article asks us to consider the billions of fossils buried in sedimentation ("laid-down-by-water rock") found all over the earth. According to geologist Dr. John

Morris, president of the Institute for Creation Research (ICR), "Sedimentary rocks, by definition, are laid down as sediments by moving fluids, are made up of pieces of rock or other material which existed somewhere else, and were eroded or dissolved and deposited in their present location."

In his book "The Young Earth" (2001, Page 51), Dr. Morris reveals that over 70% of the earth's surface rock is sedimentary rock and the remainder is volcanic igneous and metamorphic rock. Geologists have found some very odd features in these sedimentary rock layers, such as fossilized trees buried at all angles and often passing through multiple rock layers. This is obviously the result of a catastrophic marine event, and these "polystrate" fossils (poly, meaning more than one; strate, meaning rock layer) occur all over the world.

On Page 70 of his book, Dr. Morris asks us to consider the ratios of dead things that are found buried in sedimentary rock: "95% of all fossils are marine invertebrates, particularly shellfish. Of the remaining 5%, 95% are algae and plant fossils (4.74%). 95% of the remaining 0.25% consists of the other invertebrates, including insects (0.2375%). The remaining 0.0125% includes all vertebrates, mostly fish. 95% of the few land vertebrates consist of less than one bone. (For example, only about 1,200 dinosaur skeletons have been found.)"

In his article in "Creation Magazine" (Volume 24:2, Pages 54-55), Mr. David Catchpoole asks us to also consider the abundance of marine fossil remains found on top of every mountain range in the world. For example, hundreds of gigantic (300kg/650lbs) oysters have been found on top of the Andes Mountains in South America.

4. Are there other evidences that a Great Flood has occurred on earth?

In his book "In the Beginning," Dr. Walt Brown provides a list of many other evidences that the Great Flood actually occurred. He writes, "The origin of each of the following is a subject of controversy with the earth sciences. Each has many aspects inconsistent with standard explanations. Yet all appear to be consequences of a sudden and unrepeatable event – a cataclysmic flood whose waters erupted from worldwide, subterranean, and interconnected chambers with an energy release exceeding the explosion of ten billion hydrogen bombs. Consequences of this event included the rapid formation of the features listed below. The mechanisms involved are well-understood."

Dr. Brown goes on to list each of the features, which are presented below, and explains how each is related to the Flood:

- The Grand Canyon and Other Canyons
- Mid-oceanic Ridge
- Continental Shelves and Slopes
- Ocean Trenches
- Seamounts and Tablemounts
- Earthquakes
- Magnetic Variations on the Ocean Floor
- Submarine Canyons
- Coal and Oil Formations
- Methane Hydrates
- Ice Age
- Frozen Mammoths
- Major Mountain Ranges
- Overthrusts
- Volcanoes and Lava
- Geothermal Heat
- Strata and Layered Fossils

- Metamorphic Rock
- Limestone
- Plateaus
- Salt Domes
- Jigsaw Fit of the Continents
- Changing Axis Tilt
- Comets
- Asteroids and Meteoroids

<u>Logical Conclusion</u>: From the analysis of the evidence that a Great Flood occurred, it may be inferred that:

1. According to Genesis Chapters 6 through 9, God decided to destroy humanity, land animals, and the fowls of the air throughout the earth with a Great Flood, because of the wickedness, corruption, and violence of humanity.

2. According to the website <u>http://www.allaboutcreation.org/the-flood.htm (41)</u>, literally hundreds of Flood traditions have been preserved throughout the world, including Europe, Asia, Africa, Australia, and the Americas, and collectively, they serve to corroborate the biblical account of the Flood. Two of the oldest accounts of the Flood that have survived the passage of time are: China's "Hihking Classic" and Babylon's "Epic of Gilgamesh." Both of these Flood traditions are unusually consistent, considering how isolated these cultures are, and the length of time since the Flood.

3. According to geologist Dr. John Morris, president of the Institute for Creation Research (ICR), "Sedimentary rocks, by definition, are laid down as sediments by moving fluids, are made up of pieces of rock or other material which existed somewhere else, and were eroded or dissolved and deposited in their present location." In his book "The Young Earth" (2001, Page 51), Dr. Morris reveals that over 70% of the earth's surface rock is sedimentary rock and the remainder is volcanic igneous and metamorphic rock.

4. **In his book "In the Beginning," Dr. Walt Brown provides a list of many other evidences that the Great Flood actually occurred.**

D. Is it feasible that Noah's Ark could house a remnant of the land animals for over a year?

The commentary in this section about the feasibility of Noah's Ark comes from the following sources: the Book of Genesis and http://www.allaboutpopularissues.org/noahs-ark.htm (43).

1. How big was Noah's Ark?

Following is the biblical account of the construction of Noah's Ark from Genesis 6:14-16: "Make thee an ark of gopher wood; rooms shalt thou make in the ark, and shalt pitch it within and without with pitch. And this is the fashion which thou shalt make it of: The length of the ark shall be three hundred cubits (450 ft.), the breadth of it fifty cubits (75 ft.), and the height of it thirty cubits (45 ft.). A window shalt thou make to the ark, and in a cubit shall thou finish it above; and the door of the ark shalt thou set in the side thereof; with lower, second, and third stories shalt thou make it." The ark was 450 feet long by 75 feet wide by 45 feet high, or about 1,518,750 cubic feet, including the three floors.

2. Was there enough room on Noah's Ark?

Considering the fact that Noah's Ark had to accommodate Noah and his family of eight people, at least two of every kind of land animal, and seven of some animals, was the ark big enough? Did it have room for essential supplies that would last for one year? In addition to the space required for the people and the animals, there had to be enough space to store enough food to sustain the people and all the animals for more than a year. This article will study the Genesis account of the Flood, found in chapters 6 through 9, to determine if Noah's Ark is a feasible reality or a fantastic part of an ancient myth.

3. How many land animals would there need to be to provide a remnant to replenish the earth?

According to this article, the first step in determining if Noah's Ark was big enough is to determine how many land animals would need to be on the boat to provide a remnant to replenish the earth after the Flood. What kinds of animals would need to be saved? Most scholars believe that the Genesis account would exclude sea animals and insects from being loaded on the ark, because remnants of these creatures could survive outside the ark. That would leave mammals, birds, reptiles, amphibians and Noah's family.

Since God directed Noah to bring animals on the ark "after their kind," we should deal with the scientific concept of variations within a Kind. For example, most biologists would agree that wolves, coyotes, dingoes, jackels, foxes, and the hundreds of different breeds of domestic dogs could come from a single pair of original "dogs." As we have learned, the genetic code will not allow for variations from Kind to Kind (one species evolving into an entirely different species), but DNA will allow for variations within a Kind or species. Considering these variations within a Kind, there are roughly 16,000 to 25,000 distinct Kinds of mammals, birds, reptiles and amphibians now living or known to have lived in the past.

4. What is the feasibility that Noah's Ark could have existed and survived the Flood?

What is the feasibility of the design and size of Noah's Ark? Based on the dimensions given above from the Genesis account, most experts would agree that the ark contained approximately 1,500,000 cubic feet of free space, which would resemble a three-level barge the size of one- and-a-half football fields. According to this article, many feasibility studies have been conducted which have concluded that this was more than enough space to house the 16,000 to 25,000 distinct Kinds of animals along with all of their requirements for food for an entire year.

Assuming that the average size of each animal in the ark was that of a sheep, the ark could hold up to 125,000 separate animals. The ark was not only large enough for its cargo, but it was perfectly designed for stability and sea-worthiness. This has been confirmed by various hydrodynamic tests which show that it was virtually impossible to capsize this barge design in the most violent winds and waves.

Logical Conclusion: **From the analysis of the feasible that Noah's Ark could house a remnant of the land animals for over a year, it may be inferred that:**

1. **The ark was 450 feet long by 75 feet wide by 45 feet high, or about 1,518,750 cubic feet, including the three floors.**
2. **Considering the fact that Noah's Ark had to accommodate Noah and his family of eight people, at least two of every kind of land animal, and seven of some animals, it can be determined if there was enough room in the ark.**
3. **As we have learned, the genetic code will not allow for variations from Kind to Kind (one species evolving into an entirely different species), but DNA will allow for variations within a Kind or species. Considering these variations within a Kind, there are roughly 16,000 to 25,000 distinct Kinds of mammals, birds, reptiles and amphibians now living or known to have lived in the past.**
4. **Assuming that the average size of each animal in the ark was that of a sheep, the ark could hold up to 125,000 separate animals. The ark was not only large enough for its cargo, but it was perfectly designed for stability and sea-worthiness.**

This has been confirmed by various hydrodynamic tests which show that it was virtually impossible to capsize this barge design in the most violent winds and waves.

E. Who were our ancestors after the Great Flood?

Noah was 600 years old when the flood waters began to fall in about 2370 BCE and Noah's father, Lamech, had died about five years before the flood at the age of 777 years, and Methuselah, the oldest man in the Bible, died in the same year of the flood at the age of 969 years. So Noah was the last living Patriarch in the Godly lineage of Seth at the time of the flood. The only human beings alive after the flood were Noah, his wife, his three sons Shem, Ham, and Japheth, and their wives. At some time after the flood, Noah got drunk and became naked in his tent. Noah's younger son Ham saw him naked and went and told his brothers, who took a garment and covered Noah without looking at his nakedness.

When Noah woke up and found out what Ham had done, he cursed Ham's son Canaan: "And the sons of Noah, that went forth of the ark, were Shem, and Ham, and Japheth: and Ham is the father of Canaan. These are the three sons of Noah: and of them was the whole earth overspread. And Noah began to be an husbandman, and he planted a vineyard: And he drank of the wine, and was drunken; and he was uncovered within his tent. And Ham, the father of Canaan, saw the nakedness of his father, and told his two brethren without. And Shem and Japheth took a garment, and laid it upon both their shoulders, and went backward, and covered the nakedness of their father; and their faces were backward, and they saw not their father's nakedness. And Noah awoke from his wine, and knew what his younger son had done unto him. And he said, Cursed be Canaan; a servant of servants shall he be unto his brethren. And he said, Blessed be the LORD God of Shem; and Canaan shall be his servant. God shall enlarge Japheth, and he

shall dwell in the tents of Shem; and Canaan shall be his servant."
(Gen. 9:25-27).

Following is the biblical record of the descendants of Noah along
with their family trees and the territory the sons of Noah occupied
after the flood.

1. **The Descendants of Shem. The descendants of Shem settled
   in the area from Mesha toward Sephar, which is an area
   along the eastern side of the Red Sea now occupied by Saudi
   Arabia.** "Unto Shem also, the father of all the children of Eber,
   the brother of Japheth the elder, even to him were children born.
   The children of Shem; Elam, and Asshur, and Arphaxad, and
   Lud, and Aram. And the children of Aram; Uz, and Hul, and
   Gether, and Mash. And Arphaxad begat Salah; and Salah begat
   Eber. And unto Eber were born two sons: the name of one was
   Peleg; for in his days was the earth divided; and his brother's
   name was Joktan. And Joktan begat Almodad, and Sheleph,
   and Hazarmaveth, and Jerah, And Hadoram, and Uzal, and
   Diklah, And Obal, and Abimael, and Sheba, And Ophir, and
   Havilah, and Jobab: all these were the sons of Joktan. And their
   dwelling was from Mesha, as thou goest unto Sephar a mount
   of the east. These are the sons of Shem, after their families, after
   their tongues, in their lands, after their nations" (Gen. 10:21-
   31). (See **Exhibit 4a1**, The Family Tree of Shem, and **Exhibit
   4a2**, The Family Tree of Abraham, the son of Shem)

The family tree of Shem includes Abraham, who was a descendant
of Shem's son Arphaxad, and Abraham became the father of the
Nation of Israel and Arphaxad also became the father of other
nations and clans through his great grandson Eber. Shem's son
Aram had four sons and became the father of other nations and
clans. Shem's other sons: Elam, Asshur, and Lud are not mentioned
in the Bible as having a specific territory. The descendants of Shem
settled in the area from Mesha toward Sephar: "And their dwelling

was from Mesha, as thou goest unto Sephar a mount of the east" (Gen. 10:21-30). Based on an analysis of the http://bibleatlas.org/ (2) website for that period, this is an area along the eastern side of the Red Sea which is now occupied by Saudi Arabia.

2. **The Descendants of Ham.** The family tree of Ham includes his son Canaan, who settled in the area "from Sidon, as thou comest to Gerar unto Gaza; as thou goest, unto Sodom, and Gomorrah, and Admah and Zeboim, even unto Lasha," which is the area between the Dead Sea, Jordan River, Sea of Galilee and the Mediterranean Sea now occupied by Palestine: "And the sons of Ham; Cush, and Mizraim, and Phut, and Canaan. And the sons of Cush; Seba, and Havilah, and Sabtah, and Raamah, and Sabtechah: and the sons of Raamah; Sheba, and Dedan. And Cush begat Nimrod: he began to be a mighty one in the earth. He was a mighty hunter before the Lord: wherefore it is said, Even as Nimrod the mighty hunter before the Lord. And the beginning of his kingdom was Bagel, and Erech, and Accad, and Calneh, in the land of Shinar. Out of that land went forth Asshur (Assyria), and builded Nineveh, and the city Rehoboth, and Calah, And Resen between Nineveh and Calah: the same is the great city. And Mizraim begat Ludim, and Anamim, and Lehabim, and Naphtuhim, And Pathrusim, and Casluhim, (out of whom came Philistim,) and Caphtorim. And Canaan begat Sidon his firstborn, and Heth, And the Jebusite, and the Amorite, and the Girgasite, And the Hivite, and the Arkite, and the Sinite, And the Arvidite, and the Zemarite, and the Hamathite: and afterward were the families of the Canaanites spread abroad. And the border of the Canaanites was from Sidon, as thou comest to Gerar, unto Gaza; as thou goest, unto Sodom, and Gomorrah, and Admah, and Zeboim, even unto Lasha. These are the sons of Ham, after their families, after their tongues, in their countries, and in their nations" (Gen. 10:6-20). (See **Exhibit 4b**: The Family Tree of Ham)

The family tree of Ham includes his son Canaan, who settled in the area "from Sidon, as thou comest to Gerar unto Gaza; as thou goest, unto Sodom, and Gomorrah, and Admah and Zeboim, even unto Lasha" (Gen. 10:15-19). Based on an analysis of the http://bibleatlas.org/ (2) website for that period, this is the area between the Dead Sea, Jordan River, Sea of Galilee and the Mediterranean Sea, which is now occupied by the Nation of Israel. According to the http://bibleatlas.org/ (2) website, the descendants of Ham's son Mizraim became the Philistines who settled in the Gaza Strip: "And Pathrusim, and Casluhim, (out of whom came Philistim (Philistines)) and Caphtorim" (Gen. 10:13-14). And the descendants of Ham's son Cush settled in the area now occupied by Iraq and Syria and became the nations of Assyria and Babylonia: "And the beginning of his kingdom was Babel, and Erech, and Accad, and Calneh, in the land of Shinar. Out of that land went forth Asshur (Assyria), and builded Nineveh, and the city Rehoboth, and Calah, And Resen between Nineveh and Calah: the same is a great city" (Gen. 10:10-12). The Bible does not name any descendants of Ham's son Phut.

3. **The Descendants of Japheth: The Bible gives no specific territories for settlement of the seven sons of Japheth: Magog, Madaim, Javan, Gomer, Tubal, Meshech and Tiras, but the names of his descendants show that most remained in the vicinity of present-day Turkey, where Noah's ark settled after the flood: "The sons of Japheth; Gomer, and Magog, and Madaim and Javan, and Tubal, and Meshech, and Tiras. And the son of Gomer; Ashkenaz, and Riphath, and Togarmah. And the sons of Javan; Elishah, and Tarshish, Kittim, and Dodanim (Rodanim). By these were the isles of the Gentiles divided in their lands; every one after his tongue, after their families, in their nations" (Gen. 10:2-5). (See Exhibit 4c: The Family Tree of Japheth)**

The Bible gave no specific territories for settlement of the seven sons of Japheth: Magog, Madaim, Javan, Gomer, Tubal, Meshech and Tiras. However, an analysis of the http://bibleatlas. org/ (2) website reveals places that were named after Japheth's sons: Javan, Tubal, and Meshech. Some of these places can be found by locating the places that go by the name of Japheth's descendants on a map in my reference Bible, which show that most of his descendants remained in the area near present-day Turkey, where Noah's ark settled after the flood.

<u>Logical Conclusion</u>: From the scriptures about the curse Noah placed on Ham's son Canaan and our ancesters after the Flood, it may be inferred that:

1. **Noah, his wife, his three sons, Shem, Ham, and Japheth, and their wives were our only ancestors after the Great Flood (8 Persons).**
2. **Since Noah cursed Canaan by name, Canaan must have been born and was probably the firstborn and only son of Ham at the time.**
3. **Since Ham's other three sons, Cush, Mizraim, and Phut, were probably not born at the time, the curse only applied to Canaan (It is not clear why Noah chose to curse Canaan).**
4. **Since Noah gave Shem a special blessing, Shem was probably Noah's firstborn and received the firstborn's traditional blessing, which gave Shem's descendants some influence over the descendants of the other two sons. (The translation of Gen. 10:21 is not clear as to who is the older of the other two brothers).**
5. **The descendants of Ham's son Canaan would serve the descendants of the other two brothers.**
6. **The land belonging to the descendants of Canaan was later given to the descendants of Shem (Abraham) as an inheritance during the conquest of Palestine.**

7. After the Flood the descendants of Noah's sons resided in different areas near Mount Ararat where the ark settled after the Flood, which was also relatively close to the population centers before the Flood.

8. The descendants of Shem resided in the area east of the Red Sea which is now occupied by Saudi Arabia.

9. The descendants of Japheth resided in the area near where the ark settled after the Flood which is now occupied by Turkey.

10. The descendants of three of Ham's sons resided in the following areas: his son Mizraim resided in the area now occupied by the Gaza Strip (Philistia); his son Canaan resided in the area now occupied by Palestine; and his son Cush resided in the area now occupied by Syria and Iraq, which includes the area where the Tower of Babel was located. The Bible did not show any descendants for Ham's fourth son Phut.

F. Who were our ancestors before the Great Flood?

1. One of the inferences of the Theory of Creation is that every human being on earth today is a descendant of the original human beings from the time of creation. If every human being is a descendant of the original human beings from the time of creation, then there should be a genealogy that ties us all to Adam and Eve. The Books of Matthew and Luke provide a complete genealogy from Adam to Jesus Christ. Genealogies are also provided in 1 Chronicles 1:1-9:44.

There are two aspects to the genealogies in Matthew and Luke, which will give us a measure of the accuracy and truthfulness of the biblical record. In the Davidic Covenant God promised David that: "And thine house and thy kingdom shall be established for ever before thee: thy throne shall be established forever" (2 Sam. 7:16). God promised that David's throne will last forever.

However, there is a prophecy by Jeremiah the Prophet that no person in the lineage of Solomon and Coniah (Jehoiachin) will sit on David's throne. How does God overcome this prophecy against the throne of David? He continues the lineage to Jesus Christ through Nathan, the brother of Solomon, to Mary, the mother of Jesus.

2. After the reign of Solomon, God split Israel into two kingdoms, Judah and Israel, because Solomon violated the Laws of the Administration of Kings and in his old age served idol gods. Ten of the twelve tribes were split away from Rehoboam, Solomon's son, and only two tribes were left with Rehoboam, Judah and Benjamin. The other ten tribes, called Israel, chose Jeroboam to be their king. Jeroboam immediately sinned by setting up golden calves to be worshipped by the people and chose priests that were not of the tribe of Levi, to keep the people from going to Jerusalem to worship. Both kingdoms, Judah and Israel, continued to sin against God and Israel was delivered into the hands of the Assyrians in about 740 BCE.

3. The kingdom of Judah continued to survive until about 617 BCE when Judah was captured by Nebuchadnezzar, king of Babylon, and Coniah (Jehoiachin), king of Israel, was taken captive and carried to Babylon. After Coniah (Jehoiachin) was carried to Babylon, Jeremiah the prophet made the following prophecy: "O earth, earth, earth, hear the word of the Lord. Thus saith the Lord, Write ye this man childless, a man that shall not prosper in his days: for no man of his seed shall prosper, sitting upon the throne of David, and ruling any more in Judah" (Jer. 22:29-30). The final destruction of Jerusalem and the temple occurred in about 607 BCE. It appears that God has gone against His promise in the Davidic Covenant, because Jerimiah has prophesied that no person in the lineage of Solomon and Coniah (Jehoiachin) will sit on David's throne.

4. David, however, had another son, Nathan. His line was not cursed. Mary, the physical mother of Jesus, traces her lineage

back to David through Nathan (Luke 3:23-38). Notice the care and the extent to which God goes to keep His Word and to preserve its truthfulness. The virgin birth was absolutely essential not only to assure the sinless character of Jesus but also to fulfill the Davidic Covenant. Jesus receives His "blood right" to David's throne through his earthly mother, Mary, and His "legal right" to David's throne through his adoptive earthly father, Joseph. The virgin birth guarantees that one of David's line will sit on David's throne and rule forever, while at the same time preserving intact the curse and restriction on the line of descent through Coniah (Jehoiachin) and Solomon.

5. **The genealogy of Christ through Joseph, the adoptive father of Jesus, from Abraham to Jesus Christ in Matthew 1:1-17 is as follows:** "The book of the generation of Jesus Christ, the son of David, the son of Abraham. Abraham begat Isaac; and Isaac begat Jacob; and Jacob begat Judas and his brethren; And Judas begat Phares and Zara of Thamar; and Phares begat Esrom; and Esrom begat Aram; And Aram begat Aminadab; and Aminadab begat Naasson; and Naasson begat Salmon; And Salmon begat Boaz of Rachab; and Boaz begat Obed of Ruth; and Obed begat Jesse; And Jesse begat David the king; and David the king begat Solomon of her that had been the wife of Urias; And Solomon begat Roboam; and Roboam begat Abia; and Abia begat Asa; And Asa begat Josaphat; and Josaphat bagat Joram; and Joram begat Ozias; And Ozias begat Joatham; and Joatham begat Achaz; and Achaz begat Ezekias; And Ezekias begat Manasses; and Manasses begat Amon; and Amon begat Josias; And Josias begat Jechonias and his brethren, about the time they were carried away to Babylon: And after they were brought to Babylon, Jechonias begat Salathiel; and Salathiel begat Zorobabel; And Zorobabel begat Abiud; and Abuid begat Eliakim; and Eliakim begat Azor; And Azor begat Sadoc; and Sadoc begat Achim; and Achim begat Eliud; And Eliud begat Eleazar; and Eleazar begat Matthan; and Matthan begat Jacob; And Jacob begat Joseph the husband of Mary, of whom was

born Jesus, who is called Christ. So all the generations from Abraham to David are fourteen generations; and from David until the carrying away into Babylon are fourteen generations; and from the carrying away into Babylon unto Christ are fourteen generations" (Matt. 1:1-17).

6. **The genealogy of Christ through Mary, his mother, from Jesus Christ to Adam in Luke 3:23-38 is as follows:** "And Jesus himself began to be about thirty years of age, being (as was supposed) the son of Joseph, which was the son of Heli, Which was the son of Matthat, which was the son of Levi, which was the son of Melchi, which was the son of Janna, which was the son of Joseph, which was the son of Mattathias, which was the son of Amos, which was the son of Naum, which was the son of Esli, which was the son of Nagge, Which was the son of Maath, which was the son of Mattathias, which was the son of Semei, which was the son of Joseph, which was the son of Juda, Which was the son of Joanna, which was the son of Rhesa, which was the son of Zorobabel, which was the son of Salathiel, which was the son of Neri, Which was the son of Melchi, which was the son of Addi, which was the son of Cosam, which was the son of Elmodam, which was the son of Er, Which was the son of Jose, which was the son of Eliezer, which was the son of Jorim, which was the son of Matthat, which was the son of Levi, Which was the son of Simeon, which was the son of Juda, which was the son of Joseph, which was the son of Jonan, which was the son of Eliakim, Which was the son of Melea, which was the son of Menan, which was the son of Mattatha, which was the son of Nathan, which was the son of David, Which was the son of Jesse, which was the son of Obed, which was the son of Booz, which was the son of Salmon, which was the son of Naasson, Which was the son of Aminadab, which was the son of Aram, which was the son of Esrom, which was the son of Phares, which was the son of Juda, Which was the son of Jacob, which was the son of Isaac, which was the son of Abraham, which was the son of Thara, which was the son of Nachor, Which was the son

of Saruch, which was the son of Ragau, which was the son of Phalec, which was the son of Heber, which was the son of Sala, Which was the son of Cainan, which was the son of Arphaxad, which was the son of Sem, which was the son Noe, which was the son of Lamech, Which was the son of Mathusala, which was the son of Enoch, which was the son of Jared, which was the son of Maleleel, which was the son of Cainan, Which was the son of Enos, which was the son of Seth, which was the son of Adam, which was the son of God" (Luke 3:23-38). (See **Appendix 1**: The Family Tree from Adam to Jesus Christ)

This family tree shows the genealogy from Adam to David through the Godly family line of Seth, through the family line of Noah and his son Shem, and through the family of Abraham to David the king of Israel. After David, the genealogy is split between David's son Solomon and David's son Nathan by his wife Bathsheba. The genealogy from Solomon goes to Joseph the adopted father of Jesus. The genealogy from Nathan goes to Mary the mother of Jesus.

Logical Conclusion: From the scriptures about our ancesters before the Flood, it may be inferred that:

1. **The Bible provides three scriptures that link Noah's ancesters to Adam and Eve and they are: 1Chronicles 1:1-9:44, Matthew 1:1-17, and Luke 3:23-38.**
2. **1Chronicles 1:1-9:44 traces the genealogy of the Children of Israel from Adam to Saul, king of Israel.**

3. **Matthew 1:1-17 traces the genealogy of Jesus from Abraham to the birth of Jesus Christ.**

4. **Luke 3:23-38 traces the genealogy of Jesus from his mother, Mary, to Adam.**

5. **All of these scriptures together trace the ancestors of Noah to Adam, which means that Noah and his sons, humanity's ancestors after the Flood, can be traced to Adam and Eve. This makes Adam and Eve the original ancestors of humanity before the Flood.**

G. How can evolution be related to creation and the species before and after the Great Flood?

The knowledge we have gained from our scientific analysis of evolution will now be used to predict the impact of microevolution on the species from the beginning of creation to the present time.

1. Based on our earlier analysis of evolution, there are four evidences of microevolution which can occur in nature without direct human intervention and they are:

   a. <u>Genetic Drift</u> – Which occurs when a species is split into two or more groups that live in different environments and have no contact with one another and are not able to reproduce with one another. Natural selection in each of the groups will favor them in their different environments which will favor slightly different genes in each group.

   b. <u>Gene Migration (Gene Flow)</u> – Which occurs when two or more separate groups that have experienced *genetic drift* are brought back together again and allowed to reproduce. All of their genetic differences that occurred during the separation will be merged together again into one group which will create more *genetic diversity* within the group.

   c. <u>Adaptive Radiation</u> – Which occurs when there is a slow change in the genetic constitution and physical characteristics of a species from its common ancestors such that the species becomes more diversified over time due to natural selection.

d. <u>Industrial Melanism</u> – Which occurs when a species develops internal or physical differences due to natural selection that is based on a very specific characteristic of their different environments which favors their survival, such as their color, size, or location.

2. The evolution of all species before the Great Flood may be explained as follows. If there is no clear empirical evidence that one species can evolve into an entirely new and totally different species, then all of the estimated 7.2 plus million species that currently exist on earth, plus all the species that have since become extinct, must have been created from the beginning. If all of the species were created from the beginning, then all of the variations within each species must have been created from the beginning to be compatible with the environments into which they were created.

In the case of Darwin's finches, this would mean that all of the adaptations of Darwin's finches would have been created from the beginning. Since each adaptation of the finches was created in a separate environment from the others, each group of finches would have exhibited the effects of <u>*genetic drift*</u>. In the estimated 1,656 years from the biblical time of creation in 4026 BCE to the Great Flood in 2370 BCE, the predictable and unpredictable occurrences that are a natural or man-made part of the universe would have occurred, such as hurricanes, floods, earthquakes, volcanoes, droughts, human and animal migrations, and famines, which would have caused many of the groups within each species (like the finches) to come together and experience <u>*gene migration*</u> and greater <u>*genetic diversity*</u>, while other species would have become extinct.

The combining of the various groups of species over the years would have created great <u>*genetic diversity*</u> within each species and the resulting offspring within each group would have inherited some of the different characteristic of all the species within each group of species. This _genetic diversity_ within each group of species would have been evident in the pairs of animals that went into Noah's Ark at the time of the Flood and would allow them, through natural selection, to replenish the earth after the Flood with similar groups of species as before the Flood.

The Flood itself would have caused many species, such as the dinosaurs, to become extinct, and it is probable that the cultures that existed prior to the Flood in 2370 BCE would have encountered the dinosaurs and other animals that have since become extinct. When God selected the animal species to go into the ark, it is probable that He eliminated some because they were too large and others because their species was already represented by the species He selected.

3. The evolution of the human species before the Flood would have been different from the other species because this particular species started with only one pair of ancestors. When Adam and Eve were expelled from the Garden of Eden, they began to produce offspring and their offspring initially expanded and migrated to other areas near the Garden of Eden. As time passed their offspring continued to expand into clans and nations and the predictable and unpredictable occurrences that are a natural or man-made part of the universe, such as hurricanes, floods, earthquakes, volcanoes, droughts, human and animal migrations, and wars would have caused the clans and nations to become more isolated from each other, which would have resulted in _genetic drift_.

As the offspring of the original ancestors continued to expand and migrate to far-away places and developed their own cultures, the process of _adaptive radiation_ would occur such that their genetic constitutions and physical characteristics would change from their original ancestors and they would become more diversified due to natural selection. As they migrated to different environments, some would also have developed specific characteristics over time, as a result of natural selection and *industrial Melanism*, due to the specific characteristics of their environments which would favor their survival, such as their color, size, or location.

At the time of the Flood, the Bible tells us a great deal about the character and ancestry of Noah, but we know nothing about the character and ancestry of Noah's wife or the wives of Noah's three sons, nor do we know much about the character of his sons. Consequently, it is probable that the genetic constitutions, physical characteristics, and cultural norms reflected in the Flood victims, would be carried forward in the future offspring of the Flood survivors due to heredity and their individual participation in the culture of the Flood victims.

4. How did the land animals that were on Noah's Ark evolve after the Flood? In Genesis 8:17, 19, God told Noah to, "Bring forth with thee every living thing that is with thee, of all flesh, both of fowl, and of cattle, and of every creeping thing that creepeth upon the earth; that they may breed abundantly in the earth, and be fruitful, and multiply upon the earth." And Verse 19 states that, "Every beast, every creeping thing, and every fowl, and whatsoever creepeth upon the earth, after their kinds, went forth out of the ark." It is probable that just as God had gathered the 16,000 to 25,000 distinct species of land animals from all over the face of the earth to go into the ark, He likewise, at some point in time, dispersed the animals and their offspring back to the various parts of the earth to replenish the animal population of the earth.

Once those male and female pairs of land animals and their offspring, at some point in time, were dispersed back into their natural environments, the process of microevolution would begin to take place as it did with the original human species of Adam and Eve. However, before being dispersed by God back to their original environments around the earth, the animals would have to stay in one general area for a certain period of time to build up their numbers.

The gestation periods of most animals are much less than humans and the number of offspring produced at birth is much greater than humans, so the land animals would have replenished the earth at a much faster rate than humans. In the 4,388 plus years since the Flood and AD 2018+, the predictable and unpredictable occurrences that are a natural or man-made part of the universe would occur in the various environments of the different species, such as hurricanes, floods, earthquakes, volcanoes, droughts, human and animal migrations, and famines, which would cause some to adapt to their environments while others would become extinct, and the following microevolutionary processes would take place:

a. *Genetic Drift* would happen when over time the predictable and unpredictable natural or man-made occurrences would cause the species to split into two or more groups that would live in different environments and would have no contact with one another and would not be able to reproduce with one another. Natural selection in each of the groups would favor them in their different environments which would favor slightly different genes in each group.

b. *Adaptive Radiation* would happen when the slow change in the genetic constitution and physical characteristics of the separated species would occur, as a result of natural selection, such that each species would become more diversified over time than their original ancestors. The diverse characteristics that were combined in the species that went into the ark would reappear due to natural selection as these species would drift back to their original diverse environments.

c. _Industrial Melanism_ would occur in some species who would develop internal and physical differences due to natural selection that is based on a very specific characteristic of their different environments which would favor their survival, such as their color, size, or location.

d. _Gene Migration_ would occur when two or more separate groups that have experienced _genetic drift_ would be brought back together again, as a result of the predictable and unpredictable occurrences that are a natural or man-made part of the universe, and allowed to reproduce. All of their genetic differences that occurred during the separation would be merged together again into one group which would create more _genetic diversity_ within the combined group.

5. The evolution of the human species after the Flood, which took place in about 2370 BCE, would be impacted by the event that took place at the Tower of Babel in about 2239 BCE, 131 years after the Flood. To assess the impact of this particular event, the growth of the descendants of the Children of Israel during their 215-year sojourn in Egypt will be used to estimate the human population of the earth at the time of the Tower of Babel event in 2239 BCE. The total number of the Children of Israel when they entered Egypt in about 1728 BCE was 70 persons, excluding the wives and children. When they left Egypt in about 1513 BCE, 215 years later, those 70 persons had grown to a population of men 20 years or older of 603,550.

It is reasonable to assume that there would be about the same number of women 20 years or older, for a total of 1,207,100 men and women above the age of 20 years. It is also reasonable to assume that there would be about one-half this number of men, women, and children under the age of 20 years, for a grand total estimated population of men, women, and children of about 1,810,650, which we will round to 1.8 million.

What would be the approximate growth of the 8 people that survived the Flood over the period of 131 years from the end of the Flood to the Tower of Babel? If the descendants of those 8 Flood survivors had grown at the same rate as the Children of Israel over the 215-year period, their population after 215 years would have been about 205,714 persons, for an average growth rate of about 957 persons per year. If that average growth rate of 957 persons per year is applied to the 131 years from the Flood to the Tower of Babel, the total population of the earth in 2239 BCE would have grown from 8 persons to about 125,367 persons, which we will round to 125,000 persons.

When the waters from the Great Flood subsided, Noah's Ark settled in the mountains of Ararat in eastern Turkey, which is relatively close to the same general area where all the people on earth resided prior to the Flood. According to Genesis 10:1-32, the descendants of the three sons of Noah resided in different areas after the Flood. The descendants of Shem resided in the area east of the Red Sea which is now occupied by Saudi Arabia. The descendants of Japheth resided in the area near where the ark settled after the Flood which is now occupied by Turkey. The descendants of three of Ham's sons resided in the following areas: his son Mizraim resided in the area now occupied by the Gaza Strip (Philistia); his son Canaan resided in the area now occupied by Palestine; and his son Cush resided in the area now occupied by Syria and Iraq, which includes the area where the Tower of Babel was located. The Bible did not name any descendants for Ham's fourth son Phut.

According to Genesis 11:1-9, after the Flood the whole earth had only one language and one speech, and a group of people traveled to the east and settled in the area where Iraq is now located, which was called Babel. These people decided that they were going to build a city and a great tower to reach into heaven to make a name for themselves and avoid being separated from one another. When God saw what they were planning to do, He noted that because of their unity, they would be able to do anything they imagined to do. Therefore, to stop this challenge to His sovereignty, God confused their language and scattered them over the face of the earth.

Since the descendants of Noah settled in different areas after the Flood, and Babel was located in the area that the descendants of Ham's son Cush resided in, it is probable that the people involved at the Tower of Babel were the descendants of Cush. However, their challenge to God's sovereignty caused all of the estimated 125,000 descendants of Noah to be judged by God and be scattered all over the face of the earth into different language groups.

In the 1.6 plus thousands of years from the creation of Adam and Eve to the Great Flood, it is probable that all the people on earth also spoke the same language before the Flood, because they were the descendants of common ancestors, but in their isolation they would have created different forms of writing to record their experiences. And in the 131 years after the Flood the 125,000 Flood survivors would probably have migrated to all the areas that were populated prior to the Flood, which would include the more advanced nations of Egypt and Assyria. If the human population on earth before and after the Flood spoke the same language, then it would be relatively easy for the descendants after the Flood to assimilate the cultures that existed prior to the Flood and carry them forward in their offspring.

It is probable that the ancestors of Noah's wife and the wives of his three sons came from some of those other cultures. When

God caused the estimated 125,000 descendants of Noah to be scattered over the face of the earth into different language groups, some of the advanced cultures that existed prior to the Flood would have also been transported to other parts of the earth. That would explain why some of the cultures in South America resemble the ancient advanced cultures of Egypt and Assyria.

As for the case of the evolution of the human species after the Flood, let us first consider the evolution before the Flood, which would have created _genetic drift_ between all the nations and clans over the 1.6 plus thousands of years before the Flood. The Flood would have the effect of bringing many of those cultures together again in the family of Noah to create _gene migration_ within the human species, and, at the same time, create more _genetic diversity_ within the human species.

The intervention by God at the Tower of Babel in about 2239 BCE caused all of the estimated 125,000 descendants of Noah to be scattered over the face of the earth into different language groups, which began the process of _genetic drift_ again. In the 4.2 plus thousands of years since the Tower of Babel event, the predictable and unpredictable occurrences that are a natural or man-made part of the universe would have caused some members of the human species to adapt to the changes in their environments while others would have become extinct.

During those 4.2 plus thousands of years of _genetic drift_ between the language groups since 2239 BCE, the predictable and unpredictable occurrences that are a natural or man-made part of the universe have already occurred, such as hurricanes, floods, earthquakes, volcanoes, droughts, human and animal migrations, famines, wars, slave trading, and nation building, which have caused the following microevolutionary processes to take place:

a. The process of *adaptive radiation* has taken place such that the genetic constitutions and physical characteristics of the language groups have changed from their original ancestors and have become more diversified due to natural selection within their different environments.

b. Some language groups have migrated to different environments such that they have developed specific characteristics over time, as a result of natural selection and *industrial Melanism*, due to the specific characteristics of their environments, which have favored their survival, such as their color, size, or location.

c. The process of *gene migration* has occurred such that two or more separate groups that have experienced *genetic drift* are brought back together again, as a result of the predictable and unpredictable occurrences that are a natural or man-made part of the universe, and allowed to reproduce and cause the genetic differences that occurred during the separation to be merged together again into one group which has created more *genetic diversity* within certain groups of people. This process has resulted in the different races of people as we see them today.

Logical Conclusion: From the analysis of the relationship between evolution and creation of the species before and after the Great Flood, it may be inferred that:

1. **The four evidences of microevolution:** *genetic drift, gene migration, adaptive radiation,* **and** *industrial melanism* **have occurred before and after the Great Flood.**

2. **If all of the species were created from the beginning, then all of the variations within each species must have been created from the beginning to be compatible with the environments into which they were created.**

3. Since each adaptation of Darwin's finches was created in a separate environment from the others, each group of finches would have exhibited the effects of *genetic drift*.

4. In the estimated 1,656 years from the biblical time of creation in 4026 BCE to the Great Flood in 2370 BCE, the predictable and unpredictable occurrences that are a natural or man-made part of the universe would have occurred, which would have caused many of the groups within each species (like the finches) to come together and experience *gene migration* and greater *genetic diversity*, while other species would have become extinct.

5. The combining of the various groups of species over the years would have created great *genetic diversity* within each species and the resulting offspring within each group would have inherited some of the different characteristic of all the species within each group of species.

6. This *genetic diversity* within each group of species would have been evident in the pairs of animals that went into Noah's Ark at the time of the Flood and would allow them, through natural selection, to replenish the earth after the Flood with similar groups of species as before the Flood.

7. The evolution of the human species before the Flood would have been different from the other species because this particular species started with only one pair of ancestors, Adam and Eve.

8. As time passed their offspring continued to expand into clans and nations and the predictable and unpredictable occurrences that are a natural or man-made part of the universe would have caused the clans and nations to become more isolated from each other, which would have resulted in *genetic drift*.

9. As the offspring of the original ancestors continued to expand and migrate to far-away places and developed their own cultures, the process of *adaptive radiation* would occur such that their genetic constitutions and physical

characteristics would change from their original ancestors and they would become more diversified due to natural selection.

10. As they migrated to different environments, some would also have developed specific characteristics over time, as a result of natural selection and *industrial Melanism*, due to the specific characteristics of their environments which would favor their survival, such as their color, size, or location.

11. It is probable that the genetic constitutions, physical characteristics, and cultural norms reflected in the Flood victims, would be carried forward in the future offspring of the Flood survivors due to heredity and their individual participation in the culture of the Flood victims.

12. It is probable that just as God had gathered the 16,000 to 25,000 distinct species of land animals from all over the face of the earth to go into the ark, He likewise dispersed the animals back to the various parts of the earth to replenish the animal population of the earth.

13. In the 4,388 plus years since the Flood in 2370 BCE and AD 2018+, the predictable and unpredictable occurrences that are a natural or man-made part of the universe would occur in the various environments of the different species, which would cause some to adapt to their original environments, while others would become extinct.

14. The evolution of the human species after the Flood, which took place in about 2370 BCE, would be impacted by the event that took place at the Tower of Babel in about 2239 BCE, 131 years after the Flood.

15. When the waters from the Great Flood subsided, Noah's Ark settled in the mountains of Ararat in eastern Turkey, which is relatively close to the same general area where all the people on earth resided prior to the Flood.

16. According to Genesis 11:1-9, after the Flood the whole earth had only one language and one speech, and a group of

       people traveled to the east and settled in the area where Iraq is now located, which was called Babel.

17. These people decided that they were going to build a city and a great tower to reach into heaven to make a name for themselves and avoid being separated from one another.

18. When God saw what they were planning to do, He noted that because of their unity, they would be able to do anything they imagined to do. Therefore, to stop this challenge to His sovereignty, God confused their language and scattered them over the face of the earth.

19. Since the descendants of Noah settled in different areas after the Flood, and Babel was located in the area that the descendants of Ham's son Cush resided in, it is probable that the people involved at the Tower of Babel were the descendants of Cush. However, their challenge to God's sovereignty caused all of the descendants of Noah to be judged by God and be scattered all over the face of the earth into different language groups.

20. When God caused the descendants of Noah to be scattered over the face of the earth into different language groups, some of the advanced cultures that existed prior to the Flood would have also been transported to other parts of the earth. That would explain why some of the cultures in South America resemble the ancient advanced cultures of Egypt and Assyria.

21. As a result of the event that occurred at the Tower of Babel, which resulted in the different language groups and dispersion throughout the world, the ancestors of all of humanity on earth today can be traced back to Adam and Eve through Noah and his sons.

22. The process of microevolution from Noah, our common ancestor, has resulted in the different races and cultures of people that we see today who come from different parts of the earth.

Exhibit 4a1 – Biblical Genealogy of Noah's Son Shem (Family Tree)

EXHIBIT 4a1

BIBLICAL GENEOLOGY OF NOAH'S SON SHEM AFTER THE FLOOD

GENESIS 10:21-32; 1 CHRONICLES 1:17-23

SHEM	600
	100
ARPHANAD	438
	35
SALAH	433
	30
EBER	464
	34

ELAM

ASSHUR

ARAM

UZ HUL GETHER MASH

LUD

JOKTAN

ALMODAD SHELEPH HAZARMAVETH JERAH HADORAM UZAL DIKLAH OBAL ABIMADEL. SHEBA OPHR HAVILAH JOBAB

PELEG	239
	30
REU	239
	32
SERUG	232
	30
NAHOR	148
	29
TERAH	205
	70
ABRAHAM	175

"And their dwelling was from Mesha, as thou goest unto Sephar a mount of the east." (Gen. 10:21-30)

Exhibit 4a2 – Biblical Genealogy of Shem's Son Abraham (Family Tree)

BIBLICAL GENEOLOGY OF SHEM'S SON ABRAHAM AFTER THE FLOOD

GENESIS 11:10-26; 1 CHRONICLES 1:27-27; LUKE 3:34-36

Exhibit 4b – Biblical Genealogy of Noah's Son Ham (Family Tree)

EXHIBIT 4b

BIBLICAL GENEOLOGY OF NOAH'S SON HAM AFTER THE FLOOD

GENESIS 10:6-20; 1 CHRONICLES 1:8-16

HAM

CUSH | MIZRAIM | PHUT | CANAAN

HAVILAH | SABTAH | RAAMAH | SABTECHAH | NIMROD

SEBA

SHEBA | DEDAN

"And Cush begat Nimrod: he began to be a mighty one in the earth. He was a mighty hunter before the Lord. And the beginning of his kingdom was Babel, and Erech, and Accad, and Calneh, in the land of Shinar. Out of that land went forth Asshur (Assyria), and builded Nineveh, and the city Rehoboth, and Calah, And Resen between Nineveh and Calah: the same is a great city." (Gen. 10:8-12)

GENESIS 10:6-20; 1 CHRONICLES 1:8-16

MIZRAIM

LUDIM | ANAMIM | LEHABIM | NAPHTUHIM | PATHRUSIM | CASLUHIM | CAPHTORIM

"And Pathrusim, and Casluhim, (out of whom came Philistim (Philistines)) and Caphtorim." (Gen. 10:13-14)

GENESIS 10:6-20; 1 CHRONICLES 1:8-16

CANAAN

SIDON | HETH | JEBUSITE | AMORITE | GIRGASITE | HIVITE | ARKITE | SINITE | ARVADITE | ZEMBANITE | HAMATHITE

"And the border of the Canaanites was from Sidon, as thou comest to Gerar unto Gaza; as thou goest, unto Sodom, and Gomorrah, and Admah and Zeboim, even unto Lasha." (Gen. 10:15-19)

Exhibit 4c – Biblical Genealogy of Noah's Son Japheth (Family Tree)

BIBLICAL GENEOLOGY OF NOAH'S SON JAPHETH AFTER THE FLOOD

GENESIS 10:1-5; 1 CHRONICLES 1:5-7

JAPHETH

| MAGOG | MADAIM | JAVAN | GOMER | TUBAL | MESHECH | TIRAS |

| ASHKENAZ | RIPHATH | TOGARMAH |

"By these were the isles of the Gentiles divided in their lands; every one after his tongue, after their families, in their nations." (Gen. 10:1-5)

GENESIS 10:1-5; 1 CHRONICLES 1:5-7

JAVAN

| ELISHAH | TARSHISH | KITTIM | DODANIM |

"By these were the isles of the Gentiles divided in their lands; every one after his tongue, after their families, in their nations." (Gen. 10:1-5)

APPENDIX 1
Biblical Genealogy from Adam to Jesus Christ (Family Tree)

Appendix 1 – Biblical Genealogy from Adam to Jesus Christ (Family Tree).

APPENDIX 1

BIBLICAL GENEOLOGY FROM ADAM TO JESUS CHRIST

GENESIS 5:1-32; GENESIS 10:21-32; GENESIS 25:7; 35:28; 1CHRONICLES 1:1 - 4:23; MATTHEW 1:2-17; LUKE 3:23-38

CAIN	ABEL	ADAM 930	SONS	DAUGHTERS
	SONS	SETH 912 / 130	DAUGHTERS
	SONS	ENOS 905 / 105	DAUGHTERS
	SONS	CAINAN 910 / 90	DAUGHTERS
	SONS	MAHALALAEL 895 / 70	DAUGHTERS
	SONS	JARED 962 / 65	DAUGHTERS
	SONS	*ENOCH 365 / 162	DAUGHTERS
	SONS	METHUSELAH 969 / 65	DAUGHTERS
	SONS	LAMECH 777 / 187	DAUGHTERS
	SONS	NOAH 950 / 182	DAUGHTERS
HAM		SHEM 600 / 500	JAPHETH

Gen 5:1-32

	SONS		DAUGHTERS
100			
	ARPHAXAD 438		DAUGHTERS
35	SONS		
	SALAH 433		DAUGHTERS
30	SONS		
	EBER 464		DAUGHTERS
34	SONS		
	PELEG 239		DAUGHTERS
30	SONS		
	REU 239		DAUGHTERS
32	SONS		
	SERUG 232		DAUGHTERS
30	SONS		
	NAHOR 148		DAUGHTERS
29	SONS		
	TERAH 205		DAUGHTERS
70			
	ABRAM/ABRAHAM 175	NAHOR	HARAN
100			

Gen 10:21-32

SHUAH (KETURAH)	ISHBAK (KETURAH)	MIDIN (KETURAH)	ISHMAEL (HAGAR)	ISAAC (SARAH) 180	ZIMRAN (KETURAH)	JOKSHAN (KETURAH)	MEDAN (KETURAH)
				60			

JACOB (ISRAEL) — Sons and descendants (genealogy chart)

- JOSEPH (RACHEL)
- BENJAMIN (RACHEL)
- REUBEN (LEAH)
- SIMEON (LEAH)
- LEVI (LEAH)
- ESAU
- JACOB (ISRAEL)
- JUDAH (LEAH)
- ISACHAR (LEAH)
- ZEBULUN (LEAH)
- GAD (ZILPAH)
- ASHER (ZILPAH)
- DAN (BILHAH)
- NAPHTALI (BILHAH)

JUDAH (LEAH):
- ER (DIED) (CANAANITE)
- ONAN (DIED) (CANAANITE)
- PHAREZ (CANAANITE)
- SHELAH (CANAANITE)
- ZERAH (CANAANITE)

PHAREZ (CANAANITE):
- HEZRON
- HAMUL

HEZRON:
- JERAHMEEL
- RAM
- CHELUBAI

RAM:
- AMMINADAB
- NAHSHON
- SALMA
- BOAZ (RUTH)
- OBED
- JESSE

JESSE:
- ELIAB
- ABINADAB
- SHIMMA
- NETHANEEL
- RADDAI
- OZEM
- DAVID

AMNON (AHINOAM)	CHILEAB (ABIGAIL)	ABSALOM (MAACAH)	ADONIJAH (HAGGITH)	SHEPHATIAH (ABITAL)	SOLOMON (BATHSHEBA) (HITTITE)	NATHAN (BATHSHEBA) (HITTITE)	IBHAR	ELISHUA	ELIPHALET	NOGAH
ITHREAM (EGLAH)					ROBOAM	MATTATHA				NEPHEG
SHIMEA (BATHSHEBA)					ABIA	MENAN				JAPHIA
SHOBAB (BATHSHEBA)					ASA	MELEA				ELISHAMA
TAMAR (MAACAH)					JOSAPHAT	ELIAKIM				ELIADA
					JORAM	JONAN				ELIPHALET
					OZIAS	JOSEPH				
					JOATHAM	JUDA				
					ACHAZ	SIMEON				
					EZIKIAS	LEVI				
					MANASSES	MATTHAT				

AMON	JORIM
JOSIAS	ELIEZER
JECHONIAS	JOSE
SALATHIEL	ER
ZOROBABEL	ELMODAM
ABIUD	COSAM
ELIAKIM	ADDI
AZOR	MELCHI
SADOC	NERI
ACHIM	SALATHIEL
ELIUD	ZOROBABEL
ELEAZAR	RHESA

(JUDAH CARRIED TO BABYLON)

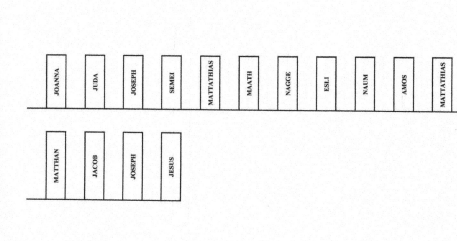

JANNA

MELCHI

LEVI

MATTHAT

HELI

JOSEPH
(MARY)

JESUS

Matt. 1:2-17

Luke 3:23-38

Printed in the United States
By Bookmasters